A Guide to

Ancient and Historic Wales

———————— • ————————

Glamorgan and Gwent

Elisabeth Whittle

London : HMSO

———————— • ————————

Front cover: *Llanthony Priory* (detail), by J M W Turner. By permission of the Trustees of the British Museum
Back cover: Arthur's Stone, Cefyn Bryn (no. 7), at sunset. Cadw: Welsh Historic Monuments

Other volumes in the series:
Dyfed

Forthcoming:
Gwynedd
Clwyd and Powys

Series Editor: Sian E Rees

While the information contained in this book is to the best of our knowledge correct at time of publication, the publisher and author can accept no responsibility for any inconvenience which may be sustained by any error or omission. Readers are also reminded to follow the Country Code when visiting the countryside monuments in this book.

HMSO publications are available from:

HMSO Publications Centre
(Mail, fax and telephone orders only)
PO Box 276, London, SW8 5DT
Telephone orders 071-873 9090
General enquiries 071-873 0011
(queuing system in operation for both numbers)
Fax orders 071-873 8200

HMSO Bookshops
49 High Holborn, London, WC1V 6HB 071-873 0011 (counter service only)
258 Broad Street, Birmingham, B1 2HE 021-643 3740
Southey House, 33 Wine Street, Bristol, BS1 2BQ 0272-264306
9–21 Princess Street, Manchester, M60 8AS 061-834 7201
16 Arthur Street, Belfast, BT1 4GD 0232-238451
71 Lothian Road, Edinburgh, EH3 9AZ 031-228 4181

HMSO's Accredited Agents
(see Yellow Pages)

and through good booksellers

Printed in the UK for HMSO
Dd 293653   C45   8/92

Contents

Editor's Foreword   *iv*
How to Use the Book   *v*
Introduction   *1*

1 Palaeolithic Caves   *3*
2 The Neolithic Period   *7*
3 The Bronze Age   *13*
4 The Iron Age   *28*
5 The Roman Period   *56*
6 The Early Medieval Period   *73*
7 The Medieval Period:
   Castles and Settlements   *85*
8 The Medieval Period:
   Ecclesiastical and Miscellaneous Sites   *149*

Appendix: Sites of Further Interest   *186*
Summary of Dates   *197*
Glossary   200
Bibliography   *203*
Acknowledgements   *208*
Index   *209*
Map   *217*

Editor's Foreword

As an archaeologist working with the preservation of our historic monuments, I have come to the firm conclusion that one of the best methods of conservation is to awaken in people an awareness of the unique contribution that ancient sites make, enriching our landscape by their quiet presence. With that aim in mind, this series of four regional guides was conceived, covering, in turn: Dyfed; Glamorgan and Gwent; Gwynedd; and Clwyd and Powys. Each volume describes 150 well preserved monuments which are accessible to the public. The volume on Dyfed covers the area roughly equivalent to the old counties of Cardiganshire, Carmarthenshire and Pembrokeshire.

The time-span covered by the volumes is from the first appearance of man in the Old Stone Age to the 16th century AD. The 16th century heralded many changes which suggested it as an appropriate termination point for a guide devoted to ancient monuments rather than to townscapes and general landscapes. Speaking somewhat casually, it marked the end of serious use of the castle in Wales, the end of the monasteries and, with the Act of Union of 1536, the political merging of Wales with England.

Inevitably there are many omissions from the book, sometimes made very reluctantly. Churches in use are not included as, despite their obvious interest and appeal, they are neither ruins nor monuments, and their very number is such that they need a guide of their own. The remains of industrial sites are a particular casualty of the cut-off date, as the vast majority of the more spectacular date from later than the 15th century. There are other sites of which the very fragility of the archaeological remains, or of the wildlife within them, render visits inadvisable. Yet more sites were left out because they were remote and difficult of access. The main omissions, however, were the many monuments which lie inaccessible to the public on private land, many of which are very fine. For this reason, an appendix has been added, listing well preserved sites for which special permission must be obtained before visiting.

Ancient sites are a tangible link with our past; they are our only link with the remotest past before literacy gave us a written history. And for the events of that written history, later sites are the stage, scenery and backdrop to the action that took place. To see these monuments makes our past come alive, if we can only clothe their stones and earthworks, battlemented walls and traceried windows with our imaginations. If this book helps the visitor to do this, its main objective will have been achieved.

Sian E Rees
Series Editor

How to Use the Book

The introduction to the book gives a brief background to the monuments of Glamorgan and Gwent. The main gazetteer is then ordered into period-based chapters, so that monuments of a class fall together, and each chapter is preceded by a brief description of the history and monuments of that period in the south-east of Wales. Each site is given a number to aid its identification on the location map.

Location

The monuments are ordered numerically in the gazetteer, and each is given the name by which it is normally known, which generally, but by no means invariably, is that found on the Ordnance Survey 1:50,000 maps. The nearest readily identifiable town or village is also given, from which the access directions start. The site type, a rough indication of its date, the Ordnance Survey 1:50,000 map number, and the site's six-figure national grid reference are also given. It is hoped that the directions alone will enable those without the 1:50,000 map to find the sites, but road and path signs, house names and the position of lay-bys change so rapidly that it is always safer to have the relevant map, if at all possible.

To locate a site on an Ordnance Survey map, first get the appropriate 1:50,000 map, the number of which is given on each entry (e.g., OS 157). Then look at the grid reference for the site, which consists of two letters and six figures (e.g., SM 750255). The letters at the beginning of the reference can usually be ignored as long as the correct map is being used, as they are a large-scale reference for the appropriate 100km grid square. Then take the first three numbers, which refer to the numbers on the top or bottom of the map; the first two of these will indicate the western line of the 1km square in which the site lies. The third will measure in tenths how far eastward within that square the site lies. Repeat the procedure with the second group of three numbers, which refer to the numbers on the right or left side of the map and increase in value northwards. Although this may sound complicated, after doing a few trial searches there should be no problem with easily locating any given site.

Accessibility

A guide to the accessibility of each site is given by the following:

U Unrestricted, i.e., access at any reasonable time free of charge.

R Restricted, i.e., access is restricted by opening hours and/or entry charge. If this symbol is used, an explanation is usually given at the end of the access direction.

Cadw standard hours

Many monuments maintained by Cadw are unrestricted, while a few operate under the 'key keeper' system by which the key may be collected from a nearby shop or house. The opening hours of the monuments with admission charges do vary slightly from site to site and according to the time of year. It is safe to assume, however, that where 'Cadw standard hours' are indicated, a monument will be open from Monday to Saturday and often part of Sunday during main daylight hours, except for Christmas Eve, Christmas Day, Boxing Day and New Year's Day. Full details of opening hours may be obtained from Cadw on request.

Monuments owned by other bodies may have similar opening times to Cadw throughout the year, in which case the phrase 'standard hours' is used. Where monuments are only open in the summer, this is indicated, with, wherever possible, a contact point, as opening dates may vary from year to year.

Disabled visitors

An attempt has been made to estimate how accessible each monument may be for disabled visitors. The entries are rated 1 to 4, this number appearing directly after the U or R at the head of each entry.

1 Easy access for all, including wheelchairs.

2 Reasonable access for pedestrians but limited access for wheelchairs.

3 Restricted access for disabled, but view of site from road or car park.

4 Access for able-bodied only.

It is also an unfortunate fact of life that field monuments tend to get covered with bracken in high summer so that some almost disappear. This has been indicated.

Abbreviations

These occur especially in the access directions:

km	kilometre	NT	National Trust
L, LHS	left, left-hand side	OS	Ordnance Survey
m	metre	R, RHS	right, right-hand side
ml	mile	tel	telephone
NCC	Nature Conservancy Council		

Welsh place-names

Any visitor to Wales will soon realise that the spelling of Welsh place-names can vary considerably, different versions of the same name being found on maps, road signs and in publications. Many Welsh place-names are compounded of two or more elements which are sometimes written as separate words, sometimes linked with hyphens and sometimes run into one. This series has attempted to use the most commonly found version of place-names, though the use of hyphens has been avoided wherever possible.

Safety

Anyone who makes periodic visits to ancient monuments will be aware of the hazards which different sorts of sites present to the unwary. Every visitor to sites in category 4 should have sensible footwear and clothing; in exposed areas, or even on country paths, sudden rain can make a walk a flounder, and mists equally suddenly can make apparently familiar terrain look strange and baffling. A pocket compass is always a good idea. Best of all, tell someone where you are going and when you expect to return.

Ruins that are officially open to the public, looked after by Cadw, the National Trust or private trusts, however hard those bodies try, may still be hazardous, especially for children, who should be supervised on higher areas of monuments and cautioned about the dangers of climbing on walls. Most monuments in categories 1, 2 and 3 are perfectly suitable for children of all ages as long as parents are aware of the hazards and avoid them. Many category 4 sites, though requiring longer walks, will also be quite suitable for older children, probably depending more on the psychological make-up and disposition of the child than on age or physique. The promise of a picnic can do wonders for enticing the most unenthusiastic visitor, and many monuments have areas for picnics nearby.

Country Code

It is, of course, most important to observe the Country Code when visiting the majority of the monuments in the book, which are situated on public footpaths through private land. Keep dogs on leads, always shut gates securely and open and shut them rather than climbing over. Keep to paths, do not drop litter and avoid any action that could start a fire. If you keep to these rules, monuments in private hands will continue to be cherished and visitors welcomed.

Further Information and Useful Addresses

A number of the monuments described in the gazetteer are owned or maintained by Cadw: Welsh Historic Monuments, a body set up in 1984 with the statutory responsibility for protecting, conserving and presenting the 'built heritage' of Wales on behalf of the Secretary of State. Many more of the sites listed in the book have been 'scheduled', or given statutory protection by the Secretary of State. Lists and maps of scheduled ancient monuments are produced by Cadw and a series of guidebooks provide detailed descriptions of the monuments it maintains. Further information can be obtained by contacting Cadw at: Brunel House, 2 Fitzalan Road, Cardiff CF2 1UY, tel: 0222-465511.

Three long-distance footpaths are of interest to those wishing to visit historic monuments. First is the Glamorgan coastal footpath, which runs (with interruptions) from Barry to Ogmore-by-Sea, and which passes several Iron Age hillforts, including Summerhouse, Nash Point and Dunraven. Second is the Wye Valley walk up the Welsh side of the Wye Valley from Chepstow to Monmouth which takes in several hillforts and Tintern Abbey. Third is the Offa's Dyke path which passes by White Castle and a hillfort and looks down on Llanthony Priory.

The Glamorgan–Gwent Archaeological Trust is the body responsible for maintaining a Sites and Monuments Record, a list of all known monuments in Glamorgan and Gwent. It carries out rescue excavation and survey work on sites which are threatened with development or erosion. The address is: 6 Prospect Place, Swansea, West Glamorgan SA1 1QP.

The following museums have collections of material from ancient monuments in Glamorgan and Gwent:

The National Museum of Wales, Cathays Park, Cardiff.

Newport Museum, John Frost Square, Newport, Gwent.

Abergavenny Museum, The Castle, Abergavenny, Gwent.

Chepstow Museum, Bridge Street, Chepstow.

Monmouth Museum, Priory Street, Monmouth.

While all possible attempts have been made to ensure that the accessibility of monuments is as described, unforeseen circumstances can alter access quite suddenly; monuments may sometimes have to be closed for short periods for repair work, and sadly, footpaths, even well established ones, do disappear from time to time. Discretion must therefore be exercised during visits and no liability can be accepted for errors in the information supplied.

Introduction

It has been said that Britain suffers from a surfeit of history. If so, one more guidebook on historical monuments would seem to be superfluous. Either this wealth of history can be ignored, and from ignorance neglected and misunderstood, or it can be studied, properly cared for and used to give a better depth of cultural understanding. This guidebook is intended to help all who would follow the latter path. The 16th-century antiquarian William Camden had the same aim, when he said in the Preface to his monumental *Britannia* that he wanted 'to restore Britain to its Antiquities, and its Antiquities to Britain', and 'to renew the memory of what was old, illustrate what was obscure, and settle what was doubtful'. It may not be possible to settle what was doubtful, but an attempt can be made on the old and obscure and on the restoration to Gwent and Glamorgan of their antiquities.

In function, the monuments can be roughly divided into two. First there are settlement remains, both secular and ecclesiastical, and secondly there are burial and commemorative sites. The preponderance of one or other type varies from period to period: settlement, even if only temporary, predominates in the Palaeolithic period, burials in the Neolithic period and Bronze Age, settlement in the Iron Age and Roman period, commemorative monuments in the early medieval period, and settlement in the medieval period (by which time burial was in churchyards and therefore outside the scope of this guidebook). This unevenness can be partly explained by methods of construction: the megalithic burial chambers of the Neolithic period and burial cairns of heaped stones of the Bronze Age survive better than their occupants' flimsier houses; the Iron Age settlements with their earthen banks are more visible than burials of the period, about which we know little and which left no upstanding monuments. The Roman period is rather different; the remains are mainly evidence of an army of occupation. The early medieval period is something of an enigma; its history is shadowy, based on garbled accounts of the lives of some of the Celtic saints who settled in the area. Monuments are scarce, and little survives of the few settlements and ecclesiastical sites that have been identified. Only the commemorative stones remain in sufficient numbers to throw any light on this period.

Several factors interact to produce a very uneven pattern of survival of sites from period to period. The first is population. A mere handful of hunting groups is thought to have been visiting or living in south-east Wales in the Palaeolithic period. Population levels crept up in the Neolithic and Bronze Age periods, and the number of Bronze Age cairns on the upland ridges in the area attests a much higher density than before. By the Roman period the population is thought to have reached the same levels as in the medieval period, but Roman and early medieval settlement remains are scant in the area.

The second factor is building materials, which have an important influence on survival. The monuments range from low earthen bumps in the ground to ruined buildings standing to a considerable height. Anything built in wood, such as early Norman castles, has completely disappeared. Slight earthen monuments, such as Roman marching camps, are easily removed by ploughing, afforestation or animal trampling, but more substantial earthworks, such as the larger Iron Age hillforts, usually prove more durable. Stone-built monuments, whether Bronze Age cairns or medieval castles, survive better than earthen ones. The ruined state of most medieval castles and monasteries is as much the result of the robbing of their stone and roof lead as of weathering and strangulation by plants.

Lastly, the location of a monument can also influence its survival. Here the geography of south-east Wales comes into play. The area is largely divided into a lowland zone of undulating farmland and an upland zone of high moorland ridges and deep, steep-sided valleys. Modern farming in the lowland zone has destroyed or reduced many of its more vulnerable earthwork monuments such as Bronze Age barrows, whereas in the upland region the Bronze Age burial cairns and barrows largely survive in uncultivated moorland. Iron Age hillforts have often escaped cultivation by being in exposed positions on hilltops, with their banks often on the edge of steep slopes. The Gower peninsula is something of a special case in that it is rich in monuments of all prehistoric periods, with Palaeolithic finds in caves, Neolithic burial chambers, Bronze Age cairns and standing stones, and Iron Age hillforts and smaller camps. Most medieval monuments occur in the lowland zone. The most visible remains from this period are the masonry castles and monasteries, but there are also humbler mottes, moated sites and the earthworks of deserted villages. Settlement has always been denser in the lowlands than in the uplands, and the medieval remains have had to take their chance, surrounded as they are by later development. Proximity of settlements to a handy abandoned castle, monastery or even Roman site has led to much haemorrhaging of stone for private purposes in the past.

Lowland south-east Wales has both suffered and benefited from its easy accessibility by sea and land from other parts of Britain. In this respect the area has more in common with the Marches of eastern Wales than with its upland interior. In the Neolithic period the Severn–Cotswold chambered tomb, whose distribution reaches into Wessex, indicates contacts to the east. The Romans and Normans, invading from England, established a firm foothold in the lowland zone, but the Normans in particular found it much harder to stamp their rule on the Welsh of the uplands. Celtic saints from further west established small monastic settlements in the lowlands early on in the early medieval period.

It is hoped that this guidebook will shed some light on these partial remains from the past, and help the visitor both to appreciate them for what they are, even though some of their secrets will remain forever hidden, and to see them as part of the wonderful surfeit of history in which the area should revel.

1

Palaeolithic Caves

The earliest evidence for human occupation of south-east Wales comprises finds of bones, both animal and human, and stone and bone artefacts of the Upper Palaeolithic period, which began some 38,000 years ago during a warm phase of the Pleistocene period, or Ice Age. Most of these finds come from caves in the Gower peninsula, a limestone area which must have held many attractions for Palaeolithic man, not least the ready-made shelters of its many natural caves. Of the 95 or so caves in the peninsula, it is estimated that about 22 show traces of occupation, some of which are Palaeolithic.

During the period known as the Early Upper Palaeolithic small groups used these caves for temporary or, in the case of Paviland (no. 1), more permanent camps. This

Reconstruction drawing of a burial at Paviland Cave, *c.*24,000 BC

was a cool but not glacial phase; the local environment was open and treeless, with low shrubby vegetation such as willow, juniper and dwarf birch. The sea was some two miles further away than it is now, with a wide level plain between it and the present sea cliffs. The population of the whole of Britain has been estimated at no more than about 500 during this period, so only very small numbers can have been present on the Gower peninsula at any one time. This makes the assemblage at Paviland all the more remarkable, for here were found thousands of artefacts and animal bones. From these bones it is deduced that man came to the Gower to hunt woolly rhino, wild horse, reindeer, mammoth and other large animals.

Around 20,000 BC Britain was once again glaciated, and the ice-sheet covering the country extended to within a few miles of the southern edge of the Gower peninsula, which was not reoccupied until slightly warmer conditions returned in about 10,000 BC. During this later phase, until about 8000 BC, known as the Late Upper Palaeolithic, the cave of Cat Hole (no. 3) seems to have been more intensively occupied than Paviland, while no occupation is recorded from Long Hole (no. 2).

There are now no visible signs of the occupation of the caves from this remote period, but visiting them helps one to envisage the living conditions of these early hunting peoples.

1
Paviland Cave, Port Eynon, Gower

Upper Palaeolithic cave
36,000–8000 BC
OS 159   SS 437859   U4

2ml (3km) NW of Port Eynon, in sea cliff. Path from B4247 at Pilton Green (signposted to cave). At the shore scramble over rocks into gully and round the headland to the right. Cave is above, about half-way up cliff, and is only accessible at lowish tide. Considerable agility required

Sollas 1913

This is one of the richest Upper Palaeolithic sites in Britain, and one of the most famous caves in British prehistory. The scramble to it is well worth the effort for it is exciting to enter a cave lived in more than 30,000 years ago. The view, very different from the one that must have been seen by the Palaeolithic occupants, is a fine one, and the peacefulness is welcome.

The main occupation of the cave dates from the Early Upper Palaeolithic phase of 36,000–25,000 BC. Some 5,042 artefacts from this phase were found in the cave, in thick occupation deposits now no longer there. The original floor level can just be discerned by looking closely at the left-hand cave wall (facing inwards). On it are the stubs of stalactites and small lumps of hardened deposits which mark the original floor level. The deposits were excavated in 1822 by William Buckland and again by W J Sollas in 1912. It was Buckland's excavation which made the discovery that was to make Paviland famous. Buried in an extended position about half-way into the cave on the left-hand side was a skeleton, minus the skull, vertebrae and parts of the right-hand side. Close to the thigh, presumably originally in

Paviland cave

raises the possibility of social stratification: was this an important member of the community, perhaps a leader of some kind?

From the number of Early Upper Palaeolithic artefacts found in the cave, and from the range of animal bones, it would appear that this was a major hunting station in the area. The artefacts are largely flint tools, but also include worked mammoth ivory; the find of a mammoth's skull with tusks suggests that the ivory may have been worked here in the cave. Animal bones found included those of woolly rhino, mammoth, bison, wolf, hyena, bear, wild horse, giant deer, reindeer and 'bovid'. Below the cave was a level plain where these could have roamed, and the lip of the cave would have been a good vantage point from which to pick out the next meal.

After an intensely cold phase the cave was again occupied in about 10,000–8000 BC. Only 27 flint artefacts, of Creswellian type, were found from this Late Upper Palaeolithic phase, indicating occasional temporary use. Mesolithic flints, a Neolithic polished axe-head and Roman pottery and coins testify to later visitors.

the pocket of a garment, were about two handfuls of small perforated shells (*Nerita littoralis*), and in contact with the ribs were 40–50 fragments of small, nearly cylindrical ivory rods and some small fragments of ivory rings. Everything, bones, shells and ivory, was lying in and stained by powdered red ochre, and the skeleton was dubbed the 'Red Lady of Paviland'. However, later study showed that in fact this was no lady, but a young man of about 25. Paviland was described by Buckland as a 'hyena's den', with the burial seen as intrusive: the notion of human existence at such a remote 'antediluvian' period was unthinkable in 1822. Radiocarbon dating has now put the 'Red Lady' burial at about 26,000 years ago, in the closing stages of the Early Upper Palaeolithic period. A well developed degree of ritual, of spiritual belief and also of personal adornment is indicated by this burial. It also

2

Long Hole Cave, Port Eynon, Gower

Upper Palaeolithic cave
36,000–25,000 BC
OS 159   SS 452851   U2

In Port Eynon take road to Overton and continue along track to W. Take footpath along cliffs to the far side of the clifftop field. Cave is seaward of this in a rocky outcrop facing S

In this natural limestone cave, which runs into the hillside some 13m, traces of occupation by man in the remote Early Upper Palaeolithic period have been found. Some 22 flint tools and bones of 'fox', wild horse and reindeer were found in the occupation deposit in the floor of the cave, which was excavated in

Long Hole cave

Cat Hole cave

1861 and again in 1969. The evidence points to a small hunting camp, perhaps used occasionally or in transit. Sea level was well below that of the present day, leaving a large level plain at the foot of the cliffs below the cave.

3
Cat Hole Cave, Parkmill, Gower
Upper Palaeolithic cave
36,000–8000 BC
OS 159   SS 538901   U2

Leave car at Parkmill on A4118 and walk N up road and track, past Parc le Breos burial chamber (no. 4). Cave is half-way up RHS of valley, reached by track and rough steps

Like the other Gower caves occupied by man in the Palaeolithic period, this is a natural limestone cave. It is an inland cave at the base of a small cliff above the flat floor of a limestone dry valley. It has a spacious chamber at its mouth, and a small passage

running some 18m into the hillside.

One flint tool, a tanged point, found in the occupation deposit testifies to its use in the Early Upper Palaeolithic period (36,000–25,000 BC). Like Long Hole cave (no. 2) it was probably merely a temporary or transit camp at that time. In the Late Upper Palaeolithic period (10,000–8000 BC), after an intervening very cold phase, the cave was again occupied, but this time the evidence points to a more intensive occupation. In total 131 artefacts were found during excavations in 1864 and 1968, including part of a finely polished bone sewing needle. Most of the artefacts were flint tools, a few of which can be positively identified as of the Late Upper Palaeolithic type known as Creswellian.

The animal bones from this phase at Cat Hole, although probably contaminated with bones from later phases of occupation, point to a cold climate fauna. They include red fox, Arctic fox, brown bear, Arctic lemming and tundra vole.

The cave continued to be occupied into the succeeding Mesolithic period, when conditions were warmer. It was used again at a much later date, in the Bronze Age, for burial, and again in the medieval period.

2
The Neolithic Period

South-east Wales in the Neolithic period, or New Stone Age (roughly the 4th and 3rd millennia BC), as in the rest of the British Isles, was warmer and wetter than today. Mixed deciduous forest covered both upland and lowland, with open heathy oak and birch woodland on the higher ground, and more dense woodland (predominantly oak, but also elm, ash, lime, hazel, yew and holly) on the lowlands. Neolithic people were farmers, with cattle, sheep and pigs to graze, and crops of wheat and barley to grow. Forest clearance began in earnest during this period, using polished flint and stone axes, some of which were acquired from the axe factories of north Wales. Elm pollen declines dramatically during the Neolithic period, suggesting the systematic exploitation of elm for fodder and fuel. We know few details of the subsistence economy but people may still have moved about the landscape from season to season, as well as having bases to which they returned. Hunting for aurochs (*Bos primigenius*), red deer, roe deer and wild pig, fishing and gathering would have supplemented the diet.

Little is known of settlement sites in the area and the most obvious evidence for Neolithic occupation comes from the 14 or so megalithic tombs of the period. These are communal tombs with a burial chamber or chambers built of massive stones and drystone walling, usually contained within a mound of stones. They are scattered along the coastal plain, with a concentration in the Gower peninsula. Their construction and distribution put most of them in the group known as Severn–Cotswold. Parc le Breos (no. 4) and Tinkinswood (no. 5) are the outstanding examples of this type in the area, exhibiting all the characteristic Severn–Cotswold features, which include trapezoidal cairns, forecourts that were probably used for ritual, drystone walling revetment, and inside, entrance passages and roughly rectangular chambers, sometimes with transepts, in which the bones of the dead were deposited. The covering mounds have often been eroded away, leaving the burial chamber exposed.

Various attempts have been made to classify and date these tombs using their layout alone, but some, like Arthur's Stone (no. 7), defy easy classification. One striking feature is the use of massive stones in the construction of the burial chamber. Although it is thought that all tombs of the Severn–Cotswold type had mounds, others, such as 'portal dolmens', a few of which are found in the area, may not have had them. A portal dolmen has a box-like chamber of stone, with or

Reconstruction drawing of a chambered tomb burial, *c.*3000 BC

without a low cairn or platform, and has a western, Irish Sea-centred distribution. Very few chambered tombs in Wales have been dated other than by analogy with examples in the Cotswolds, and none in south-east Wales has a precise date. A radiocarbon date for Penywyrlod, a chambered long cairn near Talgarth (Powys), of about 3800 BC is the closest indication that they may have been in existence as early as the 4th millennium BC. There is evidence that the tombs were in use over a long time, and in the case of Tinkinswood, possibly right to the end of the Neolithic period.

It is clear from the structure and contents of these communal tombs that they played a very important part in the life of Neolithic people. They were architecturally imposing and carefully built, and were fixed points for a scattered, partly mobile population. They contained the bones of their ancestors, and as such were the key to descent and land ownership.

4

Parc le Breos, Parkmill, Gower

Neolithic chambered cairn
4th–3rd millennium BC
OS 159   SS 537898   U2

Leave car at Parkmill on A4118 and walk N up road and track to cairn (signposted)

Lubbock 1871; Daniel 1937

Parc le Breos chambered cairn

This is the finest and best preserved chambered long cairn in south-east Wales. It is also one of the most thoroughly investigated. The chamber was excavated in 1869, with further excavation, followed by partial restoration, in 1960–1. The site lies on the floor of the picturesque dry valley of the Ilston river, which runs underground at this point.

The monument belongs to the Severn–Cotswold tradition of chambered long cairns. It is built of the local limestone and has a trapezoidal plan, with a deep concave-sided forecourt at its southern end. Around the edge of the cairn is a rubbly revetment wall, higher at the forecourt end, where it has a noticeable inward batter. Within the mound, behind this outer revetment, is an inner revetment wall. Leading into the cairn from the forecourt is a narrow passage edged with upright stones, off which are four small chambers, two on each side opposite each other. There are sill stones at the entrances to the main passage and three of the four chambers, with the two inner chambers having double sills. This careful division of space must reflect original demarcations in the ritual use of the tomb. The bones of the dead were deposited in the chambers, which are lined with uprights, with drystone walling filling the gaps between them. The badly muddled up and disarticulated bones of 20–24 individuals, including three children, were excavated. One theory to explain the state of the bones is that some bodies may have been deposited already defleshed, having been

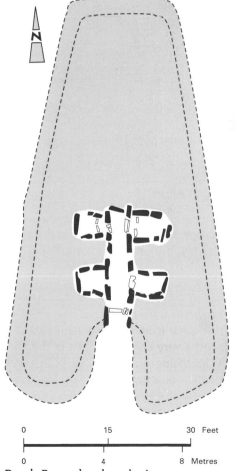

0	15	30 Feet
0	4	8 Metres

Parc le Breos chambered cairn

buried or exposed first elsewhere. The tomb was probably used over a long period.

Communal tombs of this type were usually roofed with large slabs or capstones, and it is conjectured that the passage and chambers were once covered in this way, although no sign has been found of any roof stones.

5
Tinkinswood, St Nicholas
Neolithic chambered cairn
4th–3rd millennium BC
OS 171   ST 092733   U2   Cadw

Tinkinswood chambered cairn

Take A48 to St Nicholas. In middle of village take minor road S (signed Dyffryn) for c.500m. Cairn is across field on RHS (sign at stile on road)

Ward 1915, 1916

This chambered cairn boasts the largest capstone in mainland Britain over its chamber. It weighs about 40 tons, measures 7.4m × 4.5m, and it has been estimated that at least 200 men would have been needed to lift it into position. As Edward Lhuyd stated in William Camden's *Brittania* (1695 edition), 'the Pulleys and levers, the force and skill by which 'twas done, are not so easily imagined'. That it was done about 5,000 years ago makes the feat all the more remarkable.

The cairn is located in a small, gently sloping valley in the Vale of Glamorgan. It attracted antiquarian interest as early as the late 18th century, when its appearance was rather different from now. The capstone was then on the ground surface, and the chamber was partly visible but buried, and could be entered only from the east side. The mound was ill-defined, with a heap of stones on it, much of which was removed in the 19th century. Visitors thought it 'druidical'.

In 1914 it was thoroughly excavated, and its true nature as a Neolithic communal tomb was revealed. It falls clearly into the Severn–Cotswold tradition, with its slightly

trapezoidal plan and forecourt with chamber opening off it. The mound is straight-sided, relatively squat and not as tapered as most in this group. The surface slopes gradually up towards the east, chamber end, leaving the capstone uncovered. Whether or not this was originally covered by the mound is not known. The edges of the mound are revetted with drystone walling. (Where this has been restored it is in a herringbone pattern to distinguish it from the original.) The walling was upright or leaning outwards, unlike that at Parc le Breos (no. 4), and had deliberate packing outside it to buttress it up. For the same purpose the cairn stones around the chamber were larger than on the west of the mound and sloped towards it. Within the body of the cairn, towards the western end, were found discontinuous parallel rows of small upright slabs standing on the original ground surface. These have been found in other cairns of the same type, and their purpose is obscure. On the north side of the cairn is an enigmatic intrusive stone-lined pit which contained some animal bones.

The forecourt was probably the focus of ritual activity connected with the deposition of the dead. It has curving drystone walls and a similar wall in front of the upright stones of the chamber, with a narrow stone-lined entrance at its northern end. Its surface was originally of beaten earth and gravel, with

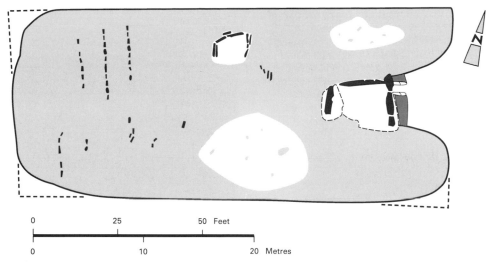

```
0            25            50  Feet
|------------|-------------|
0                   10              20  Metres
```

Tinkinswood chambered cairn

rough paving in front of the threshold. Simple pottery similar to a type known to date from about the middle of the 3rd millennium BC was found on the surface. When the tomb went out of use the forecourt was sealed with small stones.

The chamber itself is roughly rectangular, roofed by the huge capstone. Its south side has been robbed out, but the large upright slabs of the other sides are still in place. Inside and nearby were found about 920 pieces of human bone, nearly all broken. They are thought to have come from about 40 people of both sexes and all ages. As at Parc le Breos, the tomb was probably used by a small community over a long time, and there is evidence that it was in use right up to the end of the Neolithic period.

6
St Lythans Burial Chamber, St Lythans
Neolithic chambered cairn
4th–3rd millennium BC
OS 171   ST 100722   U2   Cadw

0.6ml (1km) W of St Lythans on minor road to Dyffryn. Park c.700m W of St Lythans, just past house on LHS (from St Lythans direction). Cairn is in field S of road (signposted)

Lukis 1875

This spectacular chambered tomb, with the huge slabs of its chamber standing in gaunt isolation, has not been excavated. There appears to be a low roughly rectangular

St Lythans burial chamber

mound or platform stretching out to the west of the chamber. The more or less square chamber, with a probable entrance on the east side, has three uprights and a capstone, is unusually high, and may never have been completely covered. It is, therefore, probably of portal dolmen type.

The tomb is sometimes called Maesyfelin, and in the early 19th century it was called the 'greyhound-bitch kennel' and was used as an animal shelter.

7
Arthur's Stone or Maen Ceti, Reynoldston, Gower
Neolithic chambered cairn
4th–3rd millennium BC
OS 159   SS 491906   U2   Cadw

Arthur's Stone

Take minor road from Reynoldston E towards B4271. After 0.6ml (1km) park on summit. Take track across moor to N for about 500m to cairn

Wilkinson 1870

Arthur's Stone, as its name suggests, has generated many legends. This is hardly surprising given its extraordinary nature – a giant boulder, or 'maen', perched precariously on a few small upright slabs. Its position is spectacular, and because of this superb, apparently deliberate siting it is thought that the natural boulder which forms the capstone might have been brought here from a less prominent spot nearby.

Arthur's Stone does not fit neatly into any of the established categories of Neolithic chambered tomb, and may indeed eventually prove not to be Neolithic at all. There is no clear trace of a covering cairn; a low bank of stones around the sunken area is all that survives. The chamber's eccentric capstone is a natural boulder of giant proportions. It is of local conglomerate, and is thought to have weighed between 30 and 35 tons when whole. It originally measured about 4m × 3m × 2.2m, but part has split off and now lies broken in three pieces to the west. The base of the boulder rests at the level of the original ground surface, and it is thought that to construct the burial chamber a hole was excavated beneath it and the uprights of the chamber inserted to support it. Nine uprights remain in position, but the boulder rests on only four. Those on the west side are clear of it because the capstone is broken, but the outer free-standing ones to the north and south were perhaps joined to the boulder by drystone walling. The tomb, if tomb it is, consists of two small roughly square chambers next to each other. The entrance may have been on the south side where there is a gap, but this is uncertain.

Nearby to the west is a large Bronze Age round cairn (no. 10).

3
The Bronze Age

South-east Wales appears to have prospered in the Bronze Age, which lasted for roughly the whole of the 2nd millennium BC. The climate was benign at first, with warm, dry summers, and there was ample grazing land. The local economy was largely pastoral, with sheep more important than cattle, while there is evidence of some cultivation of wheat and barley in the lowlands. It was a time of population expansion and consequent accelerated clearance of the native woodland, which led to a relatively open landscape. This was to have a disastrous effect on the uplands, where lack of tree cover and overgrazing together with a deterioration in the climate led to the spread of blanket peat towards the end of the period. But until then the uplands appear to have been fairly densely settled, with burial monuments on most of the ridgetops. In the lowlands new finds from Caldicot and the Gwent Levels are beginning to show careful woodland management similar to that already found in the Somerset Levels. Such was the increase in population at this time that it has been estimated that numbers may have reached Domesday levels by the end of the period.

The Bronze Age saw the establishment of major changes in burial custom (which had already begun in the Middle Neolithic period), from the communal chambered tombs of the Neolithic period to individual burial in round mounds of earth or stones, and from inhumation to cremation burial in pottery vessels. Most of the barrows and cairns, burial mounds predominantly of earth and stones respectively, are thought to date from the first half of the 2nd millennium BC, with some possibly continuing in use for secondary burials into the second half of the millennium. It is these barrows and cairns that are the main Bronze Age monuments in the area. Cairns are particularly well represented and well preserved on the upland ridges, often in prominent positions (for instance nos 8 and 9). On some there are so many that one can think in terms of cemeteries (no. 21). Cultivation has destroyed and reduced many of the lowland burial mounds, here usually earthen barrows, and only a few survive in anything like their original form. This was a conical earthen mound beneath which was a cremation burial. Internal structures found in excavated barrows suggest an elaborate ritual connected with burial.

Cairns come in many shapes and sizes but most are simple circular heaps of stones sometimes edged with a kerb of stones (no. 8) or drystone walling. Some

are surrounded by a bank or ditch (no. 9). In the middle there is usually a stone-lined cist containing a cremation burial in a pottery urn and sometimes a few personal possessions such as bronze daggers. Some cairns have several cists, often near the surface, suggesting secondary use. One particular variant, the ring cairn, is quite common. Instead of a mound there is a circular bank, usually now of turf-covered stones, surrounding a level area in which there is usually a sunken stone-lined burial pit or cist. A circle of upright stones may replace the bank, or may be incorporated into it as a revetment (nos 15, 16 and 19, for example). It has been speculated that the ring cairn, particularly where it is in a group of 'normal' cairns, may have acted as a ritual focus. One group of this kind occurs on Gelligaer Common (no. 8 and Appendix).

The other main category of monument in the area thought to belong to the Bronze Age is the standing stone. Standing stones are well distributed throughout the lowlands of south-east Wales, with a particular concentration in west Gower (nos 30–3). All are large, sometimes massive upright slabs of local stone, of uncertain function and date. Apart from Harold's Stones at Trellech (no. 27) and an alignment on Gray Hill (no. 16), all are isolated. The few to be excavated have produced mixed evidence. Some have a cremation burial beneath, others appear not to. Some may therefore have had a funerary or ritual purpose, while others may have had a more secular function, for instance as track markers. The dating of these stones is very problematical. Traditionally they are thought to be Early Bronze Age, but there is little clear evidence to confirm this, and indeed there are indications from elsewhere that some at least may be Neolithic – at Gavrinis in Brittany the capstone of the Neolithic tomb is part of a 14m-high standing stone.

After about 1400 BC, in the phases known as the Middle and Late Bronze Age, the climate became colder and wetter, blanket peat spread on the uplands, forcing their eventual abandonment, and social and cultural changes led to changes in settlement and burial practice. Of burials during this phase little is known, except that formal burial in cairns and barrows ceased. From evidence elsewhere in Wales it is known that settlement concentrated within larger, possibly defended hilltop settlements. One such, Coed y cymdda, Wenvoe, has been excavated in south-east Wales. There are other small hillforts in the area of similar type which could well originate in this period. By the end of the Bronze Age the population was probably organised into loose 'tribes', each occupying a distinct area.

Top left: reconstruction drawing of the preparation of an archer's grave, *c*.2000–1500 BC

Bottom left: finds from Breach Farm round barrow, South Glamorgan. (Top to bottom) left panel: accessory cup, flint knife, flint flakes; middle panel: thirteen barbed and tanged arrowheads; right panel: two stone arrowshaft smoothers, roughouts for arrowheads, bronze axe. The objects were found in a burial pit containing the cremated bones of three individuals, in the centre of a round barrow. The burial was covered with a mound of clay, around which was a low stone ring.

8
Carn Bugail, Gelligaer
Bronze Age round cairn
2000–1000 BC
OS 171   SO 100036   U2

From N take minor road W out of Pontlottyn to Fochriw and on up to Gelligaer Common. After 1ml (1.6km) cairn is on summit on RHS. From S take minor road out of Gelligaer on to common and continue until below summit

Gelligaer Common is very rich in prehistoric and historic remains and the Bronze Age is particularly well represented, with both simple round cairns and ring cairns scattered all over the ridgetop. An ancient trackway with which they may have been loosely associated runs the length of the ridge, and a later Roman road follows much the same route.

The largest and most imposing of the cairns is Carn Bugail on the very summit of the ridge. Its form suggests an Early Bronze Age date (2000–1450 BC). It consists of a circular flat-topped mound of stones laid overlapping and sloping towards the centre, with the largest ones near the top and bottom. It is edged with a kerb of larger stones laid flat, and has a stone-lined box or cist for burial in the centre. The damaged cist is visible on the top, with only one of its two side slabs remaining, and with the large oval capstone displaced to the south.

This cairn and others near it attracted the attention of early antiquaries, and there is a record that it was opened in about 1700, with urns and burnt bones being found.

Just to the north is a smaller turf-covered cairn with some large stone slabs embedded in its surface. The cist which is full of stones and has a large capstone, is exposed in the centre. Further cairns lie to the north and south and on lower ground to the south-west.

On the east slope of the summit is an early Christian standing stone (no. 79), and further south on the common are Roman practice camps (see Appendix) and medieval platform houses (nos 91 and 92).

9
Crug yr Afan, Treorchy
Bronze Age round cairn
2000–1000 BC
OS 170   SS 920954   U2

Take A4107 Treorchy to Abergwynfi road. Park at summit of ridge. Cairn on ridgetop a short distance to N

Griffith 1902

This cairn occupies a prominent position but is an unusual type for the uplands, being a ditched barrow similar to the bell barrows of Wessex which date from about 2000–1450 BC. Excavation in 1902 revealed that it is a composite mound, the two parts of which are readily discernible on the ground. The lower part, over 20m in diameter, is made of clayey soil and is surrounded by a flat ledge, or berm, and ditch. In the middle a cist was cut

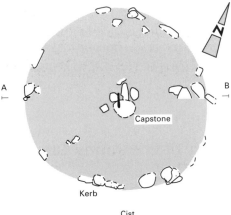

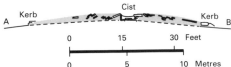

Carn Bugail round cairn

Crug yr Afan

Arthur's Stone (no. 7) to the N. Cairn is a little to the SW

Like nearby Arthur's Stone (no. 7), this cairn has a spectacular position, with sweeping views in all directions. It is a large, circular flat-topped mound of big stones, made more imposing by standing on a natural rock knoll. Excavations in the 19th century are responsible for the holes in the middle and on the east side.

There are many other smaller cairns on the Cefn Bryn ridge, in groups or on their own. Some at least may be clearance cairns associated with early fields.

into the subsoil beneath. It contained cremated bones, traces of something like bark and a small bronze dagger, grooved along its edges, of a type familiar in Early Bronze Age Wessex. On top of the clayey mound is a smaller cairn of stones, apparently originally surrounded by a ring of upright slabs. Stones of this part are visible in holes dug into the sides of the mound.

Analysis of pollen found on the site shows that when the cairn was made the surrounding area was heathy, with an open tree cover dominated by oak, a situation half-way between the earlier denser forest and the blanket peat which had smothered much of the uplands by the end of the Bronze Age.

Round cairn west of Arthur's Stone

10
Round Cairn West of Arthur's Stone, Reynoldston, Gower
Bronze Age round cairn
2000–1000 BC
OS 159   SS 490905   U2

Take minor road from Reynoldston E towards B4271. Leave car after 0.6ml (1km) and walk to

11
Carn y Defaid Round Cairns, Blaenavon
Bronze Age round cairns
2000–1000 BC
OS 161   SO 271099   U4

Take B4246 Blaenavon to Abergavenny road. 1ml (1.6km) from Blaenavon take minor road to E. Park by masts and walk S across moor for c.0.5ml (0.8km)

On this high and rather bleak moorland ridge overlooking the lowlands of Gwent stands a pair of large round cairns. Both are roughly conical, built of the material to hand, large chunks of angular limestone, and one is larger than the other. The holes in their centres are probably the result of 19th-century antiquarian curiosity; they were already there when the cairns were recorded in 1873.

12
Mynydd Caerau Round Cairns, Caerau

Bronze Age round cairns
2000–1000 BC
OS 170   SS 891944   U4

Just N of Caerau on A4063 take turn to E to Blaencaerau. At end of road turn R into entrance to Forestry Commission track. Follow track for 1.25ml (2km), keeping L at junction. Take track up to summit on LHS. A stiff climb. Do not attempt in poor visibility

This is an interesting group of nine cairns on high open moorland just below the summit of Mynydd Caerau. Three are in line NW–SE south of the summit, and the other six are in line NE–SW across it. Two of the southern group have been disturbed, but the rest are well preserved. A large group like this would suggest some kind of ancestral burial ground.

All are circular mounds of stone from 0.3 to 1.5m high. That to the south of the cairn with a Trig. Point on it is unusual, with an outer bank inside which are two level, shallowly stepped platforms with a mound about 1m high on top of them. This bears some similarity to Crug yr Afan (no. 9) and possibly ultimately to the bell barrows of Early Bronze Age Wessex. The dished tops of some of the smaller Mynydd Caeran cairns suggest disturbance (a common feature of many of the upland cairns), whether out of curiosity or for building material for sheep shelters.

13
Cefn Sychbant Round Cairns, Penderyn

Bronze Age round cairns
2000–1000 BC
OS 160   SN 986110, 985110, 979104   U1/2

Take A4059 N from Hirwaun to Penderyn. At far end of village take minor road R towards Llwyn on reservoir. Cairns are on RHS after 4ml (6.5km), two near road and one c.0.6ml (1km) to SW across moor

These three large stone cairns are typical of the many in this upland limestone area. The northernmost is a ring cairn, a circle of stones within a slight bank. Nearby to its south-west is the second, a large circular pile of stones about 1.5m high. The third is similar but slightly smaller, and has, like so many of these upland stone cairns, been partly reshaped into a modern sheep shelter. Large kerb stones are visible around its edge.

14
Pebyll, Abergwynfi

Bronze Age ring cairn
2000–1000 BC
OS 170   SS 910972   U4

Take A4107 Treorchy to Abergwynfi road. About 1.5ml (2.5km) E of Abergwynfi park on sharp bend and take Forestry Commission track for 1ml (1.6km) to the N. Cairn just to R of old track, which branches R off new one

This is a large oval ring cairn, consisting of a low stony bank with level ground inside it. On the north-east side there are traces of the original kerb on the inner face of the bank. There is an entrance on the south which may have been lined by upright slabs; three are still visible, leaning or fallen. A smaller entrance on the north-west still has one of its

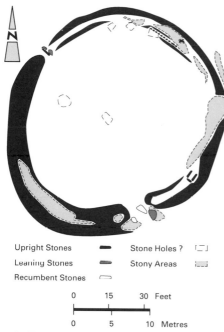

Upright Stones ▬
Leaning Stones ▬
Recumbent Stones ▭
Stone Holes ? ▣
Stony Areas ▨

| 0 | 15 | 30 | Feet |
| 0 | 5 | 10 | Metres |

Pebyll ring cairn

rectangular cist, has the distinction of being mentioned in one of Britain's earliest antiquarian books, William Camden's *Britannia* (1695 edition). This early description of the monument will still serve: 'a circle of rude stones, which are somewhat of a flat form . . . disorderly pitch'd in the ground, of about 17 or 18 yards diameter; the highest of which now standing is not above a yard in height. It has but one entry into it, which is about four foot wide'. There are 25 slabs in the circle, up to 2.5m in length, and most lean outwards slightly. In the middle of the circle is a stone cist with its east side and capstone missing. Earth, presumably from its excavation, is heaped up to the west of it. The 'entrance' is problematical, and there may not have been one. There is no trace of a covering mound.

In all respects except the use of upright stones this would appear to be a normal ring cairn, and by analogy with others in the area it should date to the first half of the 2nd millennium BC.

jamb stones in place. On the south-east of the interior is a small cist with three of its sides still intact. Three small holes to the north may indicate the positions of upright stones, long since disappeared.

15
Carn Llechart Stone Circle, Pontardawe
Bronze Age ring cairn
2000–1000 BC
OS 160   SN 697063   U2

Take A474 Pontardawe to Gwaun Cae Gurwen road. At Rhyd y fro take minor road W on to Mynydd Carn Llechart. Track off on LHS after 0.6ml (1km), cairn a 500m walk

This important ring cairn, with its unusual circle of contiguous slabs around a large

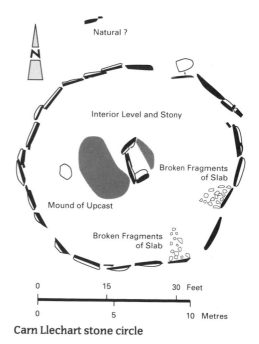

Natural ?

Interior Level and Stony

Broken Fragments of Slab

Mound of Upcast

Broken Fragments of Slab

| 0 | 15 | 30 | Feet |
| 0 | 5 | 10 | Metres |

Carn Llechart stone circle

Nearby to the west are the remains of a presumed Neolithic burial chamber (see Appendix), and there are several more Bronze Age cairns on the ridge.

16
Gray Hill Stone Circle, Llanvair Discoed

Bronze Age ring cairn
2000–1000 BC
OS 171   ST 436935   U4

Take Usk to Llanvair Discoed road to Wentwood. Park at Foresters' Oaks car park and take track to E up to Gray Hill. Continue along ridge for c.300m. Cairn is c.200m off path to S

The climb to the top of Gray Hill is rewarded on a clear day by magnificent views across the coastal plain to the Bristol Channel and beyond. In form the ring cairn is somewhat unusual, and bears similarities to Carn Llechart (no. 15), in that it consists of a circle of 13 (visible) roughly rectangular stones, some touching, some more widely separated. The stones are up to 0.5m high, some laid flat, some set on edge. Two larger stones lie flat on the ground inside the circle and may be the remains of a cist or may be fallen uprights. There is no trace of a covering mound. This part of the monument was probably, in part at least, sepulchral in purpose, by analogy with excavated similar sites elsewhere in Wales. The stones outside it may have had some other function.

To the east is a large standing stone about 1.8m high. To its south-east is a low stone, and to the north are three further large low stones. Beyond them, further north, is another standing stone about 2m high. The purpose of these outlying stones is obscure, but it has been observed that the two largest are set in line with the mid-winter sunrise.

17
Ring Cairn on Graig Fawr, Gerdinen

Bronze Age ring cairn
2000–1000 BC
OS 159   SN 628066   U2

Take minor road from Ammanford to Llangyfelach. At small hamlet of Gerdinen take footpath to W on to ridge. Site c.0.6ml (1km) to W, just to W of N–S trackway

High up on the east side of the Graig Fawr ridge, this ring cairn has lain undisturbed for about three and a half thousand years. Its arrangement is rather unusual. It has a small circle within and against the edge of a larger one. Sites of this composite kind may have had separate ritual and sepulchral functions. The outer one is an almost perfect circle, and is formed by two stony banks separated by a shallow depression, from which the stones for the banks were presumably dug. The main entrance would appear to be a gap on the

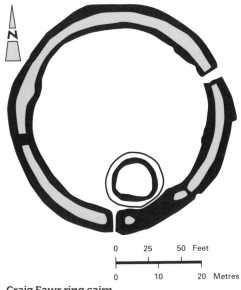

0   25   50 Feet

0   10   20 Metres

Graig Fawr ring cairn

north-east side, with a lesser one on the south side. The smaller inner circle, formed by a low bank and shallow external ditch, has no apparent entrance. A few similar sites that have been excavated were found to have a cremation burial in the inner circle, and palisades around both circles.

The Graig Fawr ridge is rich in Bronze Age burial monuments, with further cairns to the north and west of this site.

18
Penlle'rbebyll, Pontardulais
Bronze Age ring cairn
2000–1000 BC
OS 159   SN 635048   U2

Take minor road from Llangyfelach towards Garnswllt. 1.25ml (2km) N of Felindre, cairn is just to W of road near summit

| 0 | 15 | 30 | Feet |
| 0 | 5 | 10 | Metres |

Penlle'rbebyll ring cairn

This is a slightly unusual ring cairn, set near the summit of Mynydd Pysgodlyn. It comprises a horseshoe-shaped earth bank with a slight external ditch which would appear originally to have gone right around the circle. Inside the bank, lying in the gap on the south, is a smaller, roughly oval bank, with a slight gap on the east side.

The ring around the outside would appear to be a well established Bronze Age type, but the structure inside it is less easy to categorise. It may be similar in function to that at Graig Fawr (no. 17).

19
Cairn Circle on Rhossili Down, Rhossili, Gower
Bronze Age ring cairn
2000–1000 BC
OS 159   SS 421890   U2

Take B4247 to Rhossili. From end of minor road N of church public footpath leads over Rhossili Down. Cairn is just past summit, near path on RHS

Here is an unusual and interesting variant on the standard ring cairn. A circle of upright stones surrounds a level platform about 0.3m high. In some places the stones are contiguous, in others there are gaps, suggesting that perhaps the circle was originally complete. Many of the stones poke up above the level of the platform, which suggests that they may have originally supported an earth- or stone-filled rim. In the middle of the platform is a small hollow, which may be all that remains of a burial cist.

20
Merthyr Common Round Cairns, Merthyr Tydfil
Bronze Age round cairns
2000–1000 BC
OS 170   SO 077045–079032   U2

Take A4060 Merthyr Tydfil bypass. Turn E up minor road on to Merthyr Common c.1.5ml (2.5km) S of A465. First R, keep straight on, avoiding L fork. Cairns start c.0.6ml (1km) from turn, on LHS of road, and then above road on higher ground on RHS. Common road has very bad potholes, but is just passable by car

This is a group of five cairns strung out along the ridgetop of Merthyr Common and loosely associated with a trackway which may be prehistoric in origin. The northernmost three lie on the lower part of the ridge just east of the modern road. First there is a small one, then two larger, both of which are of ring cairn type, with banks of stones around the edge. The interior of the second is flat and is covered with small stones, suggesting some kind of original platform. On the higher ground to the south are two further smaller cairns, both now turf-covered.

21
Cairn Cemetery on Rhos-Gwawr, Aberdare
Bronze Age cemetery
2000–1000 BC
OS 170   SN 989010–998008   U2

Take B4277 Aberdare to Maerdy road. Park on summit above steep climb out of Aberdare. Cairns on moorland to S beginning c.500m (0.25ml) from road

Scattered over this high plateau are some 44 cairns. Small Bronze Age cairns can be very difficult to find in featureless expanses of moorland, and these are no exception. Most are small circular piles of stones, now largely turf-covered. A few are bigger and tend to be outliers of the three main groups. These groups are loosely arranged, the first below the crest of the plateau, the second straight ahead beyond the fence in undulating ground, and the third near the edge of the plateau a few hundred metres to the south of this group.

The nearest cairn to the road (SN 989010) is one of the larger ones and has a well preserved small cist exposed in the middle. Another outlier (SN 995007) is a ring cairn, with a circular stony bank around a level interior. There are several stretches of turf-covered stony bank associated with the cairns. They are low, 5–9m long, and their orientation would suggest that they were designed to give some shelter from the north-west. They raise the possibility that the Bronze Age inhabitants of this area were actually farming the ridge, and that some or all of the smaller cairns may be clearance cairns rather than burial mounds.

22
Round Barrows on Garth Hill, Pentyrch
Bronze Age round barrows
2000–1000 BC
OS 171   ST 104835   U2

Take minor road N out of Pentyrch towards Gwaelod y garth. After 500m take track on LHS which leads to public footpath up to Garth Hill. Barrows on summit

Strung out in a line along the summit of Garth Hill is the finest surviving group of Bronze Age barrows in the area. Their commanding position, and the size of the largest, suggest that this was the burial ground of important persons.

There are four large well preserved mounds and one small one, all turf-covered. They range from about 0.6m to about 4.3m high. The largest, second from the west, is imposing, and exceptionally well preserved. At its foot, on the east, is a small mound, its top hollowed out by later digging. The easternmost mound, also disturbed in the centre, is the second largest and is surrounded by a ditch.

Garth Hill, the largest barrow

23
The Beacons Round Barrows, Llanharan

Bronze Age round barrows
2000–1000 BC
OS 170   ST 017840   U1 (by car), U4 (walking)

Take A473 Llantrisant to Llanharan road. About 0.8ml (1.5km) take minor road N towards Ynysmaerdy. 1.8ml (3km) along take Forestry Commission track on LHS. Beacons c.1.25ml (2km) up track (L, R, R, R at junctions), next to track, on LHS. Access by foot, or permission to take car from Forestry Commission

Like the barrows on Garth Hill (no. 22), these two are superbly situated on a ridgetop overlooking the Vale of Glamorgan, and, it is tempting to suggest, are the burial mounds of important persons. They are high, steep-sided, and circular, slightly shaved off on their north sides by the forestry track. Their tops have been disturbed, leaving them uneven and hollowed out. The name of the barrows, and the extensive panorama they command, make it possible that they were indeed subsequently used as beacon platforms.

24
Begwns Round Barrow, Mynydd Machen, Machen

Bronze Age round barrow
2000–1000 BC
OS 171   ST 224900   U4

Take A467 from Newport to Risca. A number of possible routes by foot up to Mynydd Machen from Risca, Crosskeys or a ridge track starting at Pontllanfraith to the N. Barrow on summit at southern end of ridge

This large barrow is situated on high ground with a commanding prospect over the coastal plain. Garth Hill (no. 22), the Beacons (no. 23), and this one are all worth a visit, on a clear day, just for the views alone. The barrow is a large, steep-sided, circular mound. Small stones on the surface suggest that it is at least in part composed of stony material.

25
Wentwood Round Barrows, Llanvair Discoed

Bronze Age round barrows
2000–1000 BC
OS 171   ST 417945   U2

Wentwood, the larger of the two round barrows

Take minor road from Usk towards Llanvair Discoed. At Pen y cae mawr crossroads at top of hill (coming from Usk) turn S (R, from Usk direction). In c.500m park and walk along track to L. Barrows on LHS

These two round barrows lie on the top of the Wentwood ridge to the east of the Usk valley. The outlook is panoramic, if now hedged in by trees. The question of the original Bronze Age surroundings of these ridgetop barrows is interesting. Only at one Bronze Age cairn, Crug yr Afan (no. 9) is anything known of the surrounding environment. There it was heathy, with a light covering of mainly oak woodland. It may have been similar here, although this ridge is considerably lower than Crug yr Afan, and may always have been more densely wooded.

The barrows are two steep-sided, flat-topped, circular mounds, one slightly larger than the other. Large beech trees grow on their slopes, and there is a possibility that they were deliberately planted there, perhaps in the 19th century, as happened at other similar British sites.

26
Twyn Cae Hugh Round Barrow, Ynysddu
Bronze Age round barrow
2000–1000 BC
OS 171   ST 174915   U4

Turn S off A472 on W edge of Pontllanfraith up small road. Continue S for c.1.8ml (3km) along road and track. Site near track on LHS

This is a large, well preserved barrow on a moorland ridgetop. Large stones exposed in a hole on the north side suggest that beneath the turf surface the barrow may be at least in part constructed of stony material. This ridge, between the Rhymney and Sirhowy valleys, is rich in Bronze Age burial monuments. There are small cairns to the north-west and south-east, and at the southern end of the ridge is the imposing Begwns barrow (no. 24). This might suggest that the burials are associated with nearby settlement, or that a trackway, near which the burials were placed, ran the length of it.

27
Harold's Stones, Trellech
Bronze Age standing stones
?3000–1000 BC
OS 162   SO 499051   U2

The stones are in a field just S of B4293 on southern edge of Trellech. Access via stile from road

This is one of the very few prehistoric stone alignments in south-east Wales (see also no. 16), and as such is of great interest. The village name means – 'the village of stones'.

Three large stones of a conglomerate puddingstone, a rock found locally, are set in a 12m NE–SW alignment. The southernmost stone is the largest, but all are over 2m high. The central stone may have been shaped, and

Harold's Stones

About 1.25ml (2km) NW of Neath, on Mynydd Drumau. Public footpaths from N, S or E. Easiest access from N via minor road W out of Bryn Côch

This is an isolated large stone, standing about 4.3m high. It is of local sandstone and is incorporated into a later field wall. Its purpose, like that of most of the standing stones in the area, is obscure. It could mark a burial or a trackway, or it could have had a ritual significance.

has two cup marks on its south side. All lean at different angles, giving a slightly drunken character to the whole.

Any attempt at interpretation of the function of these stones is fraught with difficulty. A ritual, sepulchral or even astronomical function is possible, or a combination of some or all of these. Although usually ascribed to the Bronze Age, by analogy with other stone alignments such as the avenue at Avebury, Wiltshire, or the alignments of Carnac in Brittany, Harold's Stones may well be Middle to Late Neolithic. Why they are called Harold's stones is a complete mystery, but one theory is that the name may have become attached to them as a result of Earl Harold's victories in the area in the years immediately before the Norman conquest.

29
Bridgend Standing Stone, Bridgend
Bronze Age standing stone
?3000–1000 BC
OS 170   SS 902795   U1

In Bridgend turn S off A473 down Glan y parc Road towards the Leisure Centre. Stone stands in grass on S side of road in front of the Bowls Centre

This pillar-like stone now stands rather incongruously in the middle of a modern urban development. It is of sandstone, and stands about 1.8m high. The vertical grooves on the north side are natural.

In 1964 the stone was lifted from its hole, and was found to be buried some 0.8m deep, with some large packing stones around it. Beneath it were the burnt bones of an adult and some charcoal, which were either a ritual dedicatory deposit or a burial that the stone marked.

28
Carreg Bica Standing Stone, Neath
Bronze Age standing stone
?3000–1000 BC
OS 170   SS 725995   U2

30
Sampson's Jack, Llanrhidian, Gower
Bronze Age standing stone
?3000–1000 BC
OS 159   SS 477921   U2

Sampson's Jack

Take minor road from Llanrhidian towards Llanmadoc. At Oldwalls fork R, continue to Windmill Farm, on LHS. Public footpath past farm. Stone in hedge on RHS

This is one of a group of eight remaining standing stones scattered below the western end of the Cefn Bryn ridge (see also nos. 31, 32, 33). At 3.2m high it is the tallest of the group. Like the others it is of the local quartz conglomerate. It has roughly vertical sides rising to a blunt top.

31
Burry Menhir, Knelston, Gower
Bronze Age standing stone
?3000–1000 BC
OS 159   SS 464901   U2

On public footpath across Knelston Hall Farm. Start either at farm at S end, on A4118, or at minor road E of Burry at N end. 250m from N, 0.7ml (1.25km) from S end of path

Burry Menhir

Unfortunately this impressive stone fell in 1947. It is one of the largest of the group below the Cefn Bryn ridge, and would have stood 3m high. After falling its hole was excavated but only packing stones were found. There is evidence, in the form of an 18th-century estate map, that this was originally one of three stones in a row. In fact, to the south-south-east of it, in the hedge, is a small, low, upright stone which might have been part of this alignment. There are two further standing stones in the vicinity (nos 32 and 33).

32
Burry Lesser Standing Stone, Knelston, Gower
Bronze Age standing stone
?3000–1000 BC
OS 159   SS 462290   U2

As for no. 31, not far from it to W

The nearness of this stone to the Burry Menhir (no. 31) suggests that it may have been associated with it in some way. It is 1.6m high, only half the original height of the Burry Menhir, although it has been suggested that the unevenness of the top may be the result of an upper part breaking off.

33
Burry Standing Stone, Knelston, Gower
Bronze Age standing stone
?3000–1000 BC
OS 159   SS 469892   U2

As for no. 31, but c.250m N of Knelston Hall Farm, on public footpath

This standing stone is similar to the others in the area in all but shape: instead of being roughly pillar-shaped it is triangular, about 2.2m high and across the base. It is not known whether the shape of the stone had any significance for those who erected it.

Burry lesser standing stone

Burry standing stone

4

The Iron Age

The Iron Age in south-east Wales followed on from the Bronze Age without any obvious cultural or population break. Iron tools, weapons and ornaments started to appear in the first half of the 1st millennium BC, but were initially rare. The most impressive collection of Iron Age objects from the area, now in the National Museum of Wales in Cardiff, was recovered from the Llyn Fawr reservoir south of Hirwaun in 1911 when the natural lake was drained. This must have been a ritual deposit of some kind, and dates from about 600 BC. It includes, as well as bronze tools and ornaments, an iron sword from the Continent.

The main evidence for occupation of the area in the Iron Age shifts from burials, which dominate the record of the Bronze Age, to settlements. Evidence for burial in the Iron Age is scant, such as in the inner ditch at Nash Point fort (no. 43); in this period only part of the burial practice is reflected in the archaeological record. Iron Age settlements are chiefly found in, or on the fringes of, the lowlands. The uplands appear to have been less intensively utilised at this time: the distribution of hillforts inland suggests that it was the valleys which were the focus of attention. Known Iron Age settlements generally took the form of enclosures surrounded by single or multiple banks and ditches. Hilltop settlements, known as hillforts, are common, which leads one to suppose that defence was a primary consideration in their siting.

The hillforts in the area vary greatly in size and complexity. By far the most numerous are the small to medium-sized forts, home to perhaps a few families or, in the case of the smallest, a single family. There are a few larger ones in south-east Wales, but by the standards of the rest of mainland Britain they are only medium in size. The banks around the forts, built up of earth, rubble and stones, are sometimes single (univallate), sometimes multiple (multivallate). Excavation has shown that some at least had an outer revetment of drystone walling or large stones. They are almost always accompanied by an external ditch, which often has an outer or counterscarp bank, built up of material from the ditch. The ditches were usually originally steep-sided, and were sometimes cut into the underlying rock. At some forts there are several enclosures, sometimes with small univallate enclosures inside large multivallate ones (nos 45 and 52, for example). Another variant layout is that with widely spaced concentric banks (nos 38, 39 and 40, for example). These are of a type very often found on a hill-slope rather than a hilltop,

Check-Out Receipt

Alameda Free Library
Bay Farm Island Branch Library
3221 Mecarteny Road
Alameda, CA 94502
Tel: 510-747-7787
www.alamedafree.org

Checkout Date: 06-27-2015 : 13:38:21

Patron Number: xxxxxxxxxx7220

---

1 Rick Steves' Europe: Great Brit
33341004585906   Due Date: 07/18/15

Total Items: 1

Balance Due: $ 0.00

Libraries now closing at 5:00 p.m.
on Thursdays.

Reconstruction drawing of the east gate at Twyn y Gaer hillfort, *c.*400 BC–AD 100

and their entrances often face downhill, which suggests that defence was not a primary consideration in their siting. They are more frequently found across the Bristol Channel, and may indicate cross-Channel links. Several, such as nos 38 and 39, are found in the uplands. It is thought that they were chiefly concerned with stock raising, and that the outer areas were animal pens. They usually have a small central enclosure, well defended by surrounding banks and ditches, which was probably for human occupation. A further variant is the promontory fort which makes use of a natural headland for its defences, and only has banks and ditches across the neck of the promontory. This type is particularly common on the Gower peninsula, where many of the sea headlands were used in this way (nos 58–62).

There have been only a few small-scale excavations of these Iron Age hillforts in south-east Wales, and very little is known about their dating. More extensive excavations elsewhere in Wales, for instance at Moel y Gaer, Clwyd, show a considerable degree of complexity. A linear development from simple univallate forts to complex multivallate ones is only valid in the most general way: it is known, for instance, that some univallate forts, such as Twyn y Gaer (no. 50), continued in use late into the period. It is probable that by the end of the Bronze Age some small defended settlements were appearing in the area, and some of the univallate forts with simple entrances could have originated as early as this. Some forts, such as Castle Ditches (no. 34) and Llanmelin Wood (no. 56), have a preceding small univallate fort underlying a much larger one. The same may be true of small univallate enclosures within larger ones, such as at Lodge Wood (no. 52) and Summerhouse (no. 45).

Entrances may give a clue as to date: simple gap entrances are thought to be early, inturned ones later. This sequence is followed at Twyn y Gaer. It is reasonably certain that multiple ramparts represent the last phase of development of the defences of the hillfort. These can be seen at their most impressive at sites such as Lodge Wood (no. 52), Llanmelin Wood (no. 56), Sudbrook (no. 57) and Coed y Bwnydd (no. 51).

Houses found within the hillforts were round, flimsy structures, with the roof supported either by a ring of posts alone or a ring of posts and a central one. They have been found at Coed y Bwnydd (no. 51), The Knave (no. 60) and High Pennard (no. 62). They sometimes show up on the ground as level platforms or slight depressions: one is visible at The Bulwark, Llanmadoc (no. 40), and about 20 small hollows at Dunraven (no. 42) are thought to be house sites.

The Iron Age economy appears to have been mixed, with pastoralism dominating. In the Glamorgan uplands there are six simple undefended settlements, the largest of which (nos 63 and 64) are included here, which may have had a specialised pastoral function. They are so high, and in such windswept locations, that it may be they were occupied in the summer only. Their material poverty makes it unclear if they date from the Iron Age or the Roman period, or both.

One last category of prehistoric monument included in the guide is the cooking mound, of which there are very few known in the area. There may be many more, but their form – a low, rather shapeless mound – may lead them to go unrecognised. Their date is problematical, and many may, like those excavated in Dyfed, be of Bronze Age date. However, the only one excavated in the area (no. 65) dates from the Iron Age.

By the time the Romans arrived in south Wales, in the late 1st century AD, the population of the area was organised into a well defined tribe, known to the Romans as the Silures. At what stage of the Iron Age this tribe emerged is not known. Certainly the Romans found it hostile, with a military strength which took them over 25 years to break.

34
Castle Ditches, Llancarfan
Iron Age hillfort
700 BC–AD 100
OS 170   ST 059700   U2

Take minor road towards Moulton out of Llancarfan. Fork L on edge of village. At Hands Farm public footpath to site on LHS. Off path permission required from owner (Castle Lodge, further up road)

Hogg 1976

This is a large, univallate hillfort, situated on the west end of a spur in the rolling countryside of the Vale of Glamorgan. Its position is a good one for defence, with steep slopes below it on all sides but the east. An oblong area is enclosed by a single large bank and external ditch, with an outer, counterscarp bank on the west and south-west sides. The bank is high and steep on the outside, and excavation has shown that it was constructed of clay and rubble, and revetted with stone on the outside at the most vulnerable east end. The ditch was originally flat-bottomed and deepest at the east end.

The main entrance was in the middle of the

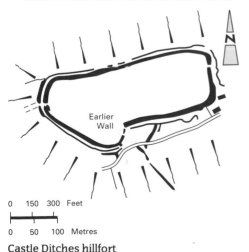

Earlier
Wall

0   150   300 Feet

0   50   100 Metres

Castle Ditches hillfort

south side, at an oblique angle. Field boundaries have obscured its original form, but there is evidence that it was at least partly inturned. Beneath the entrance traces were found of a wall which is thought to have been part of an earlier smaller enclosure, which was built not earlier than the 4th century BC. It was superseded by the large hillfort which was built not earlier than the 2nd century BC. Cultivation has removed all traces of occupation in the interior.

35
Mynydd y Castell Hillfort, Margam
Iron Age hillfort
700 BC–AD 100
OS 170   SS 806867   U4

Leave M4 at junction 38 and take A48 SE for a short distance. Turn L into Margam Country Park. Follow signs for house, and take path to its R which leads up to hillfort

From the track leading up to the fort it is easy to see why this hill was chosen for a defended settlement. Its sides are precipitous, and at its southern end a sheer rock face makes it even more impregnable. The visitor enters the site through what was probably an original entrance on the north-east. On the north side of the entrance there is a suggestion of a guard chamber, and there may have been one on the other side as well (as shown in the reconstruction drawing on the information panel). There is a secondary, much simpler entrance on the south-west side.

The hilltop is defended by a single rampart. On all but the east side this is a large scarp with a level terrace or berm outside it. On the east side, however, this becomes a massive bank, outside which is a ditch and smaller counterscarp bank.

The interior of the fort is rather surprising. There is a large sunken brick and concrete area, which is the top of a reservoir, a Scots pine plantation and some rhododendrons,

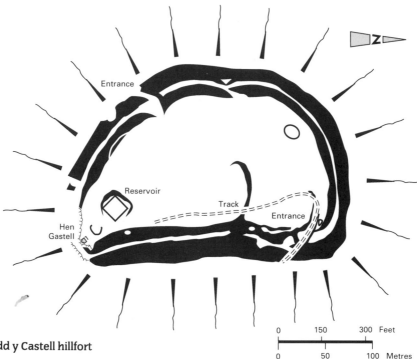

Mynydd y Castell hillfort

0 150 300 Feet

0 50 100 Metres

which bear witness to the fact that the fort was incorporated into the landscaping of Margam Park during the 19th century. Indeed, a small summerhouse, now ruined, called Hen Gastell, was in place on the southern summit of the hill by 1811. A low scarp running part of the way across the middle of the fort is thought to represent an earlier phase of settlement, with the scarp forming the northern limit of its smaller enclosure.

36
Three Forts on Hardings Down, Llangennith, Gower
Iron Age hillforts
700 BC–AD 100
OS 159   SS 434908, 437906,
437908   U4

On E edge of Llangennith take track to Hardings Down to S, or various public footpaths. Forts on top and N side of hill

Two hills at the west end of the Gower peninsula, Hardings Down and Llanmadoc Hill (see no. 40) have large hillforts on them. On Hardings Down there are three quite close together. They are all different, and may have served different purposes. Whether or not they were contemporary is not known.

The largest and most complete is the westernmost one. This has a main enclosure, roughly oval in shape, defended by a substantial single bank and ditch. Excavation showed the bank to be rubble-built, with a drystone revetment on the outside. On the weakest, east side, there are two stretches of outer rampart below the main enclosure, the outermost of which continues around towards the north as a low scarp or bank to form a partial outer enclosure. The entrance to the main enclosure is on the north-east side, where this outer scarp meets the main bank. It is a simple gap with a level track leading up to it. Excavation showed that this entrance was cobbled, its sides stone-lined, and was closed by gates supported on four large posts, the holes for which were found in the corners. Inside, the remains of two round huts were found, along with a few pieces of mid-Iron Age pottery. A further hut platform, just to the south of the northernmost one, was left unexcavated.

On the summit of Hardings Down is a semicircular rampart that appears to be an unfinished hillfort. A short stretch of isolated bank on the west side indicates its intended extent. This bank repays closer examination as there is a short stretch of stone revetment still in place on its inner face. The fort has a single bank and in places a ditch. The entrance is a simple gap in the middle of the east side. Beyond it on this side is an incomplete outer enclosure, smaller than the main one, surrounded only by a low bank or scarp. This outer annexe may have been intended for animals.

To the north of the summit is a small circular enclosure surrounded by a bank, ditch and for the most part a counterscarp bank. This smaller 'fort' would appear to be just a defended homestead for one or perhaps a few families. Its entrance, on the north-west side, is approached by a hollow way between low stony banks. Inside there is one circular hut platform on the west side up against the bank. There is another similar enclosure on Druids Moor, south-east of Hardings Down.

37
Caerau Hillfort, Cardiff
Iron Age hillfort
700 BC–AD 100
OS 171   ST 134750   U2

In Cardiff fork S off A48 Cowbridge Road down Caerau Lane in Caerau district. Turn L down Caerau Road, then straight over the wide Heol Trelai into Church Road. Park at end of road and walk up track to hillfort

This is one of the largest multivallate hillforts in south-east Wales. Its size and strategic position on the top of a steeply sloping spur overlooking the Ely and Taff valleys to the north and east suggest that here was an important settlement, perhaps the focus of the local population.

The fort follows the outline of the spur, which gives it a rather odd triangular shape, with a narrow 'nose' out to the west. The steep slopes to the north and south-west are defended by three parallel scarps. The gap at the western end is not an original entrance, but is caused by spring water seepage. The southern end of the south-east side has the most massive defences, with a huge bank and external ditch with a counterscarp bank at its southern end. The northern end of this side has been disturbed by the later construction of a medieval ringwork in the north-east corner of the fort (no. 90).

There are two entrances, quite close together on the east side. The northernmost one, where the lane to the church enters the fort, is inturned, with banks on both sides. In the south corner is another entrance up what may have been a natural gully. A low scarp cuts off a roughly rectangular area at the east end of the fort between the two entrances.

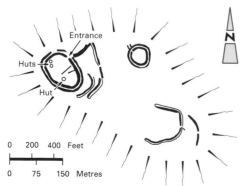

0   200   400   Feet

0   75   150   Metres

The three forts on Hardings Down

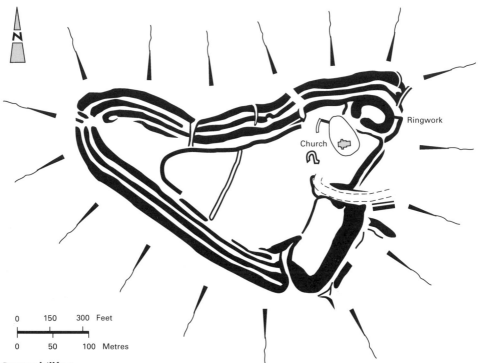

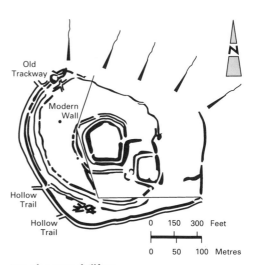

0   150   300   Feet

0   50   100   Metres

Caerau hillfort

This enclosure may either represent the earliest phase of occupation of the site, or it may have been an annexe of some sort, possibly for animals.

38
Y Bwlwarcau, Llangynwyd
Iron Age hillfort
700 BC–AD 100
OS 170   SS 838886   U4

Take A4063 Bridgend to Maesteg road. Turn W on to minor road to Llangynwyd c.1.25ml (2km) S of Maesteg. After Llangynwyd continue W for c.1ml (1.6km) until sharp LH bend. Track to site straight on up hill, for 750m

Fox and Fox 1934, Fox 1952

Y Bwlwarcau hillfort

0   150   300   Feet

0   50   100   Metres

High up on the eastward-facing slope of Mynydd Margam, this is one of the largest and best preserved forts in the area of a type which appears to have been primarily pastoral. Its hill-slope position and small central enclosure with widely spaced banks outside are best explained by a stock-raising function rather than the defence of a territory.

Y Bwlwarcau is complex. On the ground its layout is rather difficult to comprehend, so large is the area, and so many are its low banks, which stop and start in a rather confusing way. This complexity may be the result of several phases of development, but this theory has yet to be tested by excavation.

In the centre is a small, roughly pentagonal area enclosed by a bank and an impressive steep-sided ditch up to 2m deep. This was presumably the living quarters of the fort's occupants. The main entrance is a simple gap on the east side. Outside the ditch is an outer bank, ditch and low counterscarp bank, which may be earlier than the inner ones. Outside the central enclosure a much larger area is surrounded by two and in places three more or less concentric small banks and ditches. These converge on the north-west side, where an old trackway enters the area through a simple gap which may be an original entrance. Along the north side, at the top of a steep valley, the multiple banks give way to a single scarp, ditch and counterscarp bank. Cultivation and field boundaries have obscured some of the outer banks on the east side, but an entrance gap is still visible in the middle, with a hollow causeway running from it to the entrance to the inner enclosure. In the south-east corner is a rectangular enclosure, surrounded on the north, south and west by a shallow ditch and discontinuous inner and outer low banks. It is an interesting exercise to try to unravel all the complexities of this site, with its disconnected banks, tracks, gaps and all the confusion caused by the addition of later field walls and possible medieval house sites.

39
Maendy Camp, Treorchy
Iron Age hillfort
700 BC–AD 100
OS 170   SS 957955   U4

Take A4061 Treorchy to Bridgend road. On edge of Treorchy take B4223 straight on towards Ton Pentre. Take forestry track on RHS up to site (turn sharp L half way up). Path on LHS up to fort near top of track

Williams 1902

Situated on the edge of a spur overlooking the Rhondda valley, this is one of the few Iron Age hillforts in the Glamorgan uplands (see also nos 38 and 41). Its layout is of the same 'pastoral' type as that of Y Bwlwarcau (no. 38), with a small central enclosure and widely spaced low outer banks, the snake-like meanderings of which are rather difficult to follow on the ground. The main bank forms a horseshoe-shaped central enclosure, whose entrance is the wide gap on the south side, then loops back northwards to form the outer bank. On the east side it continues as a scarp at the top of the steep slope and picks up

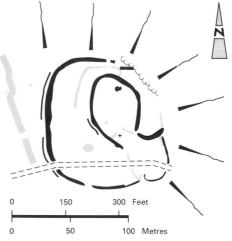

0   150   300 Feet
0   50   100 Metres

Maendy Camp hillfort

again as a bank on the north side. It continues clearly around the west side, where it is best preserved, and becomes fainter on the south side, in the middle of which is a faint inturned entrance. Further stretches of low stony bank extend from the outer to the inner ramparts on the south side, to the west of the entrances, and form an incomplete subrectangular enclosure on the north side, between the two main enclosures.

Excavation in 1901 revealed a stone pavement in the outer entrance, and a 'cist', probably a posthole, in the inner one. A hole in the ground marks its position. A Bronze Age cairn between the inner and outer ramparts on the west side was also excavated. The ramparts have been much robbed and tampered with, and may originally have been more substantial.

40
The Bulwark, Llanmadoc, Gower
Iron Age hillfort
700 BC–AD 100
OS 159   SS 443928   U4

500m S of Llanmadoc, at NW end of Gower peninsula. Footpaths up hill from edge of village. Fort on E end of ridge

Although the widely spaced ramparts of this fort suggest a primarily pastoral function, defence must have been an important consideration, or the fort would not have been situated in such a strategic and easily defensible position on the edge of the summit of Llanmadoc Hill.

The rather complex plan of the hillfort suggests that it may be the result of more than one period of building. First, in the middle is a subrectangular enclosure of almost 1 ha, surrounded by a massive bank, with an external ditch on all but the north side, and an outer, counterscarp bank along the south. A straight stretch of rampart

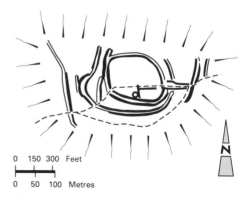

0   150 300 Feet

0   50   100 Metres

The Bulwark hillfort

adjoins the west side, at a slight angle to it. The awkward way these merge towards their north ends suggests that the inner enclosure may have been superimposed on this outer rampart. Beyond is another outer rampart on all but the steep north side. A further, straight rampart runs N–S across the saddle of the hill to the west, giving extra protection from this, the most vulnerable side.

The entrance, a simple gap, is on the east side, with a entrance way bounded by low banks running up to the fort through a series of outer banks and the main outer rampart. Just inside, on the left-hand side, a low bank and outer ditch delineate a small rectangular enclosure, with a gap near the main entrance, which may be an earlier enclosure or an animal annexe. To its west is the probable position of a circular hut platform.

41
Craig y Dinas, Pontneddfechan
Iron Age hillfort
700 BC–AD 100
OS 160   SN 913080   U4

Take A465 Swansea to Merthyr Tydfil road, and turn off N at Glyn Neath. Take B4242 E towards Pontneddfechan. Park at E end of village in old quarry. Footpath up N side of promontory to hillfort on top

In the narrow angle between the confluence of the Mellte and Sychryd rivers is a high rocky promontory, with almost sheer sides down to the rivers below. Dramatically situated on top of this is an Iron Age hillfort. Natural defences take care of all but the north-east side, where the ground slopes less steeply. Here the fort was completed by two large stony ramparts. The innermost one runs right across the promontory, with a possible entrance where a modern cart-track crosses it towards its southern end. The outer rampart, built on top of a natural scarp, encloses a roughly triangular annexe on the northern side of the promontory. At its outer end, where it turns sharply north-westwards, there is a short section of rock-cut ditch outside it. The annexe may have been for animals, with the main area behind the inner rampart reserved for human habitation.

42

Dunraven Hillfort, Ogmore-by-Sea

Iron Age hillfort

700 BC–AD 100

OS 170   SS 887727   U2

Take B4524 to Southerndown. Take minor road S out of village to beach car park. Fort is at S end of bay, on headland

The hillfort (see illustration overleaf) stands on the spectacular headland of Trwyn y Witch at the south end of Dunraven Bay. Coastal erosion has eaten into it on both sides, where there are vertical cliffs, but enough of the ramparts and interior remain intact to give a good idea of the original fort. This is the westernmost of a series of hillforts spaced out at regular intervals along the Glamorgan coast from Bridgend to Barry (see also nos 43–47).

The first part of the fort that the visitor encounters, climbing up the steep headland from the car park, is the eastern end of a small outer annexe. It is now reduced, through coastal erosion, to a narrow triangular area bounded by a bank on its south-east side.

To the south-west the ground rises steeply, and it is here that the main ramparts of the fort are situated, running eastwards from the cliff along the contours until they are cut off abruptly by a wall of the now demolished Dunraven Castle. Originally they would have continued to the other side of the promontory. The ramparts are two large parallel banks with a combined height of about 12m, which rise in giant steps up the hill. The ditches on their outer sides appear originally to have had V-shaped sections, visible in the cliff edge. The original nature of the banks is uncertain, and there is no evidence for stone revetment. The original entrance is thought to have been eroded away, and the present-day visitors' footpath cuts through a modern gap.

Immediately behind the inner rampart aerial photography has picked up the line of a bank and ditch which are not immediately apparent on the ground. This may represent an earlier phase at the site consisting of a smaller, univallate fort.

Within the ramparts, on gently sloping ground, are about ten shallow hollows which may be Iron Age house sites. To the south the ground rises more steeply to the summit of the peninsula. A low bank encloses the higher ground, within which are six further possible house platforms. On lower ground towards the Trwyn y Witch headland are a further five, and also a group of medieval pillow mounds. These low, oblong, rounded mounds were man-made rabbit warrens.

The inner end of this windswept head-land is the unlikely location of Dunraven Castle, only the footings of which remain. Here a medieval manor house was replaced at the beginning of the 19th century by a Gothic mansion. The house was demolished in 1962; its walled garden lies in the sheltered valley below.

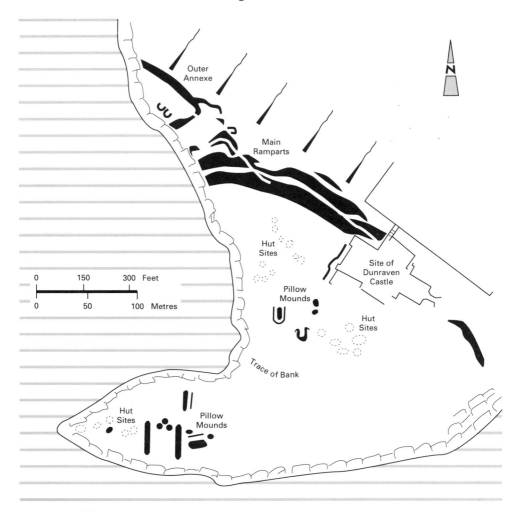

Dunraven hillfort

43
Nash Point Fort, Marcross
Iron Age hillfort
700 BC–AD 100
OS 170 SS 915684 U2

Turn S to Marcross off B4265 Llantwit Major to St Brides Major road. Continue to the sea and

park on clifftop. Fort c.500m (0.25ml) to NW along coastal path

Most of this clifftop hillfort appears to have been eaten away by coastal erosion; only a narrow tongue of the promontory is left, with a precipitous cliff on the seaward side and a steep bank down to the Marcross valley on the other. Iron Age man turned this exposed

Nash Point hillfort from the air

site into a fort by throwing banks and ditches across its now narrow neck.

The main defences consist of four parallel banks set close together. The three inner ones are steep-sided, with ditches between them. A crouched burial was found in the lower filling of the innermost ditch. The outer bank, to the north of a small gully, is much longer and gentler. It cuts off the peninsula and guards the approach, which was up the gully and along a narrow shoulder southwards to the entrance on the east side of the three inner banks. The innermost bank curves inwards next to it, making it half an inturned entrance.

Hollows in the interior are of modern origin, but the long, oblong mound is a medieval pillow mound similar to those at Dunraven hillfort (no. 42).

44

Castle Ditches, Llantwit Major

Iron Age hillfort

700 BC–AD 100

OS 170   SS 960674   U2

Take B4265 to Llantwit Major, and in centre of village take minor road S to the sea (signed to beach). Fort is above car park on its E side

In his autobiography *Some Small Harvest*, Professor Glyn Daniel, the late eminent prehistorian, recalled being summoned by his headmaster at Barry County School, who asked 'Have you seen the Castle Ditches?'. He replied that he went there to pick blackberries. The headmaster 'snorted', told him what it was, and ordered him to go and look at it in a different light. It is a large,

Aerial view of Castle Ditches

triangular, multivallate fort and its coastal position is a good defensive one, with a sea cliff on one side and a steep drop to the Col huw valley on another. Only on the east side, where the ground is level, was there a need for artificial defence. Here three large closely set ramparts were thrown up. The inner one, which is built mainly of limestone rubble from the cutting of the ditch, is the highest. The middle one, which is largely earthen, is the lowest.

The original entrance is thought to have been removed by coastal erosion, and the present-day gap at the north end of the banks probably post-dates the Iron Age. A short stretch of low bank and ditch near the western angle of the fort, along the top of the slope down to the Col huw valley, may be a remnant of an earlier univallate fort.

45
Summerhouse Fort, Llantwit Major
Iron Age hillfort
700 BC–AD 100
OS 170   SS 994665   U2

In Boverton, just E of Llantwit Major, take minor road to Boverton Mill Farm. Continue past it to car park just before end of road. Fort

c.500m (0.25ml) along public footpath. Coastal footpath passes through the fort

This coastal fort is semicircular and multivallate, with a sheer sea cliff along the straight south side. Within it is a smaller, univallate enclosure, also semicircular, which may either represent an earlier phase than the outer ramparts, or may have been contemporary. If coastal erosion has removed a substantial amount of this hillfort, as seems likely, it could originally have been circular.

The public footpath from the landward side enters the fort across a modern causeway through the two main ramparts, which are clearly visible on both sides. To the right the path runs inside them to the cliff edge, where it joins the coastal path, which crosses the ramparts to the west. The visitor can get a good idea of their size and shape here, and see how dramatically they have been cut off by erosion. Eastwards the coastal path runs through the inner enclosure, now densely overgrown, and crosses the east ramparts. Here there is a slightly different configuration, with the inner bank of the other sides becoming a scarp, and an extra bank being added below the two main ramparts. Pits dug in 1934 suggested that the middle rampart had a frontal revetment of large limestone blocks.

The 'summerhouse' of the name is an 18th-century octagonal pavilion, now a roofless shell, which stands inside the fort. It is set in an octagonal enclosure surrounded by a low wall with mock fortifications.

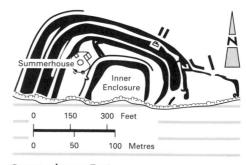

Summerhouse Fort

46
The Bulwarks, Rhoose
Iron Age hillfort
700 BC–AD 100
OS 170   ST 081663   U2

Take minor road off A4226 Barry to Llantwit Major road, towards Rhoose. After Lower Porthkerry turn L down minor road to caravan park on cliff edge. Footpath on E side to fort

Gardner 1935; Davies 1973

This large hillfort is trapezoidal in shape, bounded on the south by the sea cliff, on the east by a steep drop to a shingle beach, on the north by a steep drop to a gully (now occupied by a railway cutting) and on the west by level ground.

It is on the level west side that the main defences are found. They consist of an outer ditch and two massive closely set banks. They are heavily overgrown, and can best be seen from the footpath, which may cut through the ramparts on the site of an original entrance. In 1968 excavation in the interior revealed three rectangular buildings behind the innermost rampart. The earliest is undated, and the other two date from the 1st–2nd centuries AD

and the 3rd–4th centuries AD. This hillfort would therefore seem to have continued in use well into the Roman period.

47
Sully Island Fort, Sully
Iron Age hillfort
700 BC–AD 100
OS 171   ST 169670   U4

3km E of Barry take B4267 Barry to Penarth road. Just E of Sully turn S to Swanbridge. Walk across tidal causeway to island. Fort is on E end. Causeway only open at lowish tide. Consult tide tables at landward end before crossing

Perched on the eastern end of this small island is a hillfort unlike the large forts along the coast to the west in that it is small, with widely spaced ramparts. This would suggest a defended homestead like the promontory forts of the Gower peninsula (nos 58–62) rather than a full-scale settlement, with the outer area perhaps reserved for animals.

The outermost line of defence is a ditch, scarp and bank. The bank, which is up to 2m high, is the most substantial part. Where the promontory narrows, near its eastern end, is the inner line, which consists of a low scarp and slight outer ditch. A gap at its north end may have been an entrance. At the very end of the promontory is a small, flat-topped mound of uncertain age and purpose.

48
Mynydd y Gaer, Pencoed
Iron Age hillfort
700 BC–AD 100
OS 170   SS 973850   U2/R2

Take minor road N out of Pencoed towards Rhiwceiliog. Carry on for c.500m after Rhiwceiliog. Park just short of Coedcae Farm

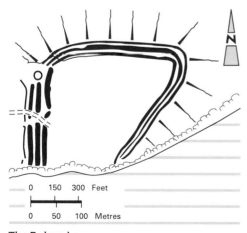

```
0    150   300  Feet
|----+----|
0    50    100  Metres
```

The Bulwarks

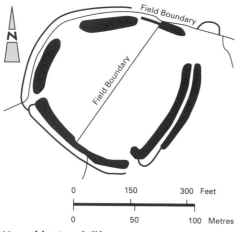

Mynydd y Gaer hillfort

700 BC–AD 100
OS 161 SO 321230 U2

Turn off A465 Abergavenny to Hereford road into Llanfihangel Crucorney. At bottom of hill turn R off Llanthony road. After c.0.6ml (1 km) turn L. Continue to end of road. Fort on moorland immediately to N

and take public footpath across moor on RHS to N side of fort (c.250m). Off-path permission from owner needed (Cadair Farch Farm).

The interesting feature of this site is the possibility that it is unfinished. It is a medium-sized hillfort in a hilltop position, from which there are panoramic views. A massive, well preserved bank with an outer ditch and counterscarp bank encloses a roughly circular area. Farming operations have interfered somewhat: field walls run along the bank on the north-west and north-east sides, the outer ditch has been destroyed at the north end of the south-west side, and a gap has been made in the west corner for access to the interior. The original entrance was probably in the south corner, where the bank has a slight inturn on its east side. The large gaps on the north-west and north-east sides are thought to be original, and lead one to suppose that the fort is unfinished.

49
Pen-twyn Hillfort, Llanfihangel Crucorney
Iron Age hillfort

Guarding the southern ends of three of the four ridges of the Black Mountains are three Iron Age hillforts: Crug Hywel (in Powys) at the southern end, Twyn y Gaer (no. 50) in the middle, and Pen-twyn at the northern end. Of the three, Twyn y Gaer is the one about which most is known. Excavations there produced evidence of occupation over a long period, and several phases of construction. Superficially, Pen-twyn would appear similar, and may well have a similar history.

This is a large oblong fort, with panoramic views over the Herefordshire plain to the east and the Black Mountains to the west. It uses the steep natural slope as a boundary on the east side. On the north side, where the ground rises gently, it is bounded by a large steep-sided bank with an outer ditch. The enclosed area to the south is divided in two by a large cross-bank, with a ditch on its

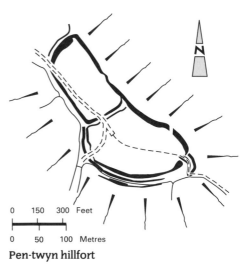

Pen-twyn hillfort

south side, which suggests that it may have formed the southern side of an enclosure built before the area to the south was enclosed within the fort. The smaller northern half may therefore be the oldest part.

The southern defences are now rather scanty on the west side, with a low bank and outer scarp next to the farm road. Along the south side are a series of scarps, of which the innermost is the highest. The outermost line of defence is just beyond the field wall at its west end, and beneath it at its east end.

The most interesting feature of the southern half is the elaborate entrance in the south-east corner. Offa's Dyke footpath passes through it, and if approached from below its cunning defensive arrangement can be fully appreciated. Visitors are channelled up a curving path flanked on the left by a high knoll and on the right by a curving bank. Gates presumably closed the entrance at the inner end.

50
Twyn y Gaer Hillfort, Llanfihangel Crucorney
Iron Age hillfort
700 BC–AD 100
OS 161   SO 294219   U2

Take B4423 off A465 Abergavenny to Hereford road into Llanfihangel Crucorney. Continue towards Llanthony for c.1.25ml (2km) to crossroads. Turn L up steep hill and continue to end of road. Fort short walk up hill ahead

Probert 1976

This is the middle of the three forts guarding the southern approaches to the Black Mountains (see also no. 49), and occupies the top of a knoll at the southern end of the Fwthog ridge from which the views are spectacular.

A bank, rock-cut ditch and counterscarp bank enclose a roughly oblong area, with an outer bank on the west. Two cross-banks,

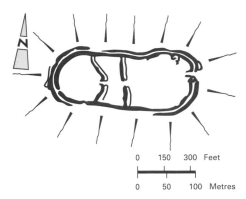

Twyn y Gaer hillfort

with ditches on their eastern sides, divide the enclosure into three parts, the easternmost part being the largest, the central the smallest. At the eastern end of the main enclosure is an inturned entrance, with its flanking banks clearly visible. The entrance in the middle bank is a simple gap, and that in the western cross-bank is slightly inturned towards the west.

Partial excavation of the site in the 1960s has given much information about its structure and development. The main bank was found to have had a drystone revetment, and in its latest phase a stone rampart walk on top. The first phase at the site, early in the Iron Age, consisted of a roughly oblong enclosure whose eastern end was the central cross-bank with the simple entrance gap. The western cross-bank was not there at this time. The area to the east was enclosed with birch fencing, and was probably an animal annexe. There is a radiocarbon date of about 400 BC for the end of this phase. Next, the eastern annexe was enclosed by a bank and ditch, and the eastern entrance made. This had a stone-revetted passageway and a gate at its inner end. Various refinements and rebuildings of the entrance took place before the last phase, when the westernmost cross-bank and ditch were built and the fort contracted to the small enclosure thus made at the west end of the site.

It is almost certain from the remains of hut platforms and the range of domestic Iron Age objects found during excavation that the site was permanently inhabited. The economy was mixed, with querns indicating cereal cultivation, and iron slag and crucibles indicating some form of iron working. In the earlier phases similarities of finds to those of the hillforts of mid-Wales and Herefordshire show a cultural affinity with the tribe of that area. In the last phase it would appear that influence from the tribe to the south, known to the Romans as the Silures, had become uppermost.

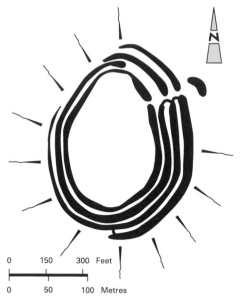

51
Coed y Bwnydd Hillfort, Bettws Newydd
Iron Age hillfort
700 BC–AD 100
OS 161   SO 365068   U2   National Trust

Coed y Bwnydd hillfort

Take minor road to Bettws Newydd either from old A40 Raglan to Abergavenny road, or A471 Usk to Abergavenny road. In village turn E up hill, fork L at 1st junction. Fort on LHS, park in layby. Entrance gate

Babbidge 1970–1, 1977

This is a smallish but well defended fort in a good defensive and strategic position on a hilltop overlooking the Usk valley. In spring it is carpeted with a succession of wild flowers, from wood anemones to bluebells.

The fort is roughly circular, and defended on all but the north-west side, where there is a steep natural slope, by multiple banks and ditches. These are most impressive along the east and south-east sides, where there are three parallel banks and an inner scarp, which becomes a bank on either side of the entrance on the level east side. The arrangement of the entrance is unusual for this area in that there is a simple gap in the defences protected by a curved outlying bank, now reduced to a low

bump in the next field. Of the three ramparts the middle is the largest. The inner one is only about half its height, while the outer is somewhere between the two. The outer ditch and bank stop rather abruptly on the south side, giving rise to speculation that this part of the fort might not have been finished.

A section cut through the ramparts on the south side during excavations in 1969–70 showed that what is now the inner scarp was originally a clay bank, built and then rebuilt on a stone footing. The outermost ditch differed from the inner two in that it appeared to have been filled in quickly, shortly after it was cut. This suggests that the outer bank and ditch were added at a late stage and were perhaps unfinished and deliberately slighted.

On the north-east side the inner bank, which now stops so abruptly, was found to have continued, and to have been revetted on the outside with a turf wall on stone footings, and on the inside with timber posts and some kind of fencing. On the top of the rampart was a walkway about a metre wide. On this side there was a further inner bank with flanking ditches deliberately filled in at a late stage, and now completely levelled off.

Behind the ramparts the excavations found evidence of occupation which indicated probable dense settlement over a considerable period. The sites of four round houses were excavated. Their walling was of wattle and daub on a stone and clay footing. One house had been rebuilt on the same site, and radiocarbon dates of around 400 BC were obtained from the second phase, which would make it contemporary with the end of the first phase at Twyn y Gaer (no. 50). If the fort was already multivallate at this early stage in the Iron Age then the development of hillforts in the area may be more complex than has previously been thought.

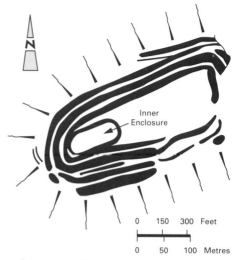

Lodge Wood hillfort

52
Lodge Wood Hillfort, Caerleon

Iron Age hillfort

700 BC–AD 100

OS 171   ST 323913   U2

On NW edge of Caerleon. From centre take Malpas road. After LH bend turn R up hill. At end of road two public footpaths cross the fort, one to W, one to NW

Modern Caerleon has crept out to and almost engulfed its prehistoric ancestor, the hillfort on the top of Lodge Wood hill. This is one of the larger and more impressive hillforts in the area, occupying a strategic position overlooking the Usk valley and the coastal plain. It was traditionally known as Belinstock, the stockaded enclosure of Beli or Belin, who may have been a local chief.

The fort is oblong, with ramparts all around it. The large gap in its south-east corner may possibly have been an original entrance. To the right is a massive bank, the only one remaining of the original three banks on all but the north end of this side. The outer

banks were destroyed by the building of Lodge Farm. The long, steep north side is defended by three high scarps. Towards its west end the outer two become banks, and as they near the end they become more and more massive. The main entrance, a simple gap in the ramparts at this narrow west end, is flanked by three huge banks, the middle the largest, the outer the smallest. To the south the arrangement of banks is somewhat confused, and may be the result of several phases of rebuilding: the outer one stops and then starts again on another alignment, and two further banks complicate matters – one very small one between the middle and outer banks, and one outside the 'outer' bank. The east end of the long south side is badly preserved, and all but a scarp continuing the middle bank has disappeared.

An interesting feature of this fort is the small elliptical enclosure enclosed by a simple bank, which lies within the hillfort at its west end. It is similar to that at Summerhouse Camp (no. 45) and may represent an earlier phase of occupation, or may just be an inner enclosure within the main one.

53
Tredegar Hillfort, Newport
Iron Age hillfort
700 BC–AD 100
OS 171   ST 289868   U2

*On W edge of Newport. Turn uphill off the main
road to Bassaleg opposite the cemetery. Turn
R into Gaer Park Avenue. Entrance at end of
road*

This is a fine large hillfort in a commanding
position on the end of the ridge, overlooking
the lower reaches of the Ebbw river, and now
a good stretch of the M4 motorway. A
motorist on the M4 approaching Newport
from the west has a good view of it.

The fort is roughly circular, with widely
spaced outer and inner enclosures. In this
respect it falls into the same category as forts
like Y Bwlwarcau (no. 38), with the outer area
thought to have been for stock. Unlike others
of this kind, however, it is in an excellent
defensive position. The inner enclosure,
disfigured by an old golf course tee and
bunker, is roughly pentagonal, and is
surrounded by a single bank and ditch, partly
destroyed on the east side, and strongest on
the west and south. Its entrance appears to
have been on the north-east side, but further
gaps of unknown origin in its east and south
sides complicate the picture.

The outer enclosure was defended by a
large bank and ditch, at their most massive on
the level north-east side. On the east they
have been partially destroyed by quarrying.
Along the steep slope on the west the bank
becomes a scarp with a ditch and an outer
counterscarp bank, while on the south side a
further outer bank and ditch branch off to
form another outer enclosure. Gaps in all
three banks on this side may be original
entrances.

In the late 17th to early 18th century the
hillfort was integrated into an ambitious

Tredegar hillfort from the air

ornamental landscaping scheme by the Morgans of Tredegar House below by being used as a focal point in the layout of avenues radiating out from the house.

54
The Bulwarks, Chepstow
Iron Age hillfort
700 BC–AD 100
OS 162   ST 538927   U2   Cadw

In Chepstow take Bulwark Road S off A48. At roundabout fork L and turn immediately L into Alpha Road. Fort at end of road

With its superb natural defences, this site closely resembles many of the other coastal forts in the area, with a steep cliff, here down to the mouth of the river Wye, forming the main part of the defences. Further strength is given by the deep ravine on the south side. Artificial defences had only to be constructed on the west and north-west sides. These consist of multiple ramparts, the innermost

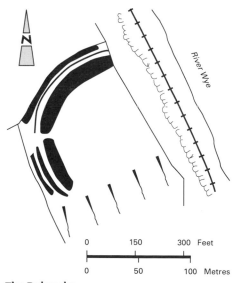

The Bulwarks

being the most massive. They are well preserved in dense scrubby woodland, and can best be seen near the present entrance.

The fort is fairly large, and in form it would appear similar to some of the forts of the late Iron Age, such as Sudbrook (no. 57) a few miles away along the coast.

55
Pierce Wood Hillforts, Chepstow
Iron Age hillforts
700 BC–AD 100
OS 162   ST 532957   U2, 536959   U4

W camp on Wye Valley Walk between Chepstow and St Arvans, c.0.6ml (1km) from Chepstow. E camp to the E of it, on end of promontory, off path

These hillforts occupy spectacular positions on the top of the cliffs which drop sheer down to the river Wye just north of Chepstow. The western one is the smaller, roughly square, and surrounded on three sides by a bank, with the cliff forming the fourth, north side. Elements of the 18th-century landscaping scheme of Piercefield Park can be found within it, including a small grotto next to the Wye Valley path on its eastern side.

The second, eastern fort is by far the more interesting, but is unfortunately the more inaccessible. It is a long, oblong enclosure lying along the top of the cliff, which forms its northern boundary. Its banks are built of large, angular stones, and although now somewhat spread, are still impressively large. On the north-east and south-east sides there is a single bank, very high and steep on the outside, quite low on the inside. Outside, a level area lies between the bank and a steep natural rock face, outside the eastern end of which there is a stretch of ditch. On the south-west where the ground is level the defences are more complicated, with the same large inner bank, a ditch, then after a gap a further earthen bank and outer ditch. These stop just short of the cliff edge, leaving a narrow passage which may have been the entrance. All that is left of the entrance through the main bank are two hollows and a high promontory to their north-west which was probably part of a guardpost. The only visible feature in the interior is a low cross-bank near the western end which runs half-way across the fort.

56
Llanmelin Wood Hillforts, Caerwent
Iron Age hillforts
700 BC–AD 100
OS 171   ST 461925,
463928   U2   Cadw

Take minor road N from A48 at Caerwent towards Llanvair Discoed. First fork R, continue for c.0.6ml (1km). Forts on RHS reached by track at end of wood: smaller one on LHS of track, larger across field and through wood to SW

Nash-Williams 1933

The questions most often asked about this site are whether this complex of enclosures was the immediate native predecessor of Roman Caerwent (no. 67) and whether it was the capital of the local tribe, the Silures, at the time of the Roman conquest. Its size, strategic position overlooking the coastal plain, its nearness to Caerwent and its demise apparently at the time of the Roman conquest all suggest that it might have been both these things.

The main enclosure is a large multivallate hillfort. It is surrounded by two, and in places three large well preserved banks, which are highest near the partly inturned entrance on the south-east side.

To the south-east of the main enclosure a series of outer, smaller banks are tacked on to

form annexes. These are subrectangular, with no apparent entrances except in the outermost one. A further earthwork, the so-called outpost, lies in woodland about 200m to the north-east, near the road. It is a small C-shaped enclosure, with a double embankment.

Extensive excavation in 1930–2 showed that the fort originated in the 3rd century BC as a smaller enclosure surrounded by a single bank and ditch, most of which is now obscured by the later banks. A small stretch of this early earthwork can be seen outside the main banks on the north-east side. The 'outpost' is thought to be contemporary with this earliest phase. Its purpose is uncertain, but may have been stock coralling. Then around 150 BC, at about the same time that the forts at Lydney (Gloucestershire) and Sudbrook (no. 57) appear to have been built, the main multivallate enclosure was constructed. The inner bank was revetted on its outside with roughly coursed stone, and the ditches were cut into the underlying rock. Evidence of settlement inside the ramparts was scanty in the area excavated but it is very likely that the fort was inhabited, and bones found showed that domestic animals and red deer were present.

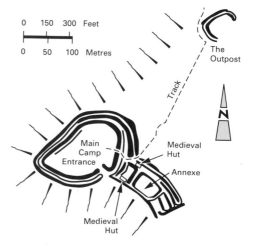

Llanmelin Wood hillforts

The third and last phase at Llanmelin, which began around 50 BC, involved the remodelling and strengthening of the entrance, which suggests an increased threat of attack. Its north-east side was cut back and refaced, and both sides were given flanking timber platforms and palisades on top of the banks. A wooden gate was placed at the inner end. The annexes were added during this phase, possibly for the coralling of animals, as there are no signs of human occupation. The whole fort seems finally to have been abandoned around AD 75.

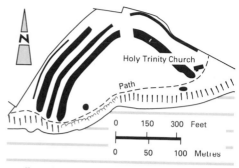

Sudbrook Fort

57
Sudbrook Fort, Portskewett
Iron Age hillfort
700 BC–AD 100
OS 162   ST 505873   U2

In Portskewett turn S by church, over railway, keep R, and park at end of road by Pumping Station. Public footpath to W to camp

Nash-Williams 1939

The Tudor antiquary William Camden described Sudbrook fort as a bow, the string of which was the cliff, and this is indeed an apt description: it has a massive curved inner bank and a straight seaward side formed by a small cliff. It is one of a series of hillforts along the shores of the Bristol Channel. Most are to the west of Cardiff, but Sudbrook, The Bulwarks (no. 54) and Lydney (Gloucestershire), are spaced out along the Channel's upper reaches.

The modern communication links across the Bristol Channel near this point suggest Sudbrook's purpose: it was strategically placed to guard the best crossing, between Aust and Portskewett, the 'Old Passage' described by early travellers such as Camden and Sir Richard Colt Hoare.

Coastal erosion has probably reduced the original area of the fort. It is enclosed by a massive, well preserved bank, with two,

possibly three smaller banks outside it on the north-west side. No outer banks are visible on the north-east, but when two cuttings were made across the ramparts in 1934–6 they were found to have continued here with two V-shaped ditches between them. The main bank on the north-west side was found to have been built up in four stages, and the inner face had two steeply sloping revetments of rough walling, one inside the other.

Inside the bank on this side two subrectangular quarry ditches were found. Finds from them indicate that the site was occupied from the mid-2nd century BC to early in the 2nd century AD, that is, from the later Iron Age into the beginning of the Roman period. They also indicate that from the mid-50s AD the site was held by the Roman army, probably to guard the ferry crossing.

Some notion of the way of life of the occupants can be gleaned from the finds, which indicated that they kept oxen, pigs and sheep (or goats), and were engaged in glass making and iron working.

58
Burry Holms Promontory Fort, Llangennith, Gower
Iron Age hillfort
700 BC–AD 100
OS 159   SS 399926   U4

Aerial view of Burry Holms at high tide

In Llangennith take minor road NW to the Burrows. Park at end of road and walk c.0.8ml (1.5km) to headland. Fort accessible only at lowish tide

Nine of the many headlands on the south and west Gower coast were defended and occupied during the Iron Age. All the sites are relatively small, and should be thought of more as defended homesteads of perhaps one or two families rather than full-scale villages. Where dating evidence has been found it appears that the sites belong to the late Iron Age, and were even occupied into the Roman period. Two such sites are on the promontories at either end of Rhossili Bay – Burry Holms at the north end, and Worms Head at the south. Burry Holms possesses marvellous natural defences, and at high tide the headland becomes an island, making the site even more impregnable.

The highest, outermost part of the headland was fortified by a high bank, ditch and outer counterscarp bank. The bank runs north–south straight across the headland,

and the ditch makes use of a natural fault. The entrance is a simple gap with a causeway across the ditch in the middle of the bank.

On the inner east end of the headland the remains of an early Christian hermitage have been found (see Appendix), and the remains of the succeeding 12th-century church and later ancilliary buildings can be seen.

59
Thurba Promontory Fort, Rhossili, Gower
Iron Age hillfort
700 BC–AD 100
OS 159   SS 422871   U4

Take B4247 towards Rhossili. At Pitton turn L into village. Coastal footpath from end of village. Thurba Head c.500m

The stretch of rocky coast between Worms Head and Port Eynon Point is particularly rich in these small defended homesteads, perched precariously on top of the cliffs. There are five in all (see also nos 60 and 61), and Thurba Camp is typical of them.

This narrow, rocky headland would seem an unpromising place to live, but there are definite signs of occupation. First, the headland is defended on its landward side by several stretches of bank and ditch. The outermost rampart is reduced to a scarp on the north-west side, and a rubbly bank with a faint outer ditch on the east. The main rampart lies behind this, and consists of a more substantial bank and ditch. Within this is a robbed wall along the edge of the summit of the plateau which may represent an earlier phase of the site. A further stretch of walling, blocking a possible way in from the south, completes the defences. Any remains there might be on the south side are obscured by quarrying and an old limekiln.

60
The Knave Promontory Fort, Rhossili, Gower

Iron Age hillfort
700 BC–AD 100

OS 159   SS 432864   U4

1.5ml (2.5km) SE of Rhossili, on coastal path. Access same as for no. 59, but further E

Williams 1939

This fort, sometimes known as Deborah's Hole camp, is the next eastwards from Thurba Camp. Its semicircular ramparts cut off an area of half a hectare on the clifftop just west of the broken cliffs called The Knave. On the landward side is a double arc of man-made defences, each arc consisting of a bank and outer ditch. The inner, rubbly bank is the

Thurba, The Knave and Paviland promontory forts

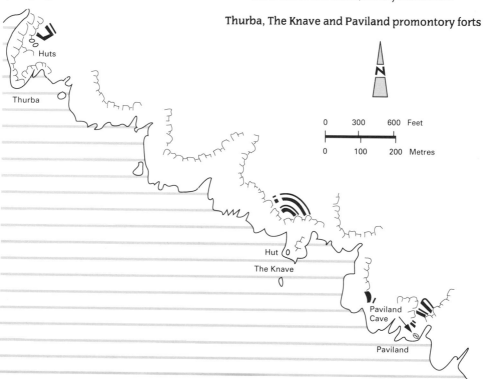

larger, reaching nearly 3m high at its east end. Entrances in both arcs are at the west end.

Inside the ramparts nothing of Iron Age date is visible, but in 1938 the site was excavated and the remains of two round huts were found. Finds indicated a mixed economy, and included pot-boilers (stones for heating and plunging into water to heat it), shells, bones of sheep (or goats) and oxen, and slingstones, possibly for defence. The ramparts were investigated and the inner bank was found to have been revetted on the inside with squarish stone blocks, and on the outside with irregular boulders. The outer bank was more crudely revetted with stone, and its external V-shaped ditch was rock-cut. Across the entrance were three postholes, indicating closure by double gates.

61
Paviland Promontory Fort, Rhossili, Gower
Iron Age hillfort
700 BC–AD 100
OS 159   SS 437860   U4

1.8ml (3km) SE of Rhossili on coastal path. Several access points to path, from Rhossili, Pilton Green or Port Eynon

This is another in the series of small clifftop forts on the coast between Worms Head and Port Eynon. It occupies the top of a long narrow headland, with deep valleys on either side and a spectacular sheer cliff on the seaward side, in which is the famous Paviland Cave (no. 1).

There are four lines of defence, and slingstones have been found here. At the seaward end a small area is enclosed by an impressive bank of rubbly limestone, outside which is a natural depression. The entrance must have been at the east end of the bank, where there is a narrow gap between it and the cliff edge. Within this enclosure are six rough platforms – possible hut sites – which

are the only signs of habitation.

Further away from the sea edge are three further lines of defence – the first an apparently unfinished rock-cut ditch, the second a shallow ditch with a low bank inside it, with an entrance towards the east end, and the third and outermost line a larger bank, again of limestone rubble, with an external ditch. The entrance may have been at the north-west end of the bank.

Nearby, to the west, is Horse Cliff camp, another small defended homestead.

62
High Pennard Promontory Fort, Bishopston, Gower
Iron Age hillfort
700 BC–AD 100
OS 159   SS 567866   U4

1.8ml (3km) SW of Bishopston, on coastal path. Access to path either at Caswell or Southgate. Fort just W of Pwlldu Head

Williams 1941

This small defended homestead is well protected naturally by cliffs and steep slopes on all sides but the north and north-east. Here it has two lines of ramparts. The inner cuts off the whole headland and is divided into two by a natural scarp which runs down the spine of the promontory. The defences consist of two parallel scarps to its north, the inner one more massive, and to the south a bank with a slight outer ditch. The entrance is in the middle of this section. The outer defences consist of a bank and outer ditch to the south of the spinal scarp.

Excavation in 1939 revealed a stone revetment and rampart on top of the northernmost scarp, and postholes showing that the entrance was closed by a pair of gates. An interesting feature found inside the rampart was a rock-cut gully leading to a pit. Its purpose is obscure, but could have been water collection. Evidence of occupation was found in the interior, showing a mixed economy of farming, gathering, fishing and hunting. The site was in use in the late Iron Age and continued to be occupied until about the 2nd century AD.

63
Blaenrhondda Ancient Village, Treherbert
Iron Age settlement
700 BC–AD 100
OS 170   SN 923018   U1/2

Take A4016 Treherbert on Hirwaun road. Site is 2.5ml (4km) N of Treherbert on open moor near road. Main part on either side of track leading down into valley

This is the largest undefended Iron Age settlement in south-east Wales. Like the few others of its kind (see also no. 64) it is on high, open moorland, and was possibly a summer settlement only, a 'hafod', for use when

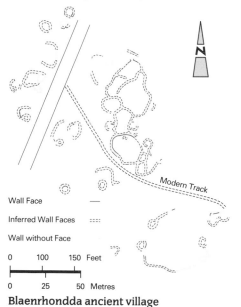

Wall Face —
Inferred Wall Faces ::::
Wall without Face

0   100   150 Feet
|————|————|

0   25   50 Metres
|————|————|

Blaenrhondda ancient village

animals were taken up to the high pastures.

The remains are an incoherent, irregular jumble of tumbled stone walls, never more than a metre high. There are large and small round houses, large and small enclosures, and stretches of walling which sometimes link up with the houses and sometimes stop abruptly in the middle of nowhere. The walling is all interlinked, forming a loose and extremely amorphous 'village'. The nucleus is to the left of the track leading down into the valley, a smaller grouping lies on the right, while there is an outlier further away to the west near the pylon line. The crude walls would originally have been drystone, probably supporting roofs of thatch.

Life at this high altitude must have been harsh, and the material poverty of the occupants was revealed by excavations in 1921 which found almost nothing, only a little iron and evidence of leather. Nothing to suggest a date was found, but pottery from a similar but smaller site in the area, Hendre'r Gelli (Ystradyfodwg), is 2nd and 3rd century AD. It is thought, therefore, that the site is Iron Age or Roman or both.

The long early medieval cross-ridge dyke of Ffos Ton Cenglau (no. 81) is visible to the north-west of the village, further up the west side of the valley.

64
Buarth Maen Ancient Village, Merthyr Tydfil
Iron Age settlement
700 BC–AD 100
OS 160   SO 013053   U4

From centre of Merthyr Tydfil take minor road W up hill to Heolgerrig. Continue up hill to summit. Walk across moor to NW c.0.6ml (1km) to site, which is on roughly level ground below the summit

This is one of the larger and better preserved of the small group of late Iron Age–Roman

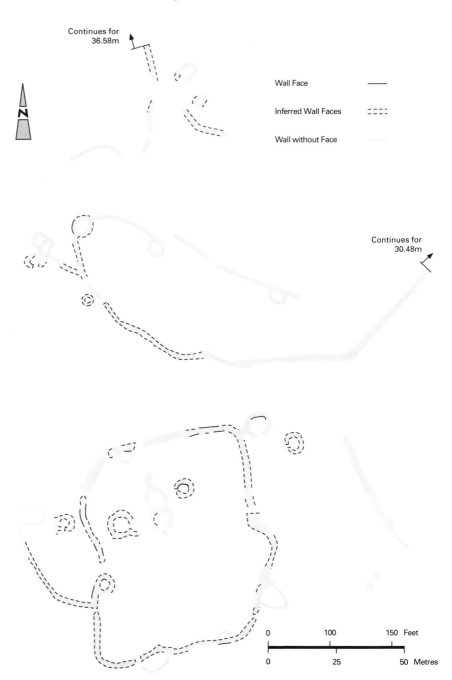

Continues for
36.58m

N

Wall Face ————

Inferred Wall Faces = = = =

Wall without Face ———

Continues for
30.48m

| 0 | 100 | 150 | Feet |
| 0 | 25 | 50 | Metres |

undefended settlements on the Glamorgan uplands. Like Blaenrhondda ancient village (no. 63), it lies on open moorland in an exposed position. It displays a similar markedly irregular and haphazard plan, although these ramblings do resolve themselves into recognisable features. There are two, possibly three larger enclosures, with small rectangular and circular huts dotted about inside and outside them and set into their walls. The walling has for the most part been reduced to lines of fallen stones, no more than half a metre high; but in places, in particular in the southernmost enclosure, the walls retain their facing stone and stand to a height of about a metre.

65

Cooking Mound East of Taff Terrace, Cardiff

Iron Age cooking site

700 BC–AD 100

OS 171   ST 134800   U2

Take A4119 and B4262 N out of Cardiff to Radyr. In Radyr turn R to station, where turn R into Junction Terrace. Continue to end, and walk a short way on public footpath to site, on RHS in woodland

Grimes and Hyde 1935

This rather shapeless, roughly oval mound, now landscaped into an amenity area, stands at the foot of a steep slope, with a small stream, necessary for the cooking operations, running along its west side. It is composed of burnt stones, charcoal and black earth, some of which is visible on the surface. Pottery fragments found during excavation in 1916 indicate occupation during or before the 1st century AD. Interestingly, all the tree species now growing in the surrounding woods, with the exception of birch, were identified in the charcoal in the mound.

The method of cooking was to fill a trough with water, heat stones over a fire, and then plunge them in the water to heat it. Food would then be cooked in the hot water. The mount is a by-product of this process, built up out of the discarded stones, charcoal and burnt earth from the fire. The absence of ordinary occupation debris, such as meat bones, suggests that the cooked food was eaten elsewhere.

Buarth Maen ancient village

5
The Roman Period

In their conquest of Britain the Romans came up against formidable opposition, one of the main sources of which was the tribe called the Silures. The Roman author Tacitus called the Silures 'swarthy, with hair mostly in tight curls'. They occupied an area roughly equivalent to the modern Gwent, Glamorgan and most of the old county of Breconshire, and it took the Romans nearly 30 years, between AD 49 and AD 77, to overpower them. The Romans moved steadily westwards into Wales, arriving in the Monmouth area in about AD 50. In AD 74 the Roman governor Julius Frontinus mounted a concerted campaign, probably using the 2nd Augustan Legion. The area to the east of a line from Cardiff to Abergavenny to Hay-on-Wye was then overrun in about two years. Thereafter Romanisation appears to have been rapid, and opposition to Roman rule crumbled in south Wales.

The Romans left their stamp on the area in two ways: through their military organisation and through civilian settlement. First, military control involved a legionary base and a system of roads, marching camps and auxiliary forts. The legionary base was initially at Usk (*Burrium*), from the mid-50s, but was soon moved to Caerleon (*Isca*, no. 66), which was founded in AD 75. Of the Usk fortress nothing remains above ground, but parts of the Caerleon fortress are visible. Caerleon was the home base of the 2nd Augustan Legion for about 200 years, although after the initial conquest it frequently campaigned elsewhere.

The road system permitted rapid military deployment to any part of the area. The main road ran along the coastal plain from Gloucester to Carmarthen, taking in Caerwent (no. 67) and Caerleon. Another road ran from Caerleon up the Usk valley and along the Tywi valley to Carmarthen, and north–south roads ran from the fort at Brecon to Neath via Coelbren, and to Cardiff via Penydarren, Gelligaer and Caerphilly. At each of these places there was an auxiliary fort, each designed to be a day's march or about 20km apart. Only small sections of Roman road are still visible (the best ones being near the fort of Coelbren, in Powys).

There are a small number of marching camps on upland ridges in south-east Wales (see no. 72 and Appendix). These are thought to date from the early phase of Roman campaigning in the area, and were used as temporary bivouacs, possibly only for one night. A small bank with a ditch outside it was thrown up to enclose a rectangular area in which the troops were housed in tents. All that can be seen of

Caerwent Roman town from the air

Caerleon amphitheatre

them are the remains of the slight banks and ditches (again the best one is in Powys, at Y Pigwn).

The auxiliary forts in the area were all built between about AD 75 and AD 90, and were only intensively occupied for 50 years at the most. By about AD 170 only Brecon and Cardiff forts were still occupied, and by then they probably had only a skeleton staff. They were 1–3ha in size, built to house 500 infantry (*cohors quingenaria peditata*), or in some cases a part-mounted cohort (*cohors quingenaria equitata*). The location of most of the forts in the area is known, but there is one 'missing' between Cowbridge and Neath which may be the *Bovium* (or *Bomium*) mentioned in a Roman text. It is thought to lie west of Bridgend, possibly near Kenfig. Some of these forts have been excavated, or partly excavated, and Gelligaer (no. 68) is the one about which most is known, and whose second, stone phase, built between AD 103 and AD 112, is thought of as a classic fort of the period.

The construction and layout of legionary fortresses and auxiliary forts were similar and more or less standard, the main difference being in the much greater size of the former. They were not built for defence, as all fighting was done outside them. All were constructed to a high standard, with the usual Roman amenities such as baths, drains, running water and heating (which was confined to the baths and sometimes the commanding officer's house). The contrast with native settlements must have been dramatic. In the 1st century construction was of earth and timber, but from about AD 100 they were built or rebuilt in stone. Gelligaer was the earliest fort in the area to be built in stone, closely followed by the long-drawn-out rebuilding of Caerleon fortress. Even in 'stone' fortresses and forts there was still much timber building, for instance in the superstructure of the barracks. The plan was rectangular with rounded corners, the so-called 'playing card' shape. This was formed by a turf- or timber-revetted earth bank, or a stone wall, with one or more external V-shaped ditches. There was an entrance gate in each side, and towers at regular intervals along the wall. The layout of the interior was tight and orderly, with the principal administrative buildings and granaries in a central block in both fortresses and forts. Barracks, officers' houses (in fortresses only) and other utilitarian buildings filled the rest of the space, with cookhouses and latrines on the fringes. Fortress baths were also within the walls, but at the forts, for instance at Gelligaer, they were in a separate annexe outside. Forts and fortresses could have many ancillary features, such as amphitheatres, parade grounds, shrines, temples, cemeteries, harbours and quays. A few of these are known in the area, most notably at Caerleon, which has a famous amphitheatre, the only completely excavated one in Britain, a parade ground, cemeteries and quays. At Gelligaer there is a parade ground, and up on the common to the north there are five 'practice camps' (see Appendix) where troops from the fort made miniature marching camps as part of their training.

Towards the end of the Roman period, when instability of rulership induced a new insecurity, some forts in Britain were adapted for defence, with higher walls, fewer and narrower entrances and towers along the walls. Forts of this kind along the south coast of Britain are known as 'forts of the Saxon shore'. The last fort at Cardiff (no. 69) was one of these, and the civilian settlement of Caerwent (no. 67) was adapted in the same way.

Hand in hand with the military occupation of south-east Wales went Romanisation of its inhabitants. At some stage in the 2nd century a tribal capital, or *civitas*, was established at Caerwent (*Venta Silurum*). This was the capital of tribal administration, run on the Roman municipal pattern, and it was occupied well into the 4th century.

Towns are known to have grown up around Caerleon fortress and Cardiff fort, and civilian settlement probably developed next to some of the other forts as well. There was, for example, a civilian settlement next to Brecon Gaer in Powys. Evidence has also been found for a certain amount of industrial activity, for instance iron working at Cardiff and Ely villa (where coal was used as a fuel for heating), and lead mining at Machen. The coastal strip of Gwent and Glamorgan was probably intensively farmed in the Roman period, and a number of villas and Romano-native farmsteads have been found in the area. The latter show that Iron Age inhabitants adopted Roman building methods and layouts on their existing farms. A number of more important houses, or villas, have been excavated, notably Whitton, Llantwit Major and Ely (see Appendix), and these show that a fairly sophisticated, fully Romanised standard of living was achieved by some of the richer local inhabitants. Although the hillforts of the Iron Age appear mostly to have been abandoned in the Roman period, a few, such as Caer Dynnaf (see Appendix) were reoccupied.

The Roman period seems to have ended in confusion and disarray at around the close of the 4th century. By this time most of the Roman troops in the area had long since been posted elsewhere (the 2nd Augustan Legion finally left at the end of the 3rd century), and only the civilian settlements were occupied. The citizens of Caerwent were the last to go, some time in the 5th century. Roman buildings were squatted in, plundered for their stone, or deliberately dismantled. The Roman occupation faded into a distant memory.

66
Caerleon Legionary Fortress, Caerleon
Roman legionary fortress
AD 74/5–mid-3rd century
OS 171   ST 338905   U1   Cadw

c. *3ml (5km) NE of Newport (B4596 road from Newport, junction 25 on M4). Park in centre of Caerleon at Fortress Baths or Amphitheatre. Cadw standard hours and entrance charge at Baths and Museum*

Wheeler and Nash-Williams 1970; Boon 1972; Moore 1979; Zienkiewicz 1986; Knight: Cadw Guide

Caerleon is one of the most important Roman sites in Britain. Beneath the centre of this unassuming village lay Isca, one of two legionary fortresses (the other was at Chester) on which depended the entire system of roads and forts designed to control the belligerent tribes of Wales. Isca was well placed to subdue the intractable Silures, who occupied south-east Wales.

Much is known about this fortress. It has been extensively excavated, first in 1843 and then intermittently from 1926 onwards. The mosaic of excavations all over modern Caerleon has enabled a very full picture of the fortress to be built up. The major areas excavated – the amphitheatre, an area of barracks and part of the baths – are exposed to view (the baths in a museum building). The rest lies under the modern village.

Isca was founded in AD 74 or 75 as a permanent base for the 2nd Augustan Legion, which was transferred to Britain from Strasbourg in AD 43. It replaced a fortress at Usk, founded in the mid-50s, as the legionary fortress in the area. It had easy access to the road network along the coastal plain, and to the sea, and unlike Usk it was not prone to flooding.

The first fortress was a substantial construction of earth and timber. It was the usual fortress size of about 20.5ha and was of standard 'playing card' shape. It had an outer V-shaped ditch, and a clay and turf rampart revetted with timber, with a wall-walk on top, wooden towers at intervals and a gateway on each side. The internal layout was the rigidly geometrical standard one of main roads between the gateways, principal buildings in the middle and barracks (60 of them for a legion of 6,000 men) in pairs filling up most of the rest of the space. An amphitheatre and baths, both built in stone from the start, followed soon afterwards, in about AD 80–90. Soon after that, in about AD 100–110, rebuilding in stone began, and continued piecemeal throughout the 2nd century (west gate about 100, barracks not before 140, headquarters 160–170). Once the area was under Roman control and there was no longer

any serious military threat in south-east Wales, occupation of Isca by the whole legion was spasmodic. Final abandonment did not come until towards the end of the 3rd century when events elsewhere led to the legion's reposting. During the two hundred or so years of its occupation a civil settlement grew up to the south-west of the fortress, between it and the river.

The best place to start a tour is on the road on the town side of the amphitheatre car park, with a cowshed to the right. This is the middle of the south-west gateway, the cowshed marking the position of one of the guard-towers. The modern road is the only one in Caerleon that exactly follows the line of an original Roman road, in this case the *via principalis*, which led to the headquarters building, or *principia*, in the middle of the fortress. This now lies under the churchyard, to the south of which were officers' houses, one of which, now underneath the Legionary Museum, has been excavated. Still by the cowshed, the playing field to the left is on the site of the parade ground. A path between this and the bank, which marks the fortress wall, leads to the area of visible barracks. There are four, of which only the nearest, lowest one is actually Roman: the other three were excavated and modern walls built to show their outlines. Although only the base of the walls remains this gives a clear idea of the sort of living quarters a legionary soldier had to put up with. The wider part was where the centurion lived in comparative comfort, but in the narrow part each pair of rooms was shared by eight men. Other features of interest in this area are the circular bases of ovens against the inner face of the rampart, and the latrine on the north-west side, which would have had wooden seats over the drain.

Back at the car park there is access via a stile to the fortress wall in the south corner. This presents an uneven appearance, with stones set higgledy-piggledy in mortar. But this is just the rubble core of what would originally have been a neatly faced wall; a little of the facing can be seen in place at its base. There were two-storey turrets at intervals along the wall. The first is marked by a large tree, the second has had its front wall robbed out, and little remains of the one in the angle, where the wall is highest, and the one on the south-east side. Further turrets can be seen in the wall to the north-west, near the barrack remains.

Outside the wall, squeezed into a narrow space between it and an existing bath-house (part of which was demolished), is the amphitheatre. It is almost complete, and a great rarity in Britain. It was completely excavated in 1926–7. Built at the same time as its larger cousin the Colosseum in Rome, it was for military parades and exercises, entertainment and religious ceremonies, and was large enough to seat the whole legion. It is oval, with the arena surrounded by massive earth banks revetted with stone and buttressed on the outside. On the inside the stone was covered with white plaster, and the arena would have been of sand. On top of the banks were tiers of wooden seats, which ran

right across the vaulted entrance passages. The main entrances were the two wide ones on the north and south sides. Their massive stone gate piers give a good idea of Roman confidence and sense of permanence. In the north entrance some of the original paving survives, very cracked. Below a grille is the drain, still in perfect working order, which runs underneath the arena. The entrance on the south-west side is the most complete, with a brickwork wall and archway over steps to the seating. The room in the middle of the entrance was the waiting room for performers, human or animal. In the entrance opposite there was originally a similar room, but what is there now is a later conversion to a shrine to an unknown deity. Above this was a box for distinguished members of the audience.

In the centre of Caerleon is the last remaining visible part of the fortress, the baths. These were entered from the main NW–SE road, roughly at the entrance to the

Caerleon barracks

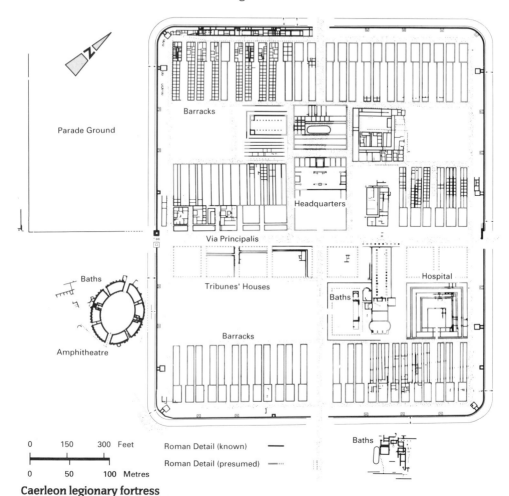

Caerleon legionary fortress

present-day car park in front of the baths building. Here was an open colonnaded court with an outdoor (cold) swimming pool on one side. This pool is the first thing encountered in the building, with part of the base of its *nymphaeum* or fountain-house at the north-west end. Beyond this are the remains of a small part of a heated changing room, two apses which housed cold plunge baths and a rectangular cold pool. In front of these are some robbed-out piers and the large baths

drain from which were recovered many small objects lost while bathing (now in the Legionary Museum). All this dates from around AD 150, a late phase in the baths' development before which there had been several alterations. The visible part of the baths is only a small fraction of the whole: to the north-west was a large exercise hall, while to the south-east were the warm and hot baths. It is interesting to note the use of dark Purbeck marble from Dorset and the extensive use of concrete, which would have made possible the wide spans of the vaulted ceilings above the baths.

The Legionary Museum in Castle Street houses some of the finds from excavations at Caerleon and Usk, and is well worth a visit. The range of objects, both military and domestic, gives a good idea of the sophistication of this outpost of Roman civilisation, and of the everyday life of the men posted here from homelands all over Europe.

We are lucky that there is anything of Roman Caerleon left; its fate after its abandonment is epitomised by the comment of an early 19th-century traveller, who was taken to a garden where an altar with a Roman inscription had just been dug up: 'we saw the venerable monument of antiquity just finished slicing into half a dozen slabs for paving'.

67
Caerwent Roman Town, Caerwent
Roman civil settlement
Late 1st century to mid-4th century
OS 171   ST 470905   U1/2   Cadw

4.4ml (7km) W of Chepstow, on A48 Chepstow to Newport road. Turn S off main road into village

Craster: Official Guide

Caerwent, or *Venta Silurum*, is the most important civilian Roman site in Wales, and the surviving stretches of its town walls are among the finest remnants of Roman masonry in Britain. It was a site that attracted the interest of early antiquaries. In the 16th century William Camden noted 'the ruinous walls, the chequer'd pavements, and the Roman coyns'. In the 17th and 18th centuries further mosaics were found and destroyed. Since 1899 over half the area within the walls has been excavated, with the result that much

is known of the layout of the Roman town. Many of the finds from these excavations are in the Newport Museum.

A settlement was established at Caerwent in the late 1st century AD, soon after the Roman conquest of south Wales. Its first occupants may well have come down to it from the nearby hillfort of Llanmelin Woods (no. 56), where occupation is known to have ceased at about this time. It lay on the main road along the coastal plain from Gloucester to Carmarthen, and may have been little more than a straggling settlement along the road to begin with. During its early years buildings were probably mainly timber-framed. At some stage in the 2nd century or beginning of the 3rd century the town became a *civitas* capital, seat of the Romanised tribal administration of the Silures, the native tribe occupying south-east Wales. It was towards the beginning of the 3rd century too that the regular grid layout of the town was established. At its peak, in the 4th century, Caerwent may have had as many as two to three thousand occupants.

From the late 2nd century the town was rectangular in shape, and was laid out on a standard Roman grid pattern. Its first defences, built sometime in the late 2nd century, consisted of an earth bank and outer ditch. The main road ran east–west through the middle, on the line of the present road but wider, and had gateways at each end. The interior was laid out in 20 blocks or *insulae*, with the main public buildings – the forum-basilica, temple and baths – situated in the middle. Shops lined the main street, and the rest of the space was taken up with houses, shops, farms and industrial and other commercial units. Near the south gate was a large building which could have been an inn. Although the basic plan was rigid and orderly, in detail it was far less rigorously geometrical. By the 4th century there were large, luxurious houses of typical Roman courtyard layout, many of which boasted wall paintings, mosaic floors and hypocaust underfloor heating.

In the second half of the 3rd century or first half of the 4th the surrounding bank was

Caerwent Roman town, south wall

(no. 69) and were for the use of archers. A further outer ditch may have been dug at the same time, the existing one filled in, and the north and south gateways blocked.

Undoubtedly the most interesting surviving part of the town is the wall. This can best be seen around the southern half of the town, being accessible for its entire length from the east to the west gate. These two gateways would have been the most important ones, probably with double archways and flanking guard-chambers. Starting at the east gate a part of the tower flanking the entrance is visible. To the south of this very little of the squared facing stone of the wall remains. What is visible is the rubble interior, roughly coursed in a herringbone pattern. In the corner is a small early Norman motte, taking advantage, like that at Cardiff fort, of already existing defences. The wall is best preserved and most impressive on the south side, where

fronted by a wall, and the gateways were rebuilt in stone. Later, in AD 350 or very soon after, towers were added to the north and south walls (six on the south side, five on the north). They are similar to those at Cardiff fort

Caerwent, layout of temple precinct

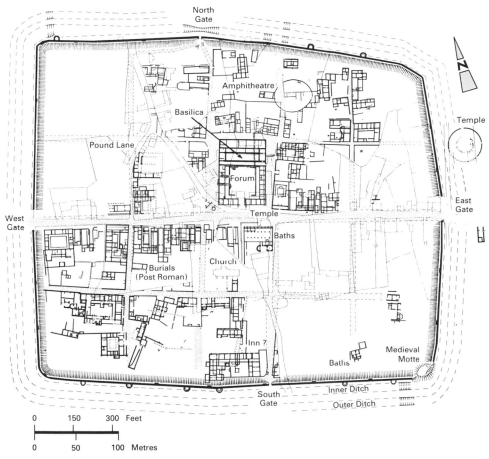

North
Gate

Amphitheatre

Basilica

Temple

Pound Lane

East
Gate

Forum

West
Gate

Temple

Baths

Burials
(Post Roman)

Church

Inn ?

Medieval
Motte

Baths

South
Gate

Inner Ditch

Outer Ditch

0   150   300 Feet

0   50   100 Metres

The layers of Roman history beneath modern-day Caerwent

it stands up to 5m high, almost to its full height. Here the facing stone survives, in places right to the top. Behind the wall is a great earth bank, part of which is the original late 2nd-century bank, and there would have been a wall-walk along the top. The blocked south gateway stands just after a farm track crosses the wall, its piers and the springing of its archway clearly visible.

A striking feature of the south wall is the six semi-octagonal hollow towers spaced out at regular intervals along its outer side. Most

are quite ruined, but one, to the west of the south gateway, stands almost to the height of the wall. Joist holes inside it show that it had three storeys, the windowless chambers of which must have been used for storage. The westernmost tower has a small blocked door in it. At the mid-point of the west side is the site of the west gate, where a beautiful old stone stile leads back on to the road. The wall continues northwards, but is less well preserved here.

The footings of some Roman buildings are

exposed in Pound Lane, which follows the line of a Roman side street (in its straight stretch) to the north of the main street. At the first site (on the right, approached from the main street) there was a complicated series of developments, culminating in what is now partly visible. This is a colonnaded shop front facing the main street, with living accommodation behind around a courtyard. Behind this again was a large house around a courtyard, part of which was possibly a rectangular walled garden. Further down Pound Lane, on the left-hand side, are the more recently excavated footings of a further large courtyard house. A timber-framed house was built on this site in the late 2nd to early 3rd century and was then demolished in the late 3rd century to make way for a larger house. In the early 4th century this was replaced by an even larger and grander house ranged around two courtyards.

A little further east down the main street is the War Memorial, built on the remains of a post-Roman platform which incorporated a statue-base of Venta Silurum's patron, Tiberius Claudius Paulinus, who was at one time commander-in-chief of the 2nd Augustan Legion at Caerleon. This inscribed plinth, originally erected shortly before AD 220, and found in 1903, now stands in the church porch. It is well worth a visit (there is also a small exhibition of Roman finds and some information). The inscription records that it was put up in honour of Paulinus, by this time governor of a province of Gaul, by the Decree of the Council of the Republic of the Community of the Silures. The town was evidently already a *civitas* capital, and civic pride was obviously burgeoning.

To continue the tour through Roman Caerwent, now move on eastwards down the main street. The baths were on the right, the forum-basilica (the market place and town hall with law courts and council chamber) on the left. The forum was on a courtyard plan and the basilica was a large colonnaded rectangular building behind it. When they were first built is not known, but the basilica was substantially rebuilt in the late 3rd

century and was dismantled in the middle of the 4th century.

Next on the left are the exposed foundations of the temple. It was built on open ground in about AD 330, and follows a plan usual in Roman temples in Celtic lands of a private inner shrine with a sanctuary-alcove, surrounded by a public ambulatory (a semicircular aisle). This was set in a walled sacred garden or *temenos* with a long entrance hall of some architectural pretension (pilasters on the walls and a tessellated floor) fronting the main Roman street. The god worshipped here is unknown, but a stone found in one of the houses, and now in the church porch, was dedicated to Mars Ocelus, a Rhineland conflation of two gods, one Roman, one Celtic, which demonstrates a degree of cultural fusion. Another find connected with religion at Caerwent was a stone head, a replica of which can be seen in the church porch, found in a house in what may have been a private shrine.

Back at the east gate, the town wall can be seen continuing northwards. The north wall is difficult to see and is partly turfed over, but behind the North Gate Inn, on its west side, the blocked north gateway is clearly visible. The piers, the springing of the arch and a small doorway made when the gate was blocked can be seen. The small lane to the east runs along the line of the town's outer ditch.

68
Gelligaer Roman Fort, Gelligaer
Roman auxiliary fort
Late 1st century to 4th century
OS 171   ST 134970   U2/R2/U3

Take B4254 to Gelligaer. In centre, fort is mostly in fields to N of main road, just NW of churchyard. View from road, or public footpath across site

Ward 1903, 1909, 1911, 1913

All that is now apparent of this extensively excavated Roman auxiliary fort (excavated intermittently from 1903 to 1919) are some low banks and ditches in grass fields to the north-west of the church. A little imagination is needed, therefore, to reconstruct a picture of Roman Gelligaer in the mind's eye.

The fort, whose original Roman name has been lost, lay on the Roman road from Brecon to Cardiff, between the forts of Penydarren and Caerphilly. The first fort here was 2.4ha in size, constructed of earth and timber and

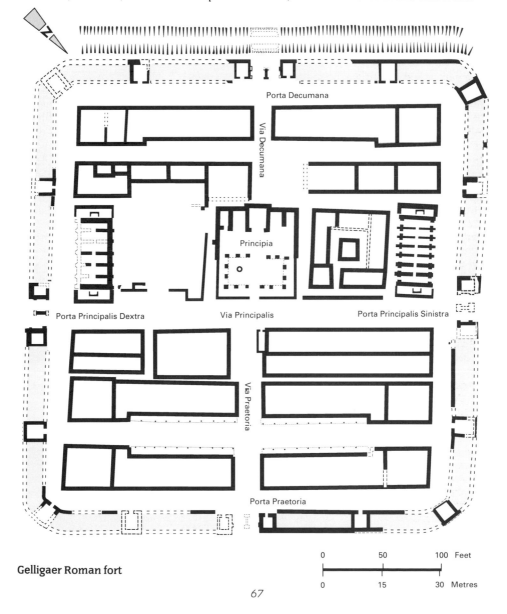

Gelligaer Roman fort

dating from the last quarter of the 1st century. It lay in the two fields to the north-west of Rectory Road, where low scarps marking its edges are just discernible. This was replaced, between AD 103 and AD 111, by a much smaller fort of 1.5ha to its south-east, in the field bounded by Rectory Road and Church Road. This was quite small as auxiliary forts go, and would have had a garrison of 500 men, probably all infantry (*cohors quingenaria*). Unlike most other auxiliary forts this one was built from the first in stone. Its basic layout was absolutely standard: a wall with towers at the angles and at intervals along the sides, surrounded a roughly square area, with a V-shaped ditch outside. The gently rolling bank and ditch in the field next to Church Road represent the wall and ditch of part of the south-west side. The bank along the far edge of the field is the north-east wall, and the gap in the middle the gateway. There was a double-arched gateway flanked by guard-chambers in the middle of each side, from which roads led to the main administrative building (*principia*) and commandant's house (*praetorium*) in the middle. These were flanked by large granaries (*horrea*). Barracks and other miscellaneous buildings filled the remaining space.

The *principia* was of standard layout, with a courtyard, a long 'audience chamber' across the back of it, and five small rooms at the back, the central one of which was the fort's 'shrine' (*sacellum*). The adjacent *praetorium* was arranged around a small courtyard. As was usual in auxiliary forts, the baths were outside the fort, in an annexe to the south-east, surrounded by a wall and shallow ditch. They had the standard suite of rooms ranging from very hot to stone cold, and excavation showed them to have been the finest known in Wales after those of Caerleon (no. 66), with painted plaster on some of the walls. There are two further parts to the complex, a pottery kiln found in the churchyard, and a roughly paved area, a presumed parade ground, to the north-east of the fort. Nearby is a cemetery, and on Gelligaer Common are several small practice camps (see Appendix).

The fort's history is difficult to determine. It would appear that it was occupied until soon after AD 160, when, like most other minor forts in the area, it seems to have been abandoned. However, finds of the 3rd and 4th centuries suggest some later, possibly civilian occupation, perhaps on a much reduced scale.

69
Cardiff Roman Fort, Cardiff
Roman fort
AD 55 to 4th century
OS 171   ST 181766   R1

In central Cardiff at S end of Cathays Park, and to the N of Duke Street. Open to public daily. Entrance charge

Simpson 1963; Webster 1981

Cardiff Castle is the most remarkable conflation of elements – a Roman fort, a Norman motte and bailey (no. 83), a medieval castle, 18th-century buildings and the late 19th-century additions and restorations of the 3rd and 4th marquesses of Bute. As the earliest structure, the Roman fort is at the bottom of this pile, but remarkably some of it is still visible.

There was a succession of four overlapping forts at Cardiff, whose original Roman name has been lost, and their occupation appears to have been more or less continuous throughout the Roman period. Cardiff's strategic position on the main east–west route along the coastal plain of south Wales, and its accessibility from the sea led to the establishment of a fort here very early on in the Roman conquest of Wales. The first fort was of earth and timber and dates from about AD 55–60 – about the same time as the founding of the legionary fortress at Usk. It was a large fort, covering a much larger area than that within the present walls, with the present enclosure towards its south-western corner. Its size suggests it was a so-called 'vexillation' fort, built to accommodate part of a legion rather than just an auxiliary force: it may have been an advance base in the campaign to subdue the Silures. Part of an axial north–south road, the remains of a large timber building and part of another even larger building to its north-east have been excavated from this phase.

The first fort appears to have been short-lived, and was replaced by a second, also of earth and timber, which dates from the last quarter of the 1st century. This was much smaller than the first fort, and was positioned in the middle of its north side, with its southern half overlapping the northern end of the present enclosure. The few parts of it that have been excavated suggest a simple fort, with civilian 'strip-houses' to the south. It too was short-lived, and was replaced, in the early 2nd century, by a third fort more or less on the same lines, which was given a slightly more elaborate south gateway. To its south iron-smelting was carried out where there had previously been houses.

In about AD 276–285 the last fort on the site was built to the south of, and overlapping the third fort. It remained in use for about a hundred years. The present-day enclosure follows the lines of this last fort: its north, east and part of its south walls were built on top of the original Roman ones in the late 19th century by the 3rd and 4th marquesses of Bute, and the west wall stands on Roman foundations. Interestingly and unusually for the Romans the enclosure is not a true rectangle, but a nine-sided polygon. The Roman parts of the walls are demarcated by a band of reddish-coloured stone on the outside, and can be seen on the south, north and east sides. On the inside a long stretch of the Roman wall is visible in a covered gallery on the south side. It is 3m thick at the base, and where best preserved is 5.2m high. It was unlikely to have been much higher. Thus the reconstructed wall is almost twice the height of the original Roman one. There is no evidence, either, for a mural gallery, and the wall towers and towers of the gates probably

Cardiff Roman fort, north gate before restoration

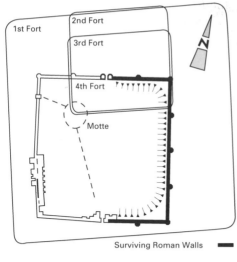

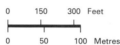

Surviving Roman Walls ■

```
0        150      300  Feet
├────────┼────────┤
0        50       100  Metres
```

Cardiff Roman fort

Little is known about the interior of the last fort, and no stone buildings have been found. Slag heaps from the earlier civil settlement were levelled to provide hard-standing for timber-framed buildings, and parts of the interior were probably farmed. This jumbled layout shows a fort very unlike the tightly organised earlier ones, and it may have been much more like a medieval walled town.

70
Neath Roman Fort, Neath
Roman auxiliary fort
c. AD 75–late 2nd century
OS 170   SS 747977   U1

On W side of Neath, just W of river Nedd, S of Neath Technical College. Bisected by A474 (Neath Abbey Road). Visible remains S of A474 opposite playing fields, in island between road and Roman Way, and on E corner of block to S (also on Roman Way)

Nash-Williams 1950; Nash-Williams 1969; Simpson 1963

The Roman fort of *Nidum*, now covered by modern roads, housing and playing fields, was discovered in 1949, when housing development took place in the area, and various parts have been excavated since then, revealing its extent, construction and two of its gateways.

It was a medium-sized (2.4ha), square auxiliary fort, situated in a strategic position on the road to Carmarthen, controlling the crossing of the river Nedd. Its history appears to be of several phases. First was a short-lived timber fort, built in about AD 75, which was soon followed, in the early 2nd century, by an earth and clay rampart and ditch. In AD 120–5 the rampart was reconstructed in stone. Stone rampart walls have been found on the south-east, south-west and possibly the north-east sides. In the north corner part of a stone angle-tower was found. The stone footings visible in two places south of the

projected above the level of the walls. Behind the wall is a large earth bank, which in its present form is medieval: the Roman bank backing the wall was much smaller. During construction there was a change of layout. At first the corners were rounded, but were changed to square, and towers were added along the walls.

The towers were solid and five-sided, and were placed at regular intervals along the walls. By extrapolation from those remaining on the east side of the fort there would have been eighteen in all. The gateways were in the middle of the north and south sides. Of the south gateway nothing remains, but its position is known. The footings of the north gateway were found and showed that it was a single narrow entrance flanked by two towers. These, and one tower in the middle of the east side, were hollow, which implies that they were guard-chambers. The present north gateway is a reconstruction by the 3rd marquess of Bute.

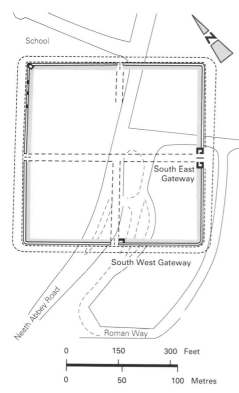

Neath Roman fort

the other side of the modern road. No evidence was found for the internal layout of the fort. After its final construction in stone it was probably short-lived: most minor forts in the area were abandoned soon after the middle of the 2nd century.

71
Knap Roman Site, Barry
Roman building
3rd–4th century
OS 171   ST 099665   U2

Take road from Barry to The Knap, to W. After mini roundabout park above beach. Site is just behind, above car parking area, at its E end

The discovery of this site during development work, and its subsequent excavation and presentation, have given the visitor an opportunity, rare in this area, to study the layout of a substantial Roman building. From the viewing platform the whole plan can be appreciated. The building, only the footings of which remain, was large, with 18 or 19 rooms arranged around a central courtyard. Immediately in front of the viewing platform is

modern road are all that remains of the south-west and south-east gateways. Of the south-west gateway, next to the main road, all that can be seen are the footings of a guard-chamber at the back of the rampart on the south-east side, and a doorway in the north-west wall. The remains of the south-east gateway are more complete and reveal the typical plan of a double roadway between two square guard-towers built on to the ends of the rampart. Outside the entrance is a section of ditch, which continues right across it, implying a bridge of some sort, probably wooden.

The only other visible part of the fort is the north-west rampart, which can be made out as a low ridge crossing the playing fields on

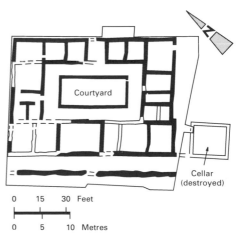

Roman building at The Knap

a long external verandah running its full length. In the centre of the courtyard was an open area which may have been laid out as a garden.

The building was constructed in the mid- to late 3rd century, and was originally part of a small settlement overlooking a harbour to the east. There is some evidence to suggest that it was never finished. Certainly it was demolished or robbed in the mid- to late 4th century. The finds from the site were few and not of a domestic character, suggesting that it may have had an official function, possibly linked with defence of the coast. In plan the house is similar to that of Roman store buildings on the Continent. Whatever its purpose, whether military, naval, or storage, it shows that buildings of standard Roman layout reached this part of Wales.

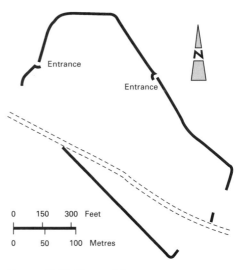

Twyn y Bridallt marching camp

72
Twyn y Bridallt Marching Camp, Ferndale
Roman marching camp
? Late 1st century
OS 170   ST 002982   U4

Take A470 to Pontypridd. From Pontypridd take B4273 to Ynysybwl. Continue N towards Mountain Ash for c.1.2ml (2km). Fork L. Continue c.1.2ml (2km) to T-junction, turn R, take 2nd forestry track on R. Camp 2ml (3.2km) along track, on open ground on LHS. Permission needed from Forestry Commission to take vehicle along track

This is one of the few remaining Roman marching camps in the area. Their slight earthwork banks have militated against their

survival, but this camp is sufficiently remote to have survived very well. It straddles a high ridge in the Glamorgan uplands and now stands in a clearing in forestry on a site sloping up from south to north. It is about 7.3ha in extent, and is roughly trapezoidal in outline – Roman regularity has been abandoned here in favour of following the contours.

The camp is enclosed by a discontinuous bank and external ditch. The bank is at its highest at the north end, where it is about 1m high. The gaps on the west and south-east sides may be partly original. There are two entrances, one on the north-west side and one on the north-east. Both are c.5m wide and of clavicular type, with a curving bank projecting inwards for a short distance from one side.

6

The Early Medieval Period

The early medieval period is the shadowy era between the withdrawal of Roman troops from Britain at the end of the 4th century and the Norman invasion in 1066. Some vestiges of Romanisation remained, such as the continued occupation of certain Roman sites, the use of Roman roads and the siting of memorial stones near them. Roman names continued in use, as did Latin and Roman capitals for inscriptions on memorial stones. But in general it was a time of reassertion of Celtic culture. It was also a time of organisation into distinct kingdoms, each with a powerful ruling dynasty, and of the introduction of Christianity. South-east Wales did not escape the attentions of the Vikings, who raided the area in the 10th century; both Llantwit Major and Llancarfan monasteries were sacked in 988.

Known settlements of the period are few. The small settlement at Dinas Powys (see Appendix), occupied from the 5th to the 7th century, is atypical in that it is unusually rich, with finds of glass and pottery from the east Mediterranean. Material culture was generally impoverished and coins and pottery disappeared. A few Gower caves, such as Lesser Garth and Minchin Hole (see Appendix), were used, and there was some continued occupation at Roman sites. At Caerwent 5th-, 6th-, 8th- and 9th-century burials have been found in the cemetery just outside the town. Trackways and Roman roads linked settlements, and a feature of the upland ridges during this period is a series of cross-ridge dykes which cross the upland trackways. These are low banks, sometimes originally revetted in stone, thought to date from the 8th and 9th centuries. Some are quite short, while some, such as Ffos Ton Cenglau (no. 81) are more than a kilometre long. From their positions, often across a narrow point on a ridge, it would appear that they acted as barriers or boundaries in some way.

At the beginning of the 5th century south-east Wales was still mainly pagan, but Christianity had seeped into Gwent in the Roman period: two of Britain's earliest martyrs, Julius and Aaron, were executed at Caerleon in the 3rd century. In the 6th and 7th centuries Celtic saints such as Cadog, Illtyd and Dyfrig established monastic settlements in the area and began the work of conversion. These settlements, or *clasau*, were usually sited in valley bottoms and were little more than a few huts for the monks, a timber church and a cemetery, all within an enclosure or *llan*. The monks, or canons, were ruled over by an abbot, but the loose organisation of these settlements bore little resemblance to that of the more rigidly controlled continental monastic orders. Most *clasau* have left no trace, and many are overlain by medieval churches and churchyards. The most well known are Llantwit Major, traditionally founded in about 500 by St Illtyd, and Llancarfan, founded in the 6th century by St Cadog.

The carved stones associated with this early church form the most important category of early medieval monument. They have been found in two main areas – in and near Margam and in the Vale of Glamorgan, in particular at Llantwit Major. Many have been removed from their original positions into the safe keeping of a church or museum. It is unclear from their find-spots whether they marked burial sites, holy places, or were memorial or commemorative stones. Burial, during this period, was not generally in a churchyard. However, the purpose of some is given away by their inscriptions – 'hic iacet', or 'here lies', must indicate a burial. The

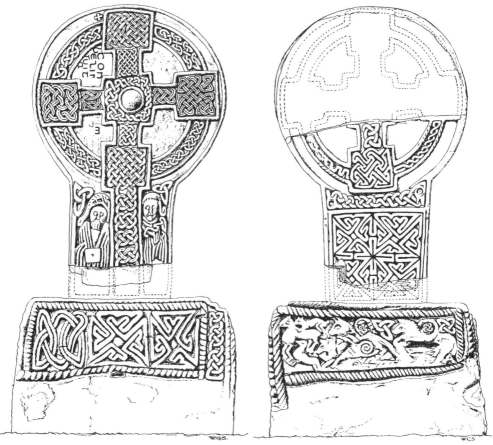

The Cross of Cynfelyn, front (left) and back (right)

stones are difficult to date, but have been sorted into a sequence using the style of inscription and decoration as a guide. The earliest, from the 6th and 7th centuries, are undressed slabs with vertical inscriptions in Latin (in Roman capitals) and also sometimes in the Irish script Ogam, written vertically in notches on the corners of the stones. The Cantusus stone, Pumpeius stone and Bodvoc stone at Margam (no. 73) are all examples of this type. The inscriptions show that these were epitaphs to nobles and churchmen of high rank. Gradually lettering changed from Roman to Carolingian (half-uncials, a more rounded script), and names became more Celtic. Crosses then began to appear, most dating from the 9th to the early 11th centuries. During the 8th and 9th centuries stones with incised crosses became more common, very few of which have an inscription. The surfaces were covered with interlaced Celtic decoration, and the form of the stones became much more elaborate and sculptured. The disc-headed crosses are a particular speciality of Glamorgan, culminating in the great cross of Cynfelyn at Margam (no. 73). In the 11th century the crosses degenerate, with simpler cruder decoration and untidy inscriptions.

During the period regional kingdoms emerged. First was Gwent, which was in existence by about 500, and next came Morgannwg, which split into two at the end of the 9th century. The kingdoms were tribal and hierarchical, with ruling dynasties, a number of lesser landholding chiefs and the church making up their organisation. Their administration was based on the hierarchy of tref, commote and cantref (which can be thought of as roughly equivalent to parish, district and county). When the Normans invaded in the late 11th century this was the society they found, with local rulers and lesser hierarchies, small scattered hamlets and, as elsewhere, a decadent church.

Key to Transcriptions

This chapter uses the following conventions in the transcriptions of early Christian gravestone inscriptions:

The inscriptions are written in capital letters. Editorial insertions within the inscriptions (also in capital letters), and the translations of the inscriptions themselves, appear in italics.

Square brackets indicate letters which are assumed, but indecipherable in the inscription.

Round brackets indicate letters or words which are inserted for comprehension or translation, but which are not present in the original inscription.

An oblique line indicates the beginning of a new line in the inscription (quite frequently in the middle of a word).

73
Margam Stones Museum, Margam

Early Christian stones

5th–11th century

OS 170   SS 801864   R1   Cadw

From junction 38 on M4 take A48 towards Bridgend. Almost immediately turn L down minor road to Margam church. Museum in small building to N of church. Entrance charge. Cadw standard hours (if locked ask for key in canteen opposite)

Radford: Official Guide; Nash-Williams 1950a

The old village school next to the abbey church (no. 125) now houses 25 carved stones, 15 of which are early Christian, ranging in date from the 6th to the 11th century. They were all found in or near Margam and Port Talbot.

The **Cantusus Stone** (Nash-Williams no. 258) is the oldest stone here. It is a Roman milestone, and was found at Port Talbot. On one side is the Roman inscription IM[*P C*]/FLA[*VA*]/L M[AXI]/MINO/INVIC/TO AU/GUS, or: *To the Emperor, Caesar, Flavius Valerius Maximinus, the unconquered Augustus*. This dates the milestone to 309–13. On the other side of the stone is an inscription dating to the second half of the 6th century, which shows that the stone was reused, upside-down, as a Christian memorial. It reads, vertically HIC IACIT CANTUSUS PATER PAULINUS, or 'Here lies Cantusus. (His) father, Paulinus (erected this stone)'.

The **Pumpeius Stone** (Nash-Williams no. 198) dates from about the middle of the 6th century. It is a simple, roughly squared pillar-stone found beside an ancient, possibly Roman road between Margam and Kenfig. It bears three inscriptions, one in Latin and two in the old Irish script of Ogam. The vertical Latin one reads PUMPEIUS/CARANTORIUS or: *Pumpeius (son of) Carantorius*. The Ogam inscriptions are the incised lines along the edge of the same face. The top one reads P[AM]P[E]S, probably *Pumpeius*; the bottom one ROLACUN MAQ ILLUNA, a different name representing an earlier or later use of the stone.

The last of the very early stones is the **Bodvoc Stone** (Nash-Williams no. 229). It was found well away from a church site, by a trackway on Margam mountain, associated with Bronze Age cairns, and is an undressed pillar-stone with no ornament. The simple incised cross at the top is probably later than the inscription. The vertical inscription reads BODVOC – HIC IACIT/FILIUS CATOTIGIRNI/PRONEPUS ETERNALI/VEDOMAV – or: *(The stone) of Bodvoc. Here he lies, son of Catotigirnus (and) great-grandson of Eternalis Vedomavus*. The recording of ancestry suggests that this stone may have commemorated a man of importance in the community, perhaps a local chief.

The circular **Pillar of St Thomas** (Nash-Williams no. 259) was found on the farm of Cwrt Isaf, Port Talbot. The form of lettering on it suggests that it dates from the 8th or early 9th century, a period from which very few stones are known in south-east Wales. On one side of the pillar are two incised crosses, and on the other a later sunken cross of Latin form. On either side of the incomplete cross are two letters, TO to the left, ME to the right. This has been interpreted as meaning *Thomae*, or *(The Cross) of Thomas*. Dedications to saints are unusual, but at Cwrt Isaf there was a later medieval chapel dedicated to St Thomas the Apostle.

The **Cross of Einion** (Nash-Williams no. 231) has always been at Margam, and from its trimming would appear to have been reused for another purpose. It is a fine disc-headed slab-cross, dated by its similarity to the cross of Rhys at Llantwit Major (no. 74) to the late 9th or early 10th century. In contrast to the earlier stones, the front is highly decorated. At the top is a wheel-cross decorated with Celtic interlaced plaits. Below is a panel of plaitwork, while the bottom section is divided into two: to the left is an inscription, and to the right two geometric designs. The Latin

The treasures of Margam Stones Museum. Left to right: the Bodvoc Stone, the Cross of Grutne and the Cross of Einion

inscription reads CRUX,X̄P̄I./ + ENNIAUN./P ANIMA./GUORGORET./FECIT, or: *The Cross of Christ. Enniaun made (or erected) it for the soul of Guorgoret.*

The **Cross of Grutne** (Nash-Williams no. 233) is a smaller pillar-cross with a circular head and splayed shaft, dating from about 900. From about 1700 until it was moved here the cross stood in the cemetery at Margam. The head is filled with a simple cross, the shaft with an inscription. The untidy lettering reads I(*N*)NOMI/NE D(*E*)I S/UM(*M*)I./ CRUX/ CRITDI/ PROP/ ARABIT/ GRUTNE/ PRO AN(*I*)MA/ AHEST, or: *In the name of the Most High God. The cross of Christ. Grutne made (it) ready for the soul of Ahest.*

The high point of the museum is the great **Cross of Cynfelyn** (Nash-Williams no. 234), which dates from the late 9th to the early 10th century. It is the largest and most elaborate of

all Welsh disc-headed slab-crosses, and when first recorded stood in the village street, outside the churchyard. It has a circular head, a narrow neck, the lower part of which is missing, and a rectangular base. All surfaces are filled with typically Celtic interlaced designs, although parts have flaked off on the back.

The cross on the front has a central raised boss and squared-off arms, and is filled with elaborate plaits, as is the circle around it. On the shaft below are two crudely depicted human figures, the left-hand one being St John, the right-hand one the Virgin Mary. The other side is similar, but without the human figures, and with the whole of the neck decorated with plaits and frets. The base has similar designs except on the back, where a hunting scene is depicted.

On the front, in the top left-hand space

between the centre and the wheel of the cross, is a Latin inscription which reads CON/BELIN/*(PO)*SUIT *(H)*A*[NC] (C)* R *(UCEM)*, or *Conbelin placed (?this cross)*. Another very faint inscription on the margin of the head reads + SODNA + CRUCEM FECIT or *Sodna made (or erected) the cross*. The cross was probably commemorative, and appears to have been instigated by Cynfelyn and put up by Sodna.

The next three stones are roughly similar in style, and date from the 11th century. They are thought to have been property markers for the church. In all three the precisely cut patterns of the earlier crosses have degenerated into more irregular wavy lines, and the cross itself has become merely a radial pattern.

The first is the **Cross from Eglwys Nunydd** (Nash-Williams no. 200), which came from the yard of the farm of that name, between Margam and Kenfig. It is a rectangular slab with a sunken 'Maltese' cross with a central circular boss in the top part and an indecipherable inscription below.

The second is the **Cross of Ilci** (Nash-Williams no. 237), which was found near Cwrt y Dafydd farm, being used with the next stone as a footbridge. It is a roughly shaped square-headed cross-slab, with radial 'cartwheel' crosses at the top, front and back, and a very worn inscription on one side. The sides are decorated with wavy lines and dots. The Latin inscription, which is horizontal, reads: ILCI. *[FE]*CIT/*[H*ANC]. CRUCE/M. I/[N] N[OM]IN/E. D*(E)*I SUMMI, or: *Ilci erected this cross in the Name of God Most High.*

The third is the **Cross of Ilquici** (Nash-Williams no. 236). It is similar in shape and layout. A very worn inscription reads: PETRI ILQUICI/[ ]A(?)CER/[ ]ER(?) [ ]C HAN/ *[C CRUCEM]*T/[ ], or: *(The cross) of Peter (?) Ilquici . . . erected this cross (? for the soul of . . .).*

The **Small Broken Wheel-Cross** (Nash-Williams no. 232) is a memorial stone found at Margam, probably dating from the 10th century. It is an irregular slab, the top of which is missing, designed to go flat on the

ground over a grave. In the upper part is a small Celtic-type Latin wheel-cross filled with plaitwork.

The **Narrow Wheel-Cross** (Nash-Williams no. 235) was also found at Margam and probably dates from the 11th century. Its cut-down sides show that it was reused as building stone. On the upper part of the front is a wheel-cross with curved arms decorated with crude and irregular plaitwork. The panel below is decorated similarly. Comparison with the earlier Cross of Einion will show how the ornament on such stones degenerated during the space of a hundred years or so.

The **Broken Wheel-Cross** (Nash-Williams no. 263) was found at Cwrt Isaf, Port Talbot. It probably dates from the 11th-12th century. It has a tapering shaft and disc head with straight-armed wheel-crosses front and back. Both sides and edges are covered with crude linear designs, debased forms of the earlier plait and fret designs.

The **Slab with a 'Maltese' Cross** (Nash-Williams no. 230) was found in a field wall on Penhydd Waelod farm near Bridgend. It is a small stone with an incised 'Maltese' cross set in a circular panel edged by double border lines with dots between. Its date lies between the 9th and 12th centuries.

The **Six-spoked Wheel-Cross** (Nash-Williams no. 262) was found by the river near Port Talbot. It may have marked a path across the sands and is a round-headed pillar-stone. On one side is an incised Latin ring-cross of 7th–9th century date, and on the other, which dates from the late 10th–11th century, is a cartwheel-type ring-cross with a central boss decorated with five sunk dots. On the shaft below is a small double-looped design.

Finally, **Carreg Fedyddiol** (Nash-Williams no. 252) is an 11th-century quadrangular cross shaft which originally stood near the holy well on Pen yr Allt farm near Bridgend. It has a large socket on top for a separate head, which is missing. All faces, except the back, which is plain, have decorated panels filled with very weathered and rather irregular interlaced patterns.

74

Early Christian Stones in Llantwit Major Church, Llantwit Major

Early Christian stones

9th–11th century

OS 170   SS 966687   U1

In the W end of St Illtyd's church, Llantwit Major, 5ml (8km) S of Cowbridge. Church is S of main through road at W end of village

Nash-Williams 1950a

In the 'West Church' of St Illtyd's church are some of the most important early Christian stones in south-east Wales. They were gathered into the church after its restoration at the beginning of the 20th century, and most were originally in the churchyard. The fine quality of the workmanship of some of these stones suggests that there was a flourishing school of sculpture based in Llantwit Major from the late 9th century onwards, and the inscriptions on them show that this was an important enough ecclesiastical centre to be the burial place of local rulers.

The most imposing stone is the tall disc-headed slab-cross which stands near the west wall (Nash-Williams no. 220). It is one of the earliest sculptured crosses in Wales and dates from towards the end of the 9th century. It is the memorial stone of Res or Rhys, put up by his son Hywel ap Rhys, who was then the ruler of the part of south Wales known as Glywysing, which stretched from the river Tawe to the river Usk.

The cross has a circular head with wheel-crosses on the front and back, and a splayed shaft. The whole is completely covered with geometric decoration of fine, regular form, carefully fitted to the shape of the stone. Below the decoration, on the front, is a Latin inscription in five horizontal lines, which reads: NI NOMINE D(E)I PATRIS ET F(ILI)/[ET (?) S]PERETUS SANTDI (H)ANC/[CR]UCEM HOUELT

PROPE/[RA]BIT PRO ANIMA RES P[A/TR]ES E(I)US, or: *In the Name of God the Father and of the Son and of the Holy Spirit. This cross Houelt (Hywel) prepared for the soul of Res (Rhys) his father.*

Next to it stands a smaller shaft, without its cross-head, (Nash-Williams no. 221). It dates from the late 9th to early 10th century. Each side is filled with a panel of well executed neat plaitwork, each one slightly different from the others.

In front of these two is a large rectangular slab dating from the late 10th century (Nash-Williams no. 222), which may once have had a separate head on top. Flaking has removed some of the decoration, which originally covered the whole stone. The Latin

Early Christian stones in Llantwit Major church. Background (left to right): late 9th–early 10th-century shaft, and memorial stone of Res (or Rhys); foreground (upright): Samson's stone

inscriptions in small panels on the front and back proclaim that this is Samson's stone. They read + SAM/SON/POSUIT/HANC C[R]UCEM + PRO AN/MIA EI/US +, or: *Samson set up this cross for his (own) soul*; and + ILT[U/TI (?)] SAM/SONI//RE/GIS SAM/UEL/ + EBI/SAR/+, or: *(for the soul) of Iltut, of Samson the king, of Samuel, and of Ebisar*. Here is conclusive proof that Llantwit Major was the burial ground of local rulers. Iltut may be St Illtud, the traditional founder of the religious community at Llantwit Major, and Ebisar also occurs on the cross-shaft in Coychurch church (no. 80). The rest of the stone is divided into panels decorated in a great variety of geometric patterns, including twists, key-patterns, plaits and interlinked rings.

Against the north wall is a large rectangular slab dating from the 10th–11th century (Nash-Williams no. 223). It may have had a separate head as there is a hollow socket in the top. The whole of the front is taken up with an untidy Latin inscription which reads: IN NOM/INE D(*E*)I SU/MMI INCI/PIT. CRU/X. SAL/UATO/RIS. QUA/E PREPA/RAUIT/SAMSO/ NI ∴ · APA/TI PRO/ANIMA/SUA : [*ET*] P/RO ANI/ MA IU/THAHE/LO REX ∴ /ET ART/MALI ˙ . ˙ ET/TEC[AI]/N +, or: *In the Name of God Most High begins the Cross of the Saviour, which Abbot Samson prepared for his own soul and for the soul of King Juthahel and (for the souls) of Artmail and Tecain*. The mention of an abbot makes it clear that there was a Celtic monastery here at the time. Down the right-hand side of the stone is a nice panel of ring-twist decoration.

Standing near Abbot Samson's stone is an entirely different one, dated by its decoration to the same period (Nash-Williams no. 224). It is a truncated, gently tapering pillar, covered with plaitwork and other geometric decoration. Incised lines divide it into four horizontal bands, and a deep straight groove runs from top to bottom. Its purpose is unknown, but it may have been part of a building of the monastery, the rest of which has long since vanished.

75
Early Christian Stones in Merthyr Mawr Churchyard, Merthyr Mawr

Early Christian stones
11th–12th century
OS 170   SS 882775   U1

In lean-to shelter on north side of churchyard. Merthyr Mawr is 2ml (3km) SW of Bridgend, and is reached by minor roads off the A48. Church in centre of village on RHS

Nash-Williams 1950a, nos 241, 242, 243, 245, 246 and 247

In a shelter behind the church a large collection of memorial stones of various dates has been gathered together from all over the churchyard. The main early Christian ones are the following: an 11th-century roughly shaped rectilinear cross-slab with a large and very weathered cross of panelled cartwheel type; the upper part of an 11th-century round-headed cross-slab with a similar cartwheel cross on the front and a plainer one on the back; a square 12th-century slab, most of one end of a cross-base, decorated with a plaitwork pattern (reused as a medieval jamb); a 12th-century pillar-stone with deeply incised T-ended crosses on both sides; a similar stone of the same date; and a badly

Merthyr Mawr early Christian stones

weathered pillar-stone of the same date with a 'Maltese' cross in a sunk circular panel on one side and a deeply incised cross with T-ended arms on the other.

This concentration of early Christian stones suggests a monastic *clas* foundation in the vicinity, perhaps on the site of the medieval church itself.

76
Cross in Llandaff Cathedral, Cardiff
Early Christian stone
Late 10th–11th century
OS 171   ST 156779   U1

Llandaff is on the W side of Cardiff. In Llandaff turn off A4119 E to the cathedral (signed). Stone in S aisle

Nash-Williams 1950a, no. 205

The original position of this stone is not known. It was found built into a well in the Bishop's Palace, and was eventually brought into the cathedral for safe keeping. It is of a type quite common in the area known as a wheel-headed pillar-cross (see also no. 78). At the top is the wheel-head with a central raised boss, four deep holes, one of which goes right through, and a cross decorated with patterns much worn down by their sojourn in the well. The rectangular shaft has plaitwork and knot decoration all over it on all sides, with four bulging attached columns in the corners. The stone is all that remains of a composite cross, of which this was the upper part. When complete the cross would have looked very similar to that at Llandough (no. 78).

77
Llangan Celtic Cross, Llangan
Early Christian stone
10th–11th century
OS 170   SS 957778   U1

Llangan Celtic cross

3ml (5km) NW of Cowbridge. From Cowbridge take A48 towards Bridgend. At Pentre Meyrick turn R (N) towards Pencoed. In 1ml (1.5km) turn L to Llangan. In Llangan turn R for church, on edge of village. Cross at W end of churchyard

Nash-Williams 1950a, no. 207

This fine, if rather worn sculptured cross is of a type known as a disc-headed slab-cross. It is cut from a single stone into a circular head on a stumpy shaft. On the west side is a depiction of the crucifixion executed in typically Celtic style. A bearded Christ occupies most of the centre. Beneath his outstretched arms are two crudely depicted kneeling figures, the one on the right piercing Christ with a spear, and the one on the left bearing the sponge. Below is an incomplete bearded figure holding a horn in the left hand, and something else in the right. On the badly flaked east side is a plain rectilinear cross. Also in the churchyard, on the south side of the church, is a fine 15th-century medieval cross (no. 136).

78

Pillar-Cross in Llandough Churchyard, Penarth

Early Christian stone

Late 10th–11th century

OS 171   ST 168733   U1

Take A4055 Cardiff to Penarth road to Llandough, 3ml (5km) S of Cardiff centre. Church on LHS in centre of village. Cross S of church

Nash-Williams 1950a, no. 206

This cross stands near the site of a Roman villa and an early monastery. It is a remarkable, almost bizarre monument, and shows how fantastical sculpture in south Wales had become by the end of the early medieval period. The whole of the surface squirms with twisted plaits and knots, and at the base there are strange figures. The shape of the cross itself is exaggerated, with bulging columns in the corners of the shaft and a great overhanging collar. In type it is a wheel-headed pillar-cross, without its cross-head, part of which was still there when the cross was drawn in the 1690s. The shape is thought to have been suggested by that of a processional cross. It is built of four pieces of local Sutton stone, comprising a pyramidal base, a two-part squared shaft and a massive collar or knop between them. There are carved figures in panels on each side of the base: on the west is a horse and rider, on the east a row of five figures each with a cross or sceptre in the right hand, and on the north and south the busts of two men. Who or what these panels depict is unknown.

Pillar-cross, Llandough churchyard

79

Gelligaer Common Standing Stone, Gelligaer

Early Christian stone

7th–9th century

OS 171   SO 103034   U2

3¹/₂ml (c.6km) N of Gelligaer. Take B4254 to Gelligaer, and continue N on to minor road across the common. Stop below highest point, and walk a short distance to the W. Stone between road and summit

Nash-Williams 1950a, no. 197

This simple, roughly rectangular leaning stone is an early Christian memorial monument, with an almost obliterated, clumsy and unenlightening inscription running vertically on the south-east angle. It reads TEF (*? or S*) ROIHI or *(The stone) of . . . oihi(?)*. The site of the stone is of interest in that it lies very close to the Roman road which runs northwards from Gelligaer Roman fort (no. 68). Early observers noticed that it lay on the south-east edge of a small horseshoe-shaped enclosure, still visible as a low uneven bank. These factors make it likely that the stone actually marks a burial, following the Roman custom of roadside tombs.

Gelligaer Common standing stone

80
Coychurch Celtic Cross-Shaft, Coychurch
Early Christian stone
11th to early 12th century
OS 170   SS 940797   R1

Stone is in church, at W end (key from Vicarage next door). Take minor road off A473 Bridgend to Pencoed road into Coychurch. Church in centre, S of road

Nash-Williams 1950a, no. 194

In a rather gloomy corner of St Crallo's church is this fine wheel-headed pillar-cross. It originally stood in the churchyard, where it was broken into three pieces by the fall of the church tower in 1877. Only the base is not covered with the twists, knots and plaits typical of Celtic decoration. At the top of the shaft, below the cross, is a band of beaded collar-moulding which is most unusual in Wales. On the back, just below it, is a clumsy inscription that reads EBI/SAR or *(? The cross)*

of Ebisar. 'Ebisar' also appears on an inscription on a late 10th-century stone in Llantwit Major church (no. 74). In the churchyard is a fine medieval cross (no. 137).

Coychurch Celtic cross-shaft

81
Ffos Ton Cenglau, Treherbert
Early medieval earthwork
8th–9th century
OS 170   SN 916031–919020   U2

Take A4061 Hirwaun to Treherbert road. About 3ml (5km) N of Treherbert park on forestry track on W side of road. Dyke runs along edge of forestry to N and S of track

This is a fine boomerang-shaped dyke, over half a mile (1km) long, across the ridgetop at the head of the Rhondda Fawr valley. Like

Ffos Ton Cenglau earthwork

most of the other Glamorgan dykes, it is aligned across the ridge, barring the east–west ridgetop route followed by the trackway called Cefn Ffordd, which crosses the dyke at its north end.

The dyke runs along a steep scarp between two precipices on the west side of the valley. It is a substantial, steep-sided bank, particularly visible to the south of the forestry track, which crosses it at a point where there may be an original gap. Stones visible on its surface and below it suggest that it was revetted on its outer, east side with a drystone wall.

82
Bwlch yr Avan Dyke, Treorchy
Early medieval earthwork
8th–9th century
OS 170   SS 921951   U2

Take A4061 Treorchy to Port Talbot road. 3ml (5km) W of Treorchy park at summit, by track to radio mast to S. Dyke near road, starting at track and running westwards

This is a well preserved section of bank and ditch which probably barred a route along the ridgetop and acted as a boundary between two neighbouring areas of jurisdiction. The dyke runs straight, east–west, across the top of the ridge, and consists of two earthen banks with a ditch in between. The southernmost bank is the more substantial.

7

The Medieval Period: Castles and Settlements

The medieval period, from 1066 to the accession of Henry VII in 1485, saw the conquest of south-east Wales by the Normans, and a complete change in its secular and ecclesiastical organisation. Most monuments of the period in the area owe their existence to the Norman conquest. The Norman barons were ambitious, warlike and land-hungry, but also pious. They built and held the majority of the mottes, moated sites and castles, established villages and boroughs, organised the church into dioceses and parishes, and founded monasteries. Ecclesiastical sites will be dealt with in chapter 8. The only category of monument from this period which owes nothing to the Normans is the platform house, a very primitive form of dwelling found in the uplands.

Immediately after 1066 some of William's most trusted followers were given a free hand in establishing Norman rule in the frontier zone of the marches of Wales. The powerful marcher lordships were created, with William fitz Osbern (d. 1071), the king's cousin and commander of the right wing at the battle of Hastings, in control of the march from Hereford to the Bristol Channel. The earliest masonry monuments of the medieval period, the rectangular keeps at Chepstow Castle (no. 98) and possibly Monmouth Castle (no. 99), date from this initial phase of conquest. Most of the coastal plain and lowlands of Gwent fell quickly into Norman hands, and victory was consolidated with the building of castles, the key to Norman success in the seizure of land. Norman castles in the area could be thought of as chess pieces in a strategic power game. The earliest castles were of the motte and bailey type, and could be thought of as the pawns in the game.

The motte and bailey castle was a simple earthwork and timber structure, quick and easy to build. It consisted of the motte, a circular, flat-topped mound surrounded by a ditch, with a timber stronghold or keep on top, and the bailey, an adjoining palisaded and sometimes embanked enclosure. In the Vale of Glamorgan and on the Gower peninsula a variant form, the ringwork, is found. This is a banked and ditched circular enclosure without a mound. This change in form may have chronological significance, or it may be that the subsoil was unsuitable for throwing up into a mound. There are a few mottes, called raised ringworks, which have a bank around the top of the mound. These earthwork and timber castles were well distributed throughout the lowland zone of south-east Wales; only a very few were built by native leaders in the uplands, most of which remained in Welsh hands until the end of the 13th century.

Of these primary castles only the earthworks remain. The largest are thought to be the earliest: Cardiff motte (no. 83) is thought to have been built in 1081, and the huge motte at Caerleon (see Appendix) is known (from the Domesday Book) to have been established by 1086. Their lifespan is thought to have been short, and most were abandoned, superseded by moated sites or converted into masonry castles by the end of the 12th century. Many of the masonry castles of the area originated as earthwork castles. At some, such as Cardiff (no. 83), Abergavenny (no. 101), Ogmore (no. 103) and Caldicot (no. 115), this is apparent on the ground; at others the earthwork phase may be more difficult to detect.

In the second generation of the Norman conquest of the area, from the 1090s onwards, the Normans pushed westwards further into Glamorgan, and, to use the chess analogy, brought out their knights and rooks. The three castles of Newcastle, Bridgend (no. 102), Ogmore (no. 103) and Coity (no. 104) mark the westward limit of this expansion. In the early 12th century the Gower peninsula was overrun by Henry de Beaumont, who established his followers in castles on the south side of the peninsula. This early hold on the whole of the lowland zone was frequently challenged by the upland Welsh: timber castles were burnt in 1135 in Gower and in 1136 in north Gwent. Rebuilding in stone must have become an urgent necessity, done when there was a lull in hostilities. The layout and earliest masonry of many castles in the area date from this 12th-century rebuilding phase.

The early Norman stone castles consisted of a courtyard surrounded by a faceted curtain wall, with living quarters and other buildings ranged around the wall's inner side. The curtain wall provided the main defensive strength of the castle. It was high and thick, plain to begin with, and after the late 12th century pierced by arrowslits. The top was battlemented, with a wall-walk behind. Keeps, such as those at Ogmore, Coity, Dinas Powys (no. 105) and Usk (no. 100), were rectangular and severe, and were incorporated into the curtain wall. There were occasional decorative adornments and concessions to comfort in these early castles: there is a blank arcade with traces of painted plaster in the hall of the keep at Chepstow, a fine fireplace in the hall at Ogmore, a decorated doorway at Newcastle, and a carved corbel from the keep at Kenfig (see Appendix) suggesting a hall of some sophistication.

The 13th century was the golden age of castle building in south-east Wales. The period was shaped by the great marcher lords of the area, the Marshals, the de Braoses, the de Clares and Hubert de Burgh, all of whom exercised great power and freedom of action. It was William Marshal who introduced new castle building ideas from France in about 1200 at his great castle of Chepstow (no. 98), which could be thought of as the king in the chess game analogy. The main innovation

Chepstow Castle, Marten's Tower and outer gatehouse

was the introduction of arrowslits and the substitution of round towers for rectangular ones in the curtain wall. Round towers were soon added to existing plain curtain walls, for instance at Grosmont (no. 112) and Usk (no. 100), and castles such as Skenfrith (no. 114) were built with them incorporated into the curtain wall from the start.

Castles played their part in various dynastic squabbles and shifting alliances. At one point Richard Marshal even teamed up with the Welsh leader Llywelyn ab Iorwerth (the Great, d. 1240) in order to drive Henry III out of the Marshal castle of Usk. However, except for the first castle at Caerphilly, their fabric was never seriously threatened; it seems that only a long siege or treachery could imperil the great castles of the 13th century. The uplands of south-east Wales were still nominally under Welsh control, however, and the de Clares planted a string of castles on their fringes – Llantrisant (no. 118), Castell Coch (no. 117), Llangynwydd (see Appendix), and eventually Caerphilly (no. 116) – from which they could control and then seize them. Another de Clare fortress, Morlais Castle (no. 119), deep in the uplands, was a provocative move in a border struggle with Humphrey de Bohun, lord of Brecon, stating de Clare's preferred border line.

But the culmination of all castle building in the area, and one of the great strongholds of Europe, was Caerphilly Castle, the queen in the chess game analogy. Once it was in place it was checkmate against Llywelyn ap Gruffudd (the Last, d. 1282) in the power struggle in south Wales. Gilbert de Clare, the 'red earl', earl of Gloucester, lord of Glamorgan (d. 1295), had won.

Caerphilly Castle

During the 13th century castle design was moving towards a cellular structure, with each cell capable of independent defence. At first this manifested itself in the free-standing round keep within the curtain wall, such as that at Skenfrith (no. 114), but this soon gave way to the strong, keep-like gatehouse, which became a heavily guarded entrance passage flanked by twin round towers. Those at Chepstow and White Castle (no. 113) are among the earliest in the area. At Caerphilly all the latest thinking was put together on a virgin site to provide the first fully concentric castle in the country, complete with immensely strong gatehouses. Castle building had entered the 'Edwardian' era, seen at its most magnificent and mature in the castles of Edward I in north Wales.

The 14th century was a period of embellishment and improvement to existing castles. New families such as the Beauchamps, Despensers and Staffords took the place of some of the old ones. A few fragments of architectural detail – traceried windows at Oystermouth (no. 109) and Caerphilly, for example – give a flavour of the period. The 15th century opened with the Welsh rebellion led by Owain Glyndŵr. Castles prepared for attack, but in the event only a few, such as Coity Castle and the Bishop's Palace at Llandaff, were seriously damaged. Glyndŵr was finally defeated near Grosmont Castle in 1405. The century saw the extensive abandonment of castles in favour of more comfortable living accommodation; semi-fortified manor houses such as Old Beaupre (no. 149) took their place. Some castles were given other uses: Caerphilly and Swansea (no. 106), for instance, were used as prisons. But one of the south-east Wales' greatest medieval monuments, Raglan Castle (no. 122), was largely built in the 15th century. It was a new concept, a fortress-palace, built not so much for defence, the need for which had largely disappeared, but as a status symbol and display of wealth.

Most castles continued to decay in the Tudor period, by which time only Abergavenny, Chepstow, Raglan, Newport, Cardiff, Swansea, Coity and Ogmore were still in good condition. The Civil War in the mid-17th century, during which many were damaged beyond repair, finally led to their total abandonment. By this time most of the chief families were living in comfortable manor houses such as Oxwich Castle (no. 150), and except for the Somerset family at Raglan, they were little disrupted by the destruction.

Monuments of medieval secular settlement, other than castles, tend to be less obvious earthworks, often hard to make out on the ground. These are the moated sites, platform houses and deserted villages, all of which form vital parts of the overall tapestry of evidence of medieval life in the area.

A moated site is a square or rectangular area, sometimes with a bank around the edge, surrounded by a flat-bottomed ditch, now very often dry, but originally filled with water. The moat was sometimes revetted in stone and was crossed by a causeway or wooden bridge. The 'island' would have been fenced or hedged around, and contained the house and ancillary buildings, or in some cases only farm buildings, orchards or gardens. Remains of buildings on them are rare, but can be seen at Horseland and Perthir (see Appendix). Moated sites might supersede those mottes that were not converted into castles, and were often of manorial or submanorial status (for instance Hen Gwrt, no. 95, and Doghill, Dyffryn, see Appendix, were manors of the bishops of Llandaff).

Moated sites appear to date largely from the 13th and 14th centuries, and in particular to the period 1275 to 1325, which was a time of general overpopulation and increasing lawlessness. There may have been a small element of defence in barricading oneself in behind a water-filled moat, but other factors such as ready availability of water, a source of fish and waterfowl, exclusion of animals, and possibly prestige value, also favoured them. Most are found in the lowland zone of the area, in particular in south-east Gwent and the Vale of Glamorgan, often near a source of water for the moat.

Platform houses are a much more primitive form of habitation found on the edges of the upland plateaus in the area. They usually occur in groups, often of two or three, and consist of levelled rectangular platforms at right-angles to the slope, with their upper ends dug into the hillside and their outer ends built out upon the upcast. The upper, or hood end often has a raised bank around it, and sometimes a ditch as well, to divert rainwash. The houses themselves have long since gone; all that remains of them are the occasional traces of walling. They date from the same period as the moated sites – the late 13th to early 14th century – when conditions such as increasing population may have led to a spread of settlement on to marginal land. The occupants' material culture was very impoverished, and scratching a living from pastoralism and a little cultivation at this altitude must have been difficult. It appears that the houses were soon abandoned, early in the 14th century, when the land came under feudal control and the climate deteriorated.

The troubles of the 14th century – plagues, Welsh raids, sand blow, climatic deterioration – all contributed to the shrinking of settlement, in particular away from marginal land. The monuments this shrinkage has left behind are the deserted villages, now only visible as faint earthworks. It has been estimated that there are 29 deserted villages in Glamorgan, 18 of which have visible earthworks. Villages were another Norman creation, part of their manorialisation of the lowlands, and most were in existence by the end of the 12th century. Some disappeared altogether, some just shrank. Only the levelled platforms of houses, the boundary banks of yards and fields, and the sunken paths of cart tracks and roads are left. So little can be seen of any of them that none has been included in the main guide; anyone with a particular interest will find the better preserved ones listed in the Appendix.

83
Cardiff Castle, Cardiff
Medieval earthwork and masonry castle
11th–19th century
OS 171   ST 181766   R1

In central Cardiff at S end of Cathays Park, and to the N of Duke Street, Open to public daily. Entrance charge

Grant 1923

Cardiff Castle possesses a very fine Norman motte surmounted by a shell-keep, which was built within the walls of the fourth Roman fort on the site (no. 69). On entering the castle the motte lies directly ahead, in the north-west quarter of the Roman enclosure. It is a large, circular mound surrounded by a deep, water-filled ditch, on top of which is a stone keep.

The first castle was built in 1081 at the instigation of William the Conqueror himself. Like its Roman predecessor it secured the lowest crossing of the river Taff, and benefited from good land and sea communications.

From it Robert Fitzhamon, who rose to eminence as a follower of William Rufus and gained the lordship of Glamorgan in the 1090s, soon overran the surrounding lowlands. Cardiff Castle then became the administrative centre of the Norman lordship of Glamorgan. This first castle consisted of the large ditched motte with a timber keep on it, and a walled ward to the north-west, which reused Roman walling on the west and south and had a cross-wall from the keep to the Roman west wall. A large earth bank was thrown up over the remainder of the Roman wall to the east to form the outer bailey. This bank completely obscured the Roman wall and bank behind it, and at a later stage a wall was built on top of it, a small part of which has been found by excavation. During restoration work begun in the 1890s the medieval bank outside the wall was removed and the Roman walls restored. We are thus left with only the inner half of the medieval bank.

The shell-keep was the work of Robert, earl of Gloucester, who was Fitzhamon's son-in-law and successor and the illegitimate son of Henry I. He held the lordship of Glamorgan from about 1113 to 1147. The importance of

Cardiff Castle, general view of keep

the castle at this time is attested by its use as the prison of Robert, duke of Normandy from 1126 to 1134. The keep consists of a simple circular shell with faceted walls which are blank on the outside and relieved only by regularly spaced putlog holes. The walls stand to their full height, with a wall-walk around the top. Buildings that stood against the inside have disappeared and only a large fireplace and corbels remain to show where they were. The lovely white stone of the keep is thought to have been quarried at Leckwith Hill just to the west of Cardiff. The gate-tower, stairs and lower gate are all 13th–14th-century additions by the de Clares and Despensers.

Cardiff Castle continued as the headquarters of the lordship of Glamorgan throughout the Middle Ages, and as such remained one of the leading castles in south Wales. It was added to and strengthened, in particular by Gilbert de Clare in the second

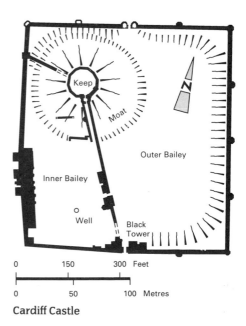

Cardiff Castle

half of the 13th century, who built the Black Tower by the south entrance (now restored) and a massive parapeted wall between it and the keep. This was demolished in the 18th century; its foundations were revealed and marked by modern low walling when the surface of the interior was lowered in the late 19th century. The outer bailey was used for the shire hall (a large rectangular 15th-century building) and houses of knights of the shire who were guarding the castle. Foundations of these buildings have been found during excavations. Further additions and alterations took place in the 15th century, when the castle was turned into a luxurious residence for the Beauchamp family by the building of new residential quarters and the Octagon Tower (its spire was added in the late 19th century) on the west side of the enclosure. Times were settled enough for a flower garden, or 'pleasance', to be made next to the private apartments south of the great hall, the outside of which can be seen from the inner ward (the interior has gone, but its vaulted basement survives). This part of the medieval castle – the Octagon Tower, the Herbert Tower (built in the late 16th century) and the rebuilt West Gate of the town – are best seen from the park outside the castle. Except for some 15th-century work, the medieval parts of the west block of the castle have been largely altered or obscured on its east side and in the interior by later rebuilding, and in particular by the fantastical works of the 3rd marquis of Bute's architect William Burges. It is in fact these that are the main attraction of Cardiff Castle today. However, the earlier contributions of William the Conqueror and Robert, earl of Gloucester, should not be overlooked.

84
Twmbarlwm, Risca
Medieval earthwork castle
12th–13th century
OS 171   ST 243926   U4

Take A467 Newport to Risca road. At N end of Rogerstone fork R towards Leisure Centre/ School. Turn R up to school, L at T-junction, continue 1.5ml (2.5km). Site a steep walk up to summit, on LHS

This is an imposing site in a spectacular position, visible for miles around. On the very top of the hill is a large motte and bailey castle, with precipitous slopes below it on all sides. The intention of its builder was obviously to guard against attack but its position is unusually inaccessible, and the castle may have been intended rather to be conspicuous and dominate the surrounding area.

The motte, a large circular mound with steep sides and a flat top, stands at the east end of the elongated summit of the hill. It was restored and landscaped in 1984 by the local authority. On its west side it is separated from the rest of the hilltop by a large rock-cut ditch with near vertical sides, on the outer lip of which is a small Bronze Age cairn. The bailey of the castle occupies the whole of the summit, and is delineated by a large bank and ditch. There are a number of gaps, particularly on the south and west sides, which may indicate that the castle was unfinished. There is also a possibility that the Normans reused an Iron Age hillfort, and that the bank and ditch date from that period.

The most likely builder of this castle is

Twmbarlwm earthwork castle from the air

Gilbert de Clare (d. 1295). Gilbert's desire for territorial aggrandisement led him to build numerous castles (see also nos 116, 117, 119). Twmbarlwm, in the lordship of Wentloog, would have been well placed to guard against and deter incursions from the north by rebellious Welshmen, and in particular Llywelyn ap Gruffudd, with whom Gilbert was in dispute over the control of the lordship of Senghenydd.

of a Norman castle here, on the ridge to the west of the Ebbw valley, on the fringes of the uplands, suggests Norman attempts to gain a foothold in the more determinedly independent uplands and to prevent Welsh incursions into the lowlands.

The juxtaposition of motte and church seen here recurs frequently in the area (see also nos 86, 88 and 90), and suggests that churches took advantage of the protection that a castle offered.

Aerial view of Twyn Tudor earthwork castle and St Tudor's Church

85
Twyn Tudor, Pontllanfraith
Medieval earthwork castle
12th century
OS 171   ST 193938   U3

1.5ml (2.5km) SE of Pontllanfraith on minor road off A472 Ystrad Mynach to Newbridge road. Take minor road to church at Mynyddislwyn. Site in second field to S on RHS. Good view from road. No public access

This large circular mound, surrounded by a ditch, is a typical Norman motte. Its sides are precipitous, its flat top is slightly dished, and there is now no sign of a bailey. The building

86
Tump Terrett Castle Mound, Trellech
Medieval earthwork castle
12th century
OS 162   SO 500054   U2

Take B4293 from Monmouth or Chepstow to Trellech. Motte is in field to SW of church. Public footpath either from NW corner of churchyard or track at S end of village

Trellech is rich in ancient monuments, three of which, Harold's Stones (no. 27), the Virtuous Well (no. 148) and this motte, are celebrated on a remarkable sundial of 1689 which now stands inside the church. The motte is a large, earthen steep-sided circular mound. The ditch

Tump Terrett castle mound

that originally encircled it survives only on the north side. All traces of the bailey have gone.

The history of the castle is obscure; but it is known to have been in existence before 1231. Trellech was within the Norman lordship of Usk, and the castle presumably had some manorial administrative function. A Norman town was planted here by the de Clares and flourished in the shadow of the castle. By 1288 its population was larger than that of Chepstow, and at the beginning of the 14th century it was one of the eight largest towns in Wales. Thereafter it declined and shrank, but its former success is attested by its large church, which has a fine late medieval cross in the churchyard (no. 141).

87
Mill Wood Castle Mound, Dingestow
Medieval earthwork castle
12th century
OS 161   SO 460104   U2

4ml (6.5km) W of Monmouth, just outside Dingestow. In Dingestow take minor road E towards Wonastow. Just past bridge over river Trothy take public footpath through wood on LHS. Motte a little way into wood, on LHS

A jungle of undergrowth now defends this large motte, but even if this prevents a closer look a good impression can be gained from the footpath. It is a typical Norman motte, circular and steep-sided, with ditches on the north and south sides. A causeway across the ditch in the north-west corner may indicate an entrance. The bailey was probably on the south side, delineated by an outer bank. The motte is in a good defensive position, with a steep drop to the river Trothy on one side and a dry ravine on the other. Strategically, it was positioned to secure the Monmouth–Raglan corridor into south Wales, and to guard the crossing of the river Trothy.

This castle was the precursor of a larger,

stone-built one, the site of which is the large rectangular mound to the west of the church. This was under construction in 1182 by Ranulf Poer, sheriff of Herefordshire, when it was attacked by Hywel ab Iorwerth, the Welsh lord of Caerleon, as part of his retaliation for the murder of Seisyllt ap Dyfnwal at Abergavenny Castle in 1175 by William de Braose.

88
Llanilid Castle Mound, Llanilid
Medieval earthwork castle
12th century
OS 170   SS 978813   U2

5ml (8km) E of Bridgend. Take A473 from Bridgend, or M4, towards Pencoed. Turn R towards Felindre opposite Pencoed. In Felindre take minor road L for c.0.5ml (0.8km) to church. Motte between church and road

This is a raised ringwork, a motte with a bank around the top. It follows the standard pattern of a steep-sided circular mound, with a ditch around it on all but the east side. A causeway across the ditch on the south side may indicate an entrance. The top of the mound is flat, and the bank around its rim 1–2m high. The bailey is thought to lie to the south, possibly including the ground that the church and churchyard now stand on. This proximity of the church and motte can be seen at several other sites in the area, such as Twyn Tudor (no. 85), Tump Terrett (no. 86), and Caerau Castle Ringwork (no. 90).

The castle was in the Norman sublordship of Ruthin, the overlords of which, from the 12th century to 1245, were the Siwards of Llanblethian and Talyfan. At some time after 1245 it was probably replaced as an administrative centre by the moated site of Gadlys (no. 97) south of the church.

89
Tomen y Clawdd, Pontypridd
Medieval earthwork castle
12th century
OS 171   ST 091865   U1

3ml (5km) SE of Pontypridd, off A473, in Church Village. In Church Village turn R at crossroads, take first L (Ffordd Gerdinan) and immediately L again. Mound at end of road in central island

The cosy domesticity of a modern housing estate makes it difficult to imagine the wild, tough times that caused this fine Norman motte to be built. Now tree-covered, it has the typical motte form of a circular flat-topped, steep-sided mound, surrounded by a ditch. The ditch is boggy in places and may have originally held water, as the motte stood at the confluence of two streams. Its history is obscure, but like Twyn Tudor (no. 85) it lies on high ground on the edge of the uplands, which were then in the hands of Welshmen unwilling to submit to Norman rule. It may have marked the northern limit of Norman control in this area.

90
Caerau Castle Ringwork, Cardiff
Medieval earthwork castle
12th century
OS 171   ST 134750   U2

In Cardiff fork S off A48 Cowbridge Road down Caerau Lane in Caerau district. Turn L down Caerau Road, then straight over the wide Heol Trelai into Church Road. Park at end of road and walk up track to Caerau hillfort. Ringwork is at the NE end

The Normans sometimes placed their castles inside existing fortifications: at Cardiff (no. 83) and Caerwent (no. 67) there are mottes within Roman forts. Here a ringwork, a variant of the

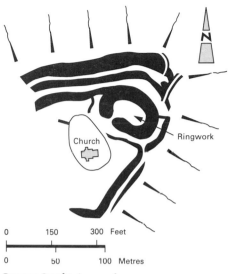

Caerau Castle ringwork

motte and bailey, was placed within an Iron Age hillfort. This both afforded extra protection from its banks and ditches, and gave an excellent strategic position overlooking the low ground now occupied by Cardiff.

The ringwork castle has no mound, only an enclosing bank, with a ditch outside it. On top of the bank there would have been a palisade, and an entrance tower would have probably doubled as a keep. Inside there might have been a hall and other utilitarian buildings. The well preserved bank is oval, with an entrance gap on the south-west side, and a slight ditch on the south. Halfway along the outside of the east side is a stone-lined spring which may have been the castle's water supply.

This is another site that demonstrates the protection afforded to churches by close proximity to a castle. The sadly ruined and vandalised 13th-century church of St Mary stands forlornly nearby, its graveyard desecrated. It is possible that the graveyard covers the area of the castle's bailey.

91
Platform Houses on the East Side of Gelligaer Common, Gelligaer
Medieval platform houses
13th–14th century
OS 171   SO 114029, 115027, 116027, 117026, 118025   U2

Take minor road on to Gelligaer Common. c.4ml (6km) N of Gelligaer park opposite a turn to the W, and walk c.500m NE. Platforms on slope below ridgetop

Fox 1939

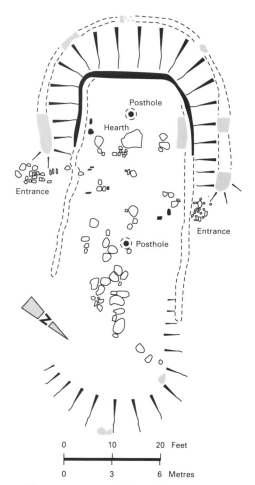

Gelligaer Common platform houses

This group of 11 well preserved medieval house platforms high up on open moorland is the largest concentration of such sites in south-east Wales. Being a little below the brow of the ridge they are difficult to see if approached from the west. However, the reeds in the northernmost group of three help, and once these are found the rest, with their bilberry-covered banks, lie at about the same height to the south-east and are easier to pick out.

All the typical features of platform houses are demonstrated by this group: their situation, their construction, their size and shape, and their pairing (at SO 115027 and SO 117026). The two northernmost are typical: their platforms are cut about 1.5m into the hillside, and the built-up outer ends jut out about 2m above the natural slope. Both have low side banks along the inner ends of the north and south sides, a feature not found on all of them.

At SO 114029 there are three, side by side. These were excavated in 1938 by Lady Aileen Fox. The central platform was found to have contained the main house. It was a rectangular building almost filling the platform, with walls of small stone slabs and turf layers, and two posts holding up the central ridge-pole. There were two doors opposite each other in the long sides,

approached by cobbled paths. Inside, at the inner end, was a hearth and a beaten earth floor, and at the outer end, vestiges of stone paving. Stone walling around the inner end prevented earth entering from the 'hood' cut into the hillside behind. The northernmost platform was found to have been occupied by a timber building of uncertain purpose. Its roof, doorways and approaches were similar to those of the central house, but inside there was only a rubbish pit and irregularly spaced postholes. These might have supported a raised wooden floor, in which case the building might have been a store. The southernmost platform contained a smaller building of similar construction in the outer part and an open yard with hearth and two post-holes, possibly for a roof or windbreak. Finds of pottery from these platforms date them to the 13th or 14th century. Lady Fox considered that this was a permanent settlement of native Welsh pastoralists eking out an existence at the fringes of habitable land.

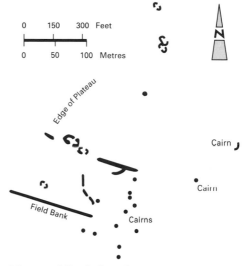

Dinas Noddfa platform houses

92
Platform Houses on Dinas Noddfa, Gelligaer
Medieval platform houses
13th–14th century
OS 171   SO 094031   U2

Take minor road N from Gelligaer on to the common. Turn L at T-junction just S of summit. Park near sharp LH bend and take track N. Site a short distance off track to W, on edge of plateau

Fox 1937

There are two groups of platform houses here, both typical in situation and form: three on a north-west-facing edge of a high moorland ridge, and two about 600m to the south, on a more westward-facing edge. Below them the ground drops steeply.

The southernmost group is of particular interest for several reasons. Both houses, one above the other, were excavated by Lady Aileen Fox in 1936; there are the remains of field walling near them; and close by to the south-east is a group of small cairns. The lower platform was found by Lady Fox to have had a roughly rectangular house occupying most of it. It had stone and turf walls, parts of which survive, turf-covered, at the western end. Its ridged roof was supported in the middle by three posts. In the middle of each

long side was an entrance with a porch, approached by a paved or cobbled path. Inside a central area of paving and a cesspit were found. At the 'hood' end a stone wall prevented soil slipping down into the house, and a drainage ditch carried rainwater away.

The upper house was smaller and yet more primitive, with turf walls revetted on the inside by stone slabs, one entrance and some stone paving. Only a whetstone and some iron slag of indeterminate age were found in the houses, which demonstrates the extreme poverty of the occupants. The low field walls to the south and the group of small cairns are thought to be earlier in date. Two of the walls run parallel to each other, aligned approximately east–west, and nearby are short stretches of curving wall. The cairns are smaller than most Bronze Age burial cairns, and could have a different purpose. The most likely explanation is that they are clearance cairns (piles of stones gathered up from the fields in order to clear them for cultivation) possibly associated with the small fields partly delineated by the turf-covered walls.

93
Platform Houses on Cefn y Brithdir, Rhymney
Medieval platform houses
13th–14th century
OS 171   SO 129030   U4

On ridge W of Rhymney valley. From the N take Fochriw road from Pontlottyn, and on edge of Pontlottyn turn L on to track at crossroads. Site c.2ml (3km) to S (fork R after 1.5ml), on RHS of track just below a Bronze Age cairn next to the track

These are three typical platform houses set close together, side by side, on the westward-facing edge of the ridge. At the same altitude on the next ridge to the west is another group (no. 91). The bracken cover in the summer makes them difficult to see: look for slight bumps in the otherwise smooth slope.

The northernmost platform is the most distinct, showing clearly the method used for creating a level base for a house: the hillside is cut away at the east end and the west end is correspondingly artificially raised using the cut-away material. All three have a slight bank defining the edge of their outer, western ends. None has been excavated, but one can expect much the same pattern of primitive houses as was found on Gelligaer Common (nos 91 and 92).

94
Carn y Wiwer Platform Houses, Ynyshir
Medieval platform houses
13th–14th century
OS 170   ST 027940   U2

5ml (8km) NW of Pontypridd. Take B4273 to Ynysybwl. 1ml (1.5km) on take LH turn to Llanwonno, where turn L. Park after 0.6ml (1km) and take forest track on RHS. Site after

c.500m, on open moorland beyond forest. Alternative track from Ynyshir

Perched on the edge of the high ridge overlooking the Rhondda Fach valley are four platform houses, disposed, as they so often are, in pairs. Faint irregularities in the smooth contours of the hillside, and reeds growing in them help reveal their presence. They are of the usual size, shape and orientation, and are well preserved.

The southernmost pair lie close together, side by side; the northern pair are similar, with one slightly higher than the other. The lower of this pair is the most impressive of all four, having a steep 'hood', with a well preserved bank around the upper end, which served to divert rainwater from the walls of the house.

To the east and north is a group of about 19 small cairns, with evidence of ploughing

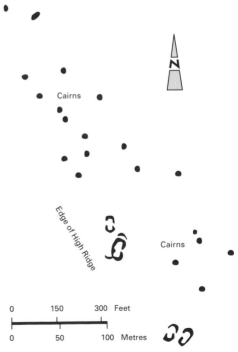

Carn y Wiwer platform houses

around them. The plough lines run north–
south, respect the cairns, and stop just short
of the platform houses (but some run right
between the southernmost platforms). The
relationship between all these elements is not
known: the mounds may be Bronze Age
burial cairns, and the ploughing may be later
than the platforms, or they could all be
contemporary, with the mounds being
clearance cairns for the fields around the
houses.

Hen Gwrt moated site from the air

95
Hen Gwrt Moated Site, Llantilio Crossenny
Medieval moated site
13th–17th century
OS 161   SO 396151   U1   Cadw

*Just N of Llantilio Crossenny in angle of
junction between B4233 Monmouth to
Abergavenny road and minor road to White
Castle to N*

Craster and Lewis 1963

It is worth pausing on the way to White Castle
(no. 113), a little way to the north, to stroll in
this peaceful enclave. As moated sites go it is
large and well preserved, and is one of the
very few in the area with water still in the
moat. What is left of the site is a large, level,
almost square island, surrounded by a wide
moat between the interior and the higher
ground outside.

Romantic connections have been made
between Hen Gwrt, or Old Court, and Dafydd
Gam, hero of Agincourt, but there is no
evidence to substantiate them. Partial
excavation of the site in 1957, along with a
plan made in about 1820, have revealed the
presence of at least two buildings on the
island, a larger post-medieval one on the
north side, and a smaller 14th-century one on
the south. When Llantilio Crossenny belonged
to the bishops of Llandaff Hen Gwrt was
probably the manor house. It appears to have

been occupied first in the early 13th century,
soon after the building of White Castle. The
moat was dug about a hundred years later,
possibly around an existing building. There
was a wooden bridge across it on the east
side, next to the main road, and some of its
supporting timbers have been found.
Occupation continued into the 14th century,
but appears to have petered out in the 15th,
when the manor buildings may have been
demoted to farm use. Damage during
Glyndŵr's rebellion may have been partly
responsible for this decline.

The second phase of occupation was
entirely different. This was during the 16th
and 17th centuries, when the site belonged to
the earls of Worcester of Raglan Castle (no.
122). The site was part of their Red Deer Park,
and the building erected, probably on the site
of or incorporating a medieval one, near the
north side of the island, was in all probability
the park's hunting lodge. The building on the
south side was levelled and a wall erected in
its place; there is evidence that a wall
completely encircled the island at this time.

The building of the now-demolished

Llantilio Court in 1775 resulted in much stone robbing and in the moving of the road, which subsequently cut off the south corner of the site.

96
Castell Moel, Bonvilston
Medieval moated site
13th–15th century
OS 170   ST 054734   U2/R2

Take A48 to Bonvilston. 0.6ml (1km) to the W turn S towards Llancarfan. After 500m stop by track on LHS which leads to Liege Castle Farm. Public footpath on LHS to site on hilltop in first field. Off-path permission from owners (Liege Castle Farm)

Castell Moel, or Liege Castle to give it its original English name, is the site of a moated manor house. It lies within the fragmentary remains of a small Iron Age hillfort. The hilltop situation is typical of a hillfort but not of moated manors, which were usually on low-lying marshy ground. However, the rectangular site was undoubtedly surrounded by a deep ditch which survives in good conditions at its northern end. The southern end, now destroyed by ploughing, was still in existence when the site was described in 1866. On the raised platform within the ditch is a rectangular sunken area, all that remains of the manor house. The hillfort scarp

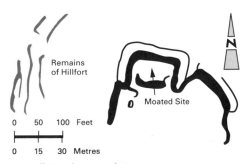

Castell Moel moated site

continues south-eastwards from the eastern side of the ditch.

The history of the house is confused, but Liege Castle is known to have been a submanor of Bonvilston, and the house could have been its administrative base. It was always owned by families with principal residences elsewhere, and was probably lived in by a retainer. Possibly built in the 13th century, it was already under the plough by the time Rice Merrick mentioned it in 1578.

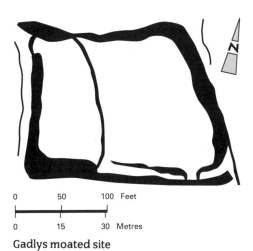

Gadlys moated site

97
Gadlys, Llanilid
Medieval moated site
13th century
OS 170   SS 979812   U2/R2

1ml (1.6km) E of Pencoed. Take minor road to Felindre out of Pencoed. In Felindre turn L to Llanilid. Park at church. Public footpath to site in field to S. Off-path permission from occupiers (Llanilid Farm)

This is probably a much ploughed-down moated site, similar in type and date to others in the area (see Appendix). It may have been the administrative centre of the sublordship of Ruthin during the 13th century, possibly superseding the ringwork castle nearby (no. 88). Its situation in low ground is a typical one for moated sites, and water could have been let into the moat from the boggy area to the north.

All that remains of the site are low banks on the west, south and east sides of a roughly rectangular area. Slight vestiges of the moat which once surrounded it are visible on the west.

98
Chepstow Castle, Chepstow
Medieval masonry castle
11th–17th century
OS 162   ST 533941   R1   Cadw

In centre of Chepstow, on W bank of river Wye, near old A48 bridge. Signposted. Entrance charge. Cadw standard hours

Perks 1967; Knight: Cadw Guide

Chepstow Castle is one of the most important and interesting castles in south Wales. It is also one of the most dramatic, lying like a great grey ship on top of a sheer cliff above the river Wye, which makes an enormous loop at this point. The castle's Welsh name, Striguil, means 'bend in the river'. Its elongated shape is the result of several phases of expansion outwards from the nucleus of the Norman keep in the middle.

From its beginning in 1067 to the Civil War in the 17th century Chepstow Castle was of great strategic importance; all through the medieval period the marcher lords of Chepstow were among the most powerful barons in the land. The castle's history is faithfully mirrored in its buildings, which also give an excellent demonstration of the development of medieval military planning and architecture.

The first phase is the Norman keep or great tower with a walled ward or bailey on either side. The keep is one of the earliest stone Norman castles in Britain, built from the start in stone between 1067 and 1071 by William fitz Osbern, lord of Breteuil, earl of Hereford, cousin and boon companion of William the Conqueror. His purpose was to guard the river crossing and consolidate his hold on south-east Wales. It was four-sided, originally two-storey, its austere surfaces mostly blank, relieved only by flat buttresses and rudimentary string courses marking floor levels, one of which uses red Roman tiles. Windows, small and round-headed, were only allowed on the secure, river side. The great hall and lord's living quarters were on the first floor, with service and storage rooms below. The original entrance is a fine round-headed, geometrically decorated doorway on the east side, which led to the hall up stairs in the wall on the left. The floor level of the hall is marked by slots for enormous joists. Inside the keep a great confusion of styles and building phases becomes apparent. Several different types of window survive in the north wall; the only Norman one left is on the extreme right. Also Norman are the blind arcades on the west and south walls, which originally continued along the south wall. Traces of painted stucco in them show that the keep's interior would have been less gloomy than its present-day appearance might suggest.

Further alterations to the keep ran parallel with building works outside it. Between 1219 and 1245 the hall and living quarters were modernised with larger windows decorated with quatrefoil tracery, and an upper chamber was added at the west end. A great arch supported this upper floor, the decorated springings of which are visible in the north and south walls. At the same time an arcaded gallery was built between the keep and the cliff edge, enabling the wards either side to be sealed off if necessary. Between 1292 and 1300 the second floor was extended along the whole length of the building, and in this part a new, distinctive style of window with a flattened or 'Caernarfon' arch was used. Only the north and west sides of this upper floor remain, but their windows are well preserved.

Chepstow Castle, the keep

A curious feature of the keep are the two small circular windows in the west wall above the arcading. These appear asymmetrically placed on the inside, although on the outside the southernmost one is in the centre of the wall, the reason being that the south wall of the keep is much thicker than the well protected north wall.

The next phase in the castle's history is its tenure by the great knight William Marshal, known as the 'flower of chivalry'. In 1189 Henry II granted him the 'damsel of Striguil', the de Clare heiress Isabella, in marriage, and

with her came many castles, including Chepstow. He strengthened the vulnerable east side by rebuilding the Middle Bailey wall on that side. This new outer wall was innovatory in Britain at the time, with the novel features of the incorporation of a round tower, an element imported from France, and true arrowslits. The gateway at the north end remained simple; all the strength was in the wall and towers. Although partly ruined and much altered in the Tudor period, when the north tower became a kitchen and buildings were put up against it, the wall still appears formidable from its outer, east side.

After William's death in 1219 his five sons continued to build until the death of the youngest, Anselm, in 1245. They strengthened existing defences, brought the keep up to date, and added the two outer cells, now called the Upper and Lower Baileys, to give the castle its present size. Another leap forward in military architecture, the great gatehouse, was built in this phase. This is the gatehouse through which the visitor now enters the castle. Visitors in the 19th century 'thundered at the portal for admission with a cannon-ball suspended by a chain'. It survives more or less intact, and its strength is immediately apparent. The windows in it are later Tudor insertions; originally its exterior was blank except for arrowslits. There was also originally a barbican and drawbridge in front. In the left-hand tower was a guardroom, in the right a prison. The gatehouse and part of the east curtain wall are the only parts of the Lower Bailey dating from this early 13th-century phase. In the Middle Bailey the south curtain wall was rebuilt, and a round tower added. The Upper Bailey was rebuilt and a rectangular tower, which stands to battlement level on its west

and south sides, added in the south-west corner. The quality of the finely moulded windows on its first floor suggests that this was accommodation for someone of high rank, perhaps William's widow, the dowager countess of Pembroke.

Outside the Upper Bailey a new ward, the Barbican, was added for purely military purposes. The rock-cut ditch which separates this from the rest of the castle was originally the outer defence on this side. This well preserved ward has a strong curtain wall which stands to battlement level, a round tower with arrowslits on four levels in the angle, and a simple gateway at the north end, converted to a three-storey gatehouse with portcullises towards the end of the 13th century.

The last great phase of building work at the castle was during its tenure by Roger Bigod III, the grandson of William Marshal's daughter Maud, from 1270 to 1306. He it was who also instigated the building of the great church at Tintern Abbey (no. 123) and the town wall (no. 144). His contribution at Chepstow was fourfold. He strengthened the Barbican gate, completed the top floor to the keep, built a domestic range along the north side of the

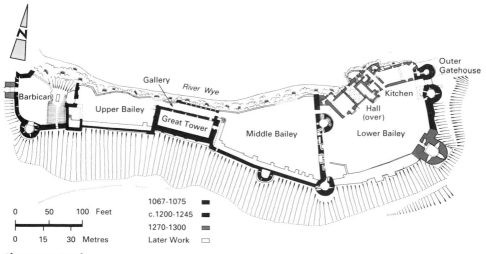

Chepstow Castle

Lower Bailey, and built the great tower on its east side known as Marten's Tower. At the west end of the domestic range was the great hall, of which little is left. Its main entrance was the storeyed porch on its south-east side, and it was also reached by steps up from a central passage off which led various service rooms and the kitchen (on the right). There are a few clues to the hall's original splendour, including traces of painted decoration, some fake ashlar walling and a fine blocked window in the north-east wall. At the end of the service passage steps lead down to a cellar beneath the hall which still retains its rib vaulting. The balcony room, from which there is a magnificent view of the river, is a Tudor addition. To the east of the kitchen was a three-storey block of private chambers, some of the windows of which retain their fine 13th-century tracery.

Marten's Tower, to the south of the entrance, is a four-storey, D-shaped tower and was the last part added to the castle by Roger Bigod III, probably replacing an earlier tower built by William Marshal's sons. It housed Bigod's own private quarters, and is another example of an advance in military planning at the castle. It was a self-contained stronghold within a stronghold, and could be separately defended if necessary, with all its entrances protected by portcullises. Its original windows, although widely splayed, narrow to slits on the outside, and each merlon of the battlements is pierced by an arrowslit. The base is strengthened with great spur buttresses. To complete the self-sufficiency there is a small chapel at the top, with beautiful floriated carving around its east window. The battlements at the top are very well preserved, with carved stone figures above the arrowslits, and the tower boasts two late-medieval doors. The large windows facing inwards date from the 16th and 17th centuries when the need for defence had passed. In the 17th century this tower was used as a prison for the regicide Henry Marten from 1660 to 1680, and it is from him it now takes its name.

Bigod had made the castle virtually

impregnable, and this immense strength deterred would-be attackers, including Owain Glyndŵr. Its life became for the most part uneventful except for the murder here of Roger Vaughan of Tretower Court by Jasper Tudor in 1471. The castle did not see military action until the Civil War, when it was twice held by Royalists, twice bombarded and twice surrendered to the Parliamentarians. Artillery bombardment breached the curtain wall of the Lower Bailey, and after the war, when the castle was garrisoned first by Parliamentarians and then by Royalists, the south curtain wall was greatly thickened, the south towers filled with earth and the parapets strengthened and given wider rectangular openings, all in an effort to strengthen it against mortar fire. The two inner walls of the rectangular tower in the Upper Bailey were demolished to ease access to the now much wider wall-walk. But the castle was not to see any more action, and at the end of the 17th century its active life came to an end. It now stands as a memorial to the great men of the Middle Ages who made it one of the strongest and most innovatory castles in the land.

99
Monmouth Castle, Monmouth
Medieval masonry castle
12th–14th century
OS 162   SO 506129   U1   Cadw

In centre of Monmouth, W of Agincourt Square. Park and walk up Castle Hill Road to castle on far side of Parade Ground. Signposted

Taylor: Official Guide

Only a fragment is left of this once important castle; the curtain wall, gatehouse and great round keep, which stood until the Civil War where the Great House now stands, have all completely vanished. All that is left is the ruined Great Tower and Hall. These stand on the edge of a precipitous slope down to the river Monnow, on the west side of what was the castle ward. This was roughly circular, surrounded on the west and north by the river and on the east and south by a wall and ditch, which is still partly apparent in back gardens behind Agincourt Square. Half-way along Castle Hill Road was the entrance, consisting of a bridge and strong gatehouse.

William fitz Osbern chose this strategic position, guarding crossings of the Wye and Monnow rivers, for one of his marcher castles sometime between 1067 and 1071, when he died. The Great Tower is similar in style to that at Chepstow, and was certainly built by about 1150. What can be seen are parts of its east and south sides. The west side fell in 1647, the north-west side remains but cannot be seen from the town side, and a house lies over the rest. This was a fine early Norman rectangular two-storeyed building with the hall and main apartments on the first floor and a cellar or undercroft below. The east wall displays some Norman features: the small round-headed windows, the fragment of simple string course and the flat pilaster buttress in the south-east corner, one of a series which originally continued all along the wall. The entrance was at first-floor level on the south side.

The castle was held uneventfully by Norman lords as the headquarters of an independent lordship until 1267, when it was granted with the Three Castles (nos 113, 114, 115) to Henry III's son Edmund 'Crouchback', when he became earl of Lancaster. He immediately built the large rectangular building to the south of the Great Tower, known as the Hall. It was a single-storey building containing one large room used for the holding of courts. It continued in use as such right up to the 17th century.

All the walls, except the north, stand almost to their full height. The entrance was the gap in the wall in the north-east corner, on the west side of which a moulded base of a door jamb is visible. The fireplace was in the middle of the north wall, and there were windows,

Monmouth Castle, The Great Tower

now blocked, in the south wall. A later medieval window, also blocked, was inserted in the east wall.

In the mid-14th century, during the lordship of Henry of Grosmont, 1st duke of Lancaster, the upper part of the Great Tower was transformed by the insertion of large Decorated windows. The elaborate frame of one of these is visible in the east wall. The original entrance was replaced by a tall door, and the tower was reroofed. At this stage 12th-century corbels of carved heads were reset high up in the east hall, where they are still visible. This tower was almost certainly the birthplace of the future Henry V on 16 September 1387.

The end came for the castle in the Civil War, when it changed hands three times and was eventually slighted by the Parliamentarians. A local man's diary for 1647 records that on 30 March the townsmen and soldiers began pulling down the round tower, which stood where Great Castle House now stands, and that on 22 December 'about twelve o'clock, the Tower in the Castle of Monmouth fell down, upon one side, whilst we were at sermon'. William Gilpin, a visitor in the late 18th century, exclaimed that 'the transmutations of TIME are often *ludicrous . . . it is now converted into a yard for fatting ducks!'*

100
Usk Castle, Usk
Medieval masonry castle
12th–14th century
OS 171   SO 377011   R2

*In centre of Usk, 10ml (16km) N of Newport.
Access off A472 N up track opposite Fire
Station. Private ownership: open by
appointment (tel. 02913 2563). Ring bell at
gate for entry*

Knight 1977

Usk Castle keep

Though it never played a leading role in the
history of the area, all through the medieval
period the holders of Usk Castle were either
royal or of high rank. The Normans
established a castle here probably soon after
William fitz Osbern overran the area between
1066 and 1071. Its position was a strategic
one, as it had been for the Romans a
thousands years earlier.

The earliest stone building is the four-sided
keep, which rises up dramatically within the
gardens of Castle House. This was probably
the work of the de Clares, who held the
lordship of Usk from 1115 to 1174 – a castle is
first mentioned at Usk in 1138. Although
much altered, enough of the original survives
to show that this was a typical Norman keep.
It is in an offensive position, jutting out from
the curtain wall, and is rectangular, austere,
with few windows and immensely thick walls.
It stands to its full height, and its walls are
now punctured by doors and windows from
four phases of building, in the 12th, 13th,
14th and 15th centuries. The 12th-century
keep had three storeys, with an unlit
basement and entrance by wooden stairs on
the inner side of the first floor.

In 1174 the castle fell to the Welsh lord of
Caerleon, Hywel ab Iorwerth, and was in the
hands of the Crown for a while after that. It
was during this time, in 1185, that the
considerable sum of £10.3s. was spent on
strengthening it, probably because of Welsh
restiveness at the time. A substantial garrison

was recorded as being in residence – 10
archers, 10 residents, 15 'mobile' sergeants,
four watchmen, a chaplain and a clerk.

The major part of the castle was built in the
early 13th century, probably by William
Marshal (see Chepstow castle, no. 98),
between 1212 and 1219. He transformed Usk
into a major castle, a demonstration of his
great power to the Welsh and to his
neighbouring antagonist Reginald de Braose.

As at Chepstow, the very latest French ideas
on military layout were used here, albeit
slightly tentatively. The castle was given a
strong curtain wall with round towers at four
of the eight angles of its squashed octagonal
shape. The curtain wall is for the most part
well preserved, standing almost to its full
height in places. The entrance is a simple
arched gateway to the north of the keep. Its
portcullis slot is visible but no details of any

gatehouse, if there was one, survive. Of the round towers only that on the south-west side, the so-called 'Garrison' tower, survives to any extent. That in the west corner was destroyed by 14th-century rebuilding, the north tower was rebuilt in the late 13th century, and only the foundations of the south tower remain.

The 'Garrison' tower is impressive, particularly from the outside, where its battered base and great height can best be appreciated. It is similar in concept and style to the slightly later keeps at Caldicot Castle (no. 115) and Skenfrith Castle (no. 114) – a stronghold capable of independent defence. There are four floors, marked on the outside by ashlar offsets. The lowest has been buried on the inner side by later raising of the ground level. At third-floor level there is a ring of beam holes which would have supported a wooden fighting gallery or hoard. A blocked

doorway at this level would have led on to it. There are arrowslits on the two lower floors, as there were originally on the upper floors. The entrance was at first-floor level, reached by wooden stairs. On the second floor are late 13th-century doors giving access to the wall-walk, and a narrow mural passage to a garderobe of the same date (beware the sheer drop). The trefoil-headed windows of the upper floors also date from the late 13th-century alterations.

After William Marshal's death in 1219 his sons held the castle until 1245. It was during this time that the keep was modified to provide more lordly apartments. The castle's strength was demonstrated when Henry III, in his quarrel with Richard Marshal, laid siege to it in 1233 but failed to take it.

The next building phase was after 1262, when Gilbert de Clare held the castle. He instigated the alterations to the 'Garrison'

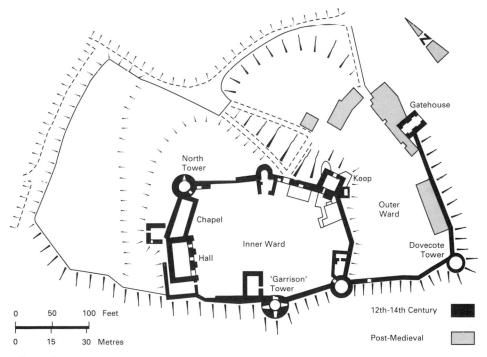

Usk Castle

tower, and rebuilt the north tower: according to an account of 1289 it was 'new' and was used to house Gilbert's treasure. It survives more or less intact, and is a three-storey D-shaped tower, with stone stairs on the inner side and a garderobe tucked into the south-east corner. On the first floor was a well appointed room with a fireplace, a window on the inner side, and some cruciform arrowslits on the outer side. Very little survives of the second floor, but an 18th-century print shows that it had corbelled-out battlements like those on the 'Garrison' tower. The door to the outside is modern. The 1289 document throws some light on life of the castle in Gilbert's time; it mentioned the falconer's wages of 18d. a week, and the purchase of a cocker dog for the large sum of 16s.

In 1314 the last Gilbert de Clare died at the battle of Bannockburn, and Usk Castle passed to his sister Elizabeth de Burgh (d. 1360). The castle then entered a phase of much greater domestic comfort, with the building of the hall block, square tower and chapel along the north-west side of the inner ward. The hall, probably built in the 1320s, is ruinous, but its layout is clear. The entrance was at the west end, with a ground-floor door into the service basement and a door above into the screens passage of the first-floor hall. Three ragged openings on the inner side mark the position of windows. The large fireplace in the north-west wall is a 15th-century addition. To the south-west was the service block, now completely gone. Adjoining the hall to the north-east was the chapel, a simple single-storey building of which very little remains. Now called St George's chapel, it is used as a family burial ground and should be treated with respect. A square block for domestic chambers was added outside the curtain wall.

In 1368–99 the lordship of Usk was held through marriage by the earls of March. They built the outer ward and gatehouse on lower ground to the south-east of the inner ward, and the small north-east angle-tower next to the entrance of the inner ward, of which only the foundations remain. The roughly rectangular outer ward is now entirely occupied by the gardens of Castle House. It may have been levelled, scarped and palisaded as an outer bailey in the early Norman period, but was not enclosed in stone until this late 14th-century phase. The gatehouse, a vaulted passageway with a single large room over it, is now incorporated into the later Castle House, and is not open to the public. The curtain wall runs south-westwards from the house to a small circular tower, the 'Dovecote' tower, which is the most visible part of the castle from the town. It has been altered since the 14th century but stands to its full height, with two storeys and a basement. The curtain wall between it and the south corner of the inner ward is largely intact, but is less substantial than the earlier walls.

The last major event in the castle's life was the decisive defeat of Glyndŵr's son's forces at Pwll Melyn (Yellow Pool) not far to the north in 1405. At that time the castle was in royal hands, and Richard, duke of York used it as a favourite retreat. In the third quarter of the 15th century Sir William Herbert of Raglan Castle (no. 122) held Usk. He did some modernising work on the keep and the hall and built lodgings against the inner side of the inner ward, of which only the foundations remain. After his death in 1469 the castle was abandoned and fell into decay.

101
Abergavenny Castle, Abergavenny
Medieval masonry castle
12th–14th century
OS 161   SO 299139   U1

On S side of centre of Abergavenny. Take Castle Street to car park. Castle a short walk to the S. Museum opening hours as advertised

Enough remains of this castle to show that it must have been impressive indeed, with very high walls which the 16th-century historian Leland said were 'likely not to fall'. Alas, most of them have, the victims of Civil War slighting and general plunder.

From its early beginnings this was an important castle, the headquarters of the Norman lordship of Abergavenny, used for accommodation by kings if they were in the locality. It stands on a spur above the river Usk, in a good position to secure the valley and prevent Welsh incursions into the lowlands.

The approach to the castle is through the gatehouse, which is its youngest part, added in about 1400 possibly in response to the threat from Owain Glyndŵr. It has a long, narrow passageway, originally vaulted and with rooms above which must have been

Abergavenny Castle

comfortable, judging from the large window and fireplace on the south side.

To the right of the gatehouse is an impressive stretch of curtain wall standing almost to its full height and retaining most of its facing stone. It is the main remnant of the castle of the second half of the 12th century, built when William de Braose held the lordship of Abergavenny. This was a turbulent time, and the castle was the scene of two particularly treacherous incidents. In 1175 William de Braose murdered Seisyllt ap Dyfnwal, lord of Castell Arnallt, a Welsh stronghold a few miles to the south-east, here on Christmas Day. In retaliation the Welsh lord of Caerleon, Hywel ab Iorwerth, burnt the castle in 1182 and went on to destroy Dingestow Castle (now reduced to a grassy mound). William Camden, the 16th-century antiquary, said that Abergavenny Castle 'has been oftener stain'd with the infamy of treachery, than any other castle in Wales'. Only fragments of the rest of the curtain wall remain, mainly on the east side where the stub of a rectangular projecting tower is visible. Built into a later cottage, now part of a museum, is a fragment of a tower, and on the north side the curtain wall is much reduced and was landscaped into a rock garden in the late 19th century.

Within the walls, the circular mound, on which the rather incongruous Victorian 'keep' of 1819 sits, is the oldest part of the castle. It is the motte thrown up by Hamelin de Ballon, Norman conqueror of this area, before 1090. Early in the 12th century de Ballon founded the Benedictine priory of Abergavenny. Soon afterwards a stone keep was built on the motte, and the present building probably stands on its foundations. During the 12th century the hall, which was between the gatehouse and the tall ruined towers to the west, remained a timber building.

There was much building during the 13th and 14th centuries, when the castle was held by the Hastings family. The most prominent remains from this period are the towers in the west corner, one circular and one semi-octagonal. Only their outer walls survive, but these stand four storeys high in places. On the left, on the south side, is a small rectangular garderobe tower with an arched outlet at the bottom. The broken end of the curtain wall is attached to it. The octagonal tower has large window openings, mostly now without their dressed stone surrounds, and the base of a spiral staircase. The uppermost floor, with a complete, round-arched window, may have been the chapel. The strength and high quality of these towers can best be appreciated from the outside.

Attached to the eastern end of the towers is a cross-wall which divided the castle ward into two. Its northern end was one wall of the hall block, and has a doorway which led into the rooms below the hall. Further along is a fine small lancet window and the base of a spiral staircase. The stretch of walling standing on its own nearby was part of a free-standing building.

The hall stood where the present ground level is sunken, and was a large rectangular room at first-floor level, its floor where the curtain wall narrows slightly. Its inner wall has completely gone. It was entered by external stairs at the north-east end, where the steps and doorway are visible.

In the middle of the lawn is an underground room, thought to have been a dungeon. It is suitably dark and damp, with a vaulted ceiling, and is reached by steep, narrow steps.

102
Newcastle, Bridgend
Medieval masonry castle
12th–16th century
OS 170   SS 902801   R2   Cadw

From centre of Bridgend take A473 Laleston road. Turn 1st R up St Leonard's Road after junction with A4063. Up hill, turn R at T-junction. Castle at end of road. Entrance door behind car park. Key (enormous) from shop or no. 1 The Square (row of cottages adjacent). Entrance charge

The castles of Newcastle, Ogmore (no. 103) and Coity (no. 104) were established at the western limit of early Norman penetration into south Wales and were built to consolidate the Normans' hold on the area. Newcastle is strategically placed on a high bluff above the Ogmore valley to guard the river crossing below.

The original castle, first mentioned in 1106, marked the western limit of Robert Fitzhamon's conquests. It is thought to have been an earthwork castle of ringwork type, and its location is unknown. It could have been on the site of the present castle, in which case its palisade may have underlain the later stone curtain wall. The round-cornered stone building, the foundations of which are visible in the south-east corner of the interior, could, on stylistic grounds, date from this initial phase, and might have been a keep; in the 19th century a stony mound was recorded here which was interpreted by G. T. Clark as the ruins of a free-standing keep. Rebuilding in stone probably took place during an unsettled phase in the 1180s, when the king himself, Henry II, held the castle. The layout and style of stonework are of this period, and the fact that it was in royal hands would explain its superior quality.

Apart from refurbishments in the south tower in the late 16th century the castle is virtually untouched since the late 12th century: in 1217 it was given to the Turbervilles, lords of Coity, who had little use for it as their main seat was nearby Coity Castle (no. 104).

The castle's most outstanding feature is its complete Norman doorway, which greets the visitor approaching the castle from the south. It is late 12th-century, contemporary with the curtain wall. On the inside it is quite plain, but the outside is given fine decorative treatment. Sutton stone is used, as it is for the high-quality ashlar facing still in place around it, and also for all other quoins and dressings in the castle. A round-headed arch over attached columns with crude Ionic capitals frames the doorway, around which is a shallower segmental arch surrounded by

Newcastle, the Norman doorway

sunken rectangular panels and 'pellet' decoration. This is a rare survival from the period, and no other decoration of the kind is known in Glamorgan. The steps in front are modern.

Once inside the curtain wall, the circuit of which is complete, the nature of the castle becomes apparent. It is a courtyard castle, roughly circular in plan, with two mural towers built into the curtain wall on the south and west sides, and originally a few buildings on the edge of the north and east sides. The curtain wall, which was built in straight sections, is impressive and stands to its full height on the west side. On the outside it was strongly battered at the base, and this batter is still visible, although most of the facing stone has gone from the lower parts of the walls, and from all of the east wall.

The square mural towers were a new development in military planning when built, but were soon to be superseded by round towers. The south tower is the better preserved, standing in parts three storeys high. It was much altered for domestic use in the late 16th century, when Tudor windows and fireplaces were inserted. Only the ground floor of the west tower survives. Very fragmentary foundations of a detached building at the north end, and the more

complete foundations of two buildings against the east curtain wall are visible. The smaller, northernmost one of these is thought to be early 13th-century, while the larger, southernmost one is possibly the keep of the initial phase.

103
Ogmore Castle, St Brides Major
Medieval masonry castle
12th–14th century
OS 170   SS 882769   U2   Cadw

Take B4524 Ewenny to Ogmore-by-Sea road. 1ml (1.6km) W of Ewenny turn R down narrow lane to castle. Signposted. Cadw standard hours

In this peaceful spot by the river Ewenny stand the ruins of the second of the three early Norman castles in the vicinity (see also Newcastle, no. 102, and Coity, no. 104). Pushing westwards in the early years of the 12th century William de Londres set up his stronghold here, in a strategic spot by a ford over the tidal river (now marked by ancient stepping stones). He built an earthwork castle whose inner ward was surrounded by a deep ditch designed to fill with water at high tide. It was also defended by a ring-bank with a palisade on top, and the initial castle was probably wooden. The outer ward or bailey is a D-shaped area tacked on to the west side of the inner ward, with banks around the edge of the west and south, and partly surrounded by a shallow ditch. Originally it would have had a palisade around the edge and wooden buildings.

There were three building phases of the stone castle, albeit all close together in date. First came the early 12th-century keep, then a 12th-century building, the so-called cellar, and then in the early 13th century the curtain wall, gateway and all other buildings in the inner ward.

Ogmore Castle, inner ward

The keep is the rectangular building to the left of the entrance to the inner ward. This is one of the oldest Norman stone buildings in south-east Wales. Its west wall is the highest remaining part of the castle; the other walls stand only to basement level. Like all Norman buildings it has an austere simplicity. A first-floor entrance on the east side led into the great hall, whose floor level is marked by the large sockets for floor beams in the west wall. This wall has two windows, small and round-headed, still with some of their ashlar Sutton stone dressing, and a fine fireplace, also in Sutton stone, flanked by columns with simple capitals; with the austerity went a certain degree of comfort and aesthetic appreciation. When the curtain wall was built another storey was added, as indicated by the clear demarcation line on the external wall faces between the old and the new work. Also added was the latrine tower, which juts out at the north end of the hall, and whose spiral staircase is visible high up on the inside of the west wall. It had latrines (or garderobes) on each floor.

The next building phase is represented by the remains of the so-called cellar, opposite the keep, of which only the basement survives. This is entered down steps which lead into a barrel-vaulted passage. Its free-standing position, slightly in from the curtain wall, suggests that it might have been respecting an existing bank which was levelled when the curtain wall was built, and the spoil from it used to build up the level of the interior. At this juncture more steps had to be added to the entrance, up to the new level, and the join is clearly visible as an upstanding sill.

The rest of the stonework of the castle dates from the early 13th century. The most important part is the curtain wall, which is built in straight sections as at Newcastle and Coity. It had no towers, and the entrance on the west was a simple gate-tower. In parts of the east and south sides it survives almost to its full height, still with its wall-walk at the top. At the north end of the east side a small opening with jambs on either side was originally a doorway. The footings of several rectangular buildings are ranged around the edge of the ward. The large rectangular building overlooking the river might have been a hall. To the north of the keep is a replica of a pre-Norman inscribed stone found during clearance work.

On leaving the inner ward there are two further interesting features, the stone footings outside the gateway, under the present wooden bridge, for the drawbridge mechanism, and the walls across the ditch. These linked the curtain wall, with which they are contemporary, with the presumed palisade around the outer ward. The holes in the bottom are to let sea water in.

The simple rectangular building against the north side of the outer ward dates from the 14th century and is thought to have been a courthouse. It was built partly over a dismantled limekiln, the lower part of which is visible at its west end. A visitor at the beginning of the 19th century noted that manor courts were still held 'in a thatched hovel near it [the castle], which appears like an overgrown pig-sty.'

104
Coity Castle, Coity
Medieval masonry castle
12th–16th century
OS 170   SS 923816   R2   Cadw

On N side of centre of Coity, 1.5ml (2.5km) NE of Bridgend. Key from no. 94 Heol West Plas, on corner of Castle Meadows, opposite west end of castle. Entrance charge

The ruins of Coity Castle dominate the centre of the village. It is worth walking into the field to its north, on a public footpath which starts by the churchyard, to get a good overall view of it. This is also the view that Owain Glyndŵr's men had when they besieged Sir Laurence Berkerolles here in 1404–5. Two attempts were made to relieve him, one by Prince Henry (later Henry V), which failed, and one by Henry IV.

Coity Castle was probably first established by the Norman knight Payn Turberville at the beginning of the 12th century. With Newcastle (no. 102) and Ogmore Castle (no. 103) it acted as an outpost at the western extremity of expansion under Fitzhamon. It quickly became the centre of an important lordship, held first by the Turbervilles, and subsequently by the Berkerolles and Gamages, who occupied it until 1584. It was the principal residence of the Turbervilles and Berkerolles.

There were five main phases of building – the earthwork castle of about 1100, the late 12th-century keep and curtain wall, the major rebuilding in the 14th century, the 15th-century rebuilding after Glyndŵr's siege and Tudor improvements. The first castle was an earth and timber castle-ringwork, with the bailey occupying the later outer ward to the west. The ringwork and its great steep-sided ditch, which would have originally completely encircled it, are very reminiscent of those of Grosmont Castle (no. 112), which is of similar date. To appreciate this impressive Norman earthwork walk straight through the outer and inner wards and over the bridge beyond to the outer bank on the east side. This is also a good place from which to see part of the next phase of building, the great faceted curtain wall.

The curtain wall was built, along with the rectangular keep on the west side of the inner ward, some time in the 1180s. The layout and building method are similar to but less lavish than at Newcastle (no. 102). The quoins of Sutton stone at the angles are a distinctively Norman feature. Part of the east side is particularly well preserved, with the wall-walk and some of the parapet still in place. On the south side the curtain wall was raised in the 14th-century rebuilding, and a straight stretch on the north side was rebuilt in the first decade of the 15th century after being demolished in the Glyndŵr siege.

The long occupation of this castle led to many rebuildings and alterations, so much so that it is confusing for the layman but fascinating for the medieval masonry

Coity Castle

enthusiast. The Norman keep, with its 12th-, 14th- and 16th-century parts, is a good illustration of this jumble. The Norman work is characterised by reddish rubble masonry and bold Sutton stone quoins. In the 14th century, when the castle was largely rebuilt, vaulting was inserted into the lower storeys and an annexe added to the north-east. In the early 16th century a third floor was added. The west wall, the only one to survive above ground floor level, rises to an impressive height. The octagonal central pier of the 14th-century vaulting, still with its fine squared facing stone and the springing of eight vaulting ribs, stands in the middle. The original entrance was at first-floor level at the north end of the inner east side, and would probably have given access to a hall. The annexe survives to a considerable height and is built of different, more evenly cut stone, with more effort at coursing. Its windows,

fireplaces and garderobes indicate some degree of comfort.

The range of buildings along the south side of the inner ward also belongs to the 14th-century rebuilding. Here again detective work is needed to sort out the sequence. Some apparently nonsensical features such as the spring of a great arch almost touching the curtain wall, and a passage that leads nowhere, are better understood if one realises that a chapel tower was planned here but never built. Reuse of stone, including tomb-slabs, and an overlay of Tudor alterations further complicate the picture. The large room in the centre was a first-floor hall, with three windows in the curtain wall and a vaulted basement. To the north runs a vaulted corridor leading to a grand stairway. To the west were service rooms, that nearest the hall having the base of a circular malting kiln in it. To the north-east of the stairs is the first-floor chapel, added in the 15th century. The parapet wall-walk was made to climb up over its gable end. To the south-east of the hall a very tall and magnificent garderobe tower was built jutting out from the curtain wall. Access to it is from the east end of the hall. It had three floors, two of which survive, on each of which there were garderobes. Below is an 8m drop to the cesspit.

There are two gatehouses to the inner ward. That on the west side is 14th-century and very little of it survives. That on the north-east is 15th-century and is a small gem, surviving almost complete. Running from it to the chapel is a ruined wall, behind which was probably a yard of some kind. In front of it are the foundations of a rectangular building of unknown date and purpose.

To the west of the inner ward is a larger, roughly rectangular outer ward surrounded by a ruined curtain wall. This is probably the area of the 12th-century bailey, although no trace of its earthworks survives. The walls were mainly built in the 14th century and were added to in the 15th century. There is a small, square 15th-century gatehouse straddling the curtain wall at the west end, but only part of the northern side survives to first-floor level. On the north side the lower half of a tower survives, and opposite it, on the south side, are the foundations of a similar tower converted into a gatehouse in the 15th century. A small bridge crosses the ditch in front of it. To the east is a 15th-century stretch of walling across the filled-in ditch of the first castle which has a row of eight cross-loops set close together in it.

The only building remains in the outer ward are those of a large 15th-century barn set against the south wall. It had buttresses and a large porch on its north side. Its presence suggests that the outer bailey may have been little more than a farmyard by this time. In the south-west corner, in the garden of a house, are the ruinous foundations of another tower which was replaced in the 15th century by a plain door to its east, and a small turret, now a garden shed, which may have been a mill.

105
Dinas Powys Castle, Dinas Powys
Medieval masonry castle
12th century
OS 171   ST 153716   U2

Take A4055 Cardiff to Barry road to Dinas Powys. In village turn R (W) at LH bend. Turn L at T-junction into Mill Road, and 1st R into The Lettons Way. Path up to castle on RHS

Only the curtain wall of Dinas Powys Castle remains standing, and much of that is ruinous; but from the outside the castle still has the appearance of a defensive stronghold. Its position on the southern end of a narrow ridge, with steep slopes below on all but the south-east side, gave it great natural strength. The castle was the centre of the lordship of Dinas Powys, and was held by the Norman de Sumeri family certainly in the mid-12th century and possibly earlier; the lordship was probably acquired by Roger de Sumeri soon after the initial Norman conquest of the area. The first castle was probably the multivallate castle-ringwork half a mile away on the hill flanking Cwm George. The present castle replaced this and had a rectangular keep just to the north of the courtyard castle, now reduced to a pile of overgrown rubble. The curtain-walled castle dates to around 1200 or slightly earlier, and was occupied into the 13th century and possibly later.

The very ruined north-west half of the early 12th-century keep stands in a thicket just beyond the north curtain wall. It appears to have been a typical early Norman keep, rectangular, with very thick walls, and it extended up to and possibly slightly beyond the curtain wall. When this was built a doorway, now a ragged gap, was made into the keep's basement. To the north-west is an outwork around the edge of the hilltop, possibly contemporary with the keep. It consists of a curving bank within which the ground is very disturbed by quarrying, probably for stone for the castle; when the curtain wall was built it had to follow the awkward quarry faces.

The castle of about 1200 is stylistically similar to Newcastle (no. 102), Ogmore (no. 103) and Coity (no. 104), with a straight-sectioned curtain wall without corner towers enclosing a roughly rectangular area. The main entrance on the south-east side was originally a simple round-headed archway; now it is merely a ragged gap, with a draw-bar hole on its west side. There is a postern gate on the north-east, with an arched doorway and draw-bar holes on both sides. The north-east and north-west curtain walls are high and well preserved, with much of their facing stone still in place. Putlog holes are the only relieving feature in their otherwise blank surfaces. The south-west wall is in poor condition and has lost most of its facing stone. The south-east side has the only window gaps in the castle and a fine east corner with large dressed Sutton stone alternating quoins. There are few traces of the buildings which must have ranged around the inside of the walls.

106
Swansea Castle, Swansea
Medieval masonry castle
13th–14th century
OS 159   SS 657931   U1

In Swansea city centre, above W bank of river Tawe, between Castle Bailey Street and The Strand. No access to inside

Morgan 1914; Evans 1983

Swansea Castle is now so hemmed in by modern buildings and roads that it is hard to imagine its original surroundings, or indeed its original form. It stands on a clifftop, below which the river Tawe originally flowed, and its position was strategic: it commanded the lowest crossing of the river, the main east–west route in south Wales, and a good

harbour. What is visible now is only a small part of the latest castle on the site, which in its heyday in the late 13th century stretched from Welcome Lane in the north to Caer Street in the south, and from the clifftop in the east almost to Princess Way in the west.

Swansea Castle's history was a turbulent one: it suffered in many Welsh raids, and changed hands many times. It was a Norman castle, first mentioned in 1116 as being attacked by the Welsh. It was established by Henry I's friend Henry de Beaumont, first earl of Warwick, as the seat of administration of the marcher lordship of Gower, which Henry bestowed on him in about 1106. This first castle was of motte and bailey type, and nothing of it remains above ground. The west side of its deep ditch has been excavated to the north of the present remains. It was rebuilt in stone on the same site, probably after being razed by the Welsh in 1217. Nothing remains above ground of this stage either, but the west side of the curtain wall has been found, together with a mural tower. To the south-west of this small castle, called the 'Old Castle', a large roughly rectangular outer bailey was walled in stone in the 13th century.

The 'New Castle', of which the present-day remains were part, lay in its south-east corner, built on the site of an earlier graveyard. This 'New Castle' dates from the late 13th to early 14th century, by which time Edward I's pacification of Wales had deprived it of any military importance. It continued as an administrative centre but at a reduced level. Its holders, then the de Braoses, preferred to live at Oystermouth Castle, and inevitable decline set in. Stripped of their usefulness, the various gates and towers of the bailey – Harold's Gate, Donald's Tower, Bokynham Tower and Singleton Tower – were sold off in the early 14th century.

The visible remains consist of the north and south blocks, probably the work of William de Braose II and William de Braose III, connected by a short stretch of much-altered curtain wall. The curtain wall originally continued up Castle Bailey Street on the west, and west

Swansea Castle, arcading in the south block

contrasting smooth Sutton stone purely for decoration, is so like those built for Bishop Henry de Gower, bishop of St David's (1328–47) at the bishops' palaces of St David's and Lamphey, that it is tempting to attribute this one to him as well. However, there are no records of his involvement, and if he was its instigator it was in a private capacity, perhaps for Lady Alenora de Mowbray, wife of Lord John de Mowbray who then held the castle. It is known that the bishop's masons were working on the Hospital of St David nearby in 1332. The parapet, best seen from Castle Lane to the south, originally ran along the inside as well as the outside walls. On the gable ends of the east wing the arcade is blind, with passages behind lit by single windows at each end.

The small rectangular tower to the north has been much altered in post-medieval times, but retains a few original features such as cross arrowslits. On the ground floor are three vaulted chambers, with four rooms above them inserted in the late 18th century when the block was turned into a debtors' prison. It had probably been used as a prison for a long time before, and still has a grim air. Other usable parts of the castle had very heterogeneous uses at the beginning of the 19th century – as a town hall, poor-house, a new market house, store cellars, a blacksmith's and other shops, a Roman Catholic chapel (in the hall) and a dovecote.

from the north block to enclose a roughly rectangular area, with an entrance on the west side. The well preserved south block, which occupied most of the south side of the 'New Castle', is the most spectacular part, with its picturesque arcaded parapet on top of the outside walls. This was probably a slightly later addition to the main building, which was a residential block. The two large windows on the south side are the windows of the first-floor hall, and below them are the narrow windows of three barrel-vaulted chambers. In the angled wing to the east was a sub-basement with great battered walls, from which there was access to the river. On the first floor was a solar, or private chamber, reached by steps on the west side. At the west end of the block is a spectacular circular garderobe tower standing to its full height, and in the south-east angle is a small turret with an arrowslit.

The lovely arcaded parapet of pointed arches, built of the local sandstone and

107
Neath Castle, Neath
Medieval masonry castle
12th–14th century
OS 170   SS 753978   U1

In centre of Neath, on E bank of river, adjoining Glamorgan Street and Castle Street. Large (supermarket) car park to W. No access to interior

Neath Castle was one of the minor Norman castles in the lordship of Glamorgan. Like the

Neath Castle gatehouse

Romans before them (see Neath Roman fort, no. 70), the Normans chose this strategic spot, guarding the river crossing, for a stronghold. The main surviving feature of the castle is the great twin-towered gatehouse on its west side. This belongs to the latest phase in its 250-year history.

The first castle was a castle-ringwork known to have been built here in the 12th century by Robert, earl of Gloucester. The roughly oval, raised enclosure to the east of the gatehouse probably dates from this period. The castle was much harried by the Welsh, and was rebuilt in stone sometime in the early 13th century, possibly after being destroyed by Llywelyn ab Iorwerth in 1231. The ruined curtain wall is part of this castle, although it has been much tampered with since. It had two projecting round towers, the stump of one of which is visible on the east side. There was a simple gatehouse on the site of the present one, and the flight of steps well below present ground level in front of the present gatehouse led up to this 13th-century one.

The castle was again severely damaged in 1321–2 by enemies of the unpopular lord of Glamorgan, Hugh le Despenser. It was the 14th-century rebuilding after this attack that gave it its magnificent gatehouse. Only the

fronts of the great D-shaped towers and the arch between them survive. The steps of the old gateway, now uncovered again, were buried and a drawbridge used instead. Blocked windows and the springing of the arch over the gateway still retain their dressed Sutton stone surrounds which contrast nicely with the dark local sandstone of the walls. Jutting out from the front of the right-hand tower is the broken end of the town wall. The interior of the castle can be glimpsed through a gateway on the south side, but foundations of buildings ranged around the curtain wall are all that can be seen.

108
Loughor Castle, Loughor
Medieval masonry castle
12th–13th century
OS 159   SS 564980   U2/U3

On W edge of Loughor, just before bridge, on S side of A484 Loughor to Llanelli road

Lewis 1975

The tiny picturesque castle of Loughor, or Llwchwr in Welsh, is a Norman castle, placed in a strategic position on the western edge of the lordship of Gower guarding the lowest crossing of the river Loughor. The Romans too found this a strategic spot, and the castle was built in the south-east corner of the Roman auxiliary fort of *Leucarum*. It was founded early in the 12th century by Henry de Viliers. At this stage an oval area on the highest part of the spur above the river was enclosed by a ditch, now gone, and the edge heightened by a bank. Thus, despite its motte-like appearance, the earliest castle was really a castle-ringwork. Excavation has revealed that a flimsy rectangular kitchen occupied the east side of the interior. Of the other buildings, which would have been of timber, nothing is known.

The castle's history, like that of all castles in

the area, was a turbulent one, and there are four further stages of rebuilding. In the mid- to late-12th century further timber buildings and possibly a stone tower, predecessor to the present one, were built, and in the late 12th to early 13th century two stone buildings were constructed in the middle. A stone curtain wall was built before 1215; its foundations were found during excavation, but standing nowhere more than 1.5m high. The slight lip around the edge of the mound marks its position.

A small stone tower on the west side of the mound dates from the late 13th century or about 1300, the last building phase at the castle, perhaps during the lordships of William de Braose II and III. The presence of a fireplace in the north wall, and garderobe in the south, both on the first floor, indicates that the tower was residential. Its thick walls stand to first-floor level, and there was originally another floor above. The whole of the south-east corner, complete with spiral stair, lies on its side, having fallen in the 1940s. Adjoining the tower to the south was the entrance gateway. The castle was made redundant by Edward I's pacification of Wales and fell into decline.

Loughor Castle from the east

109
Oystermouth Castle, Oystermouth
Medieval masonry castle
12th–14th century
OS 159   SS 613883   R2

Take A4067 Swansea to the Mumbles road to Oystermouth. In centre turn R up Newton Road (signed to castle) and then 1st R (signed). Entrance charge. Open daily, standard hours

This is the Gower peninsula's finest castle, standing on a small hill with a magnificent view over Swansea Bay. It is well preserved, intricate and exciting to explore.

Oystermouth Castle was founded by William de Londres of Ogmore Castle (no. 103) early in the 12th century. Of this first castle, which was probably a ringwork and bailey on the highest part of the hill, there is now no trace. The castle later came to the chief lords of Gower, and its history became intimately connected with that of Swansea Castle (no. 106).

The earliest stone building of the castle, the keep, dates from the 12th century. This is the building straight ahead of the entrance. It has been much altered and incorporated into a later block, of which it now forms the southern half. Originally it was a free-standing, rectangular building, entered through an arched doorway, now blocked, to the right of the present entrance porch. The great hall would have been on the first floor. Twice the Welsh burnt this early castle, first in 1116 and later in 1215.

In the 13th century the de Braoses were lords of Gower and held the castle, and towards the end of the century Oystermouth rather than Swansea became their principal residence. Edward I paid a brief visit here in December 1284. The de Braoses rebuilt the castle in stone, and most of what remains today dates from this period. On the east and west sides is a high and impressive curtain wall with a wall-walk along the top. At its

Above: Oystermouth Castle

Right: Oystermouth Castle, the south window of the chapel

north-east end this leads to a garderobe and then rises to a small tower from which the panoramic view is magnificent, but the view downwards is only for those with a head for heights. This is a good place from which to appreciate the lovely south window of the chapel. On its north side the castle is enclosed by the outside walls of several residential blocks. From the outside the walls are severe and formidable, relieved only by the white valerian growing on them, and by the windows of the chapel. It is well worth walking right around the outside to appreciate this.

The castle entrance on the south side is an arched passage flanked by what were originally two half-round towers. These have had their fronts hacked off, and the remainder patched and tidied up. Blocked doorways and floor beam sockets can be seen in the exposed back walls. When this truncation took place is not known, but it may have been during the Civil War in the 17th century. Inside the castle the southern part is an open courtyard, with the remains of two long, rectangular buildings against the curtain walls on either side of the entrance.

The rest of the castle buildings fill its northern end. Behind the keep is a rectangular room with small windows and a fireplace in the south wall. Above this was the lord's private apartment, or solar, and below is a basement. A narrow passage leads through to the top floor of the north-west block, thought to be the earliest stone addition to the castle after the keep. It is a high, three-storey block with a barrel-vaulted basement, and similar middle floor, now held up by a modern pillar. In the south-east corner there is a fascinating narrow passage, dimly lit by narrow slits, which leads back to the keep. It skirts round a spiral staircase which can be glimpsed through the slits. To the west of the keep is a small guardroom, next to which is a passageway leading to the west and north-west blocks. The north end of the west range is a three-storey residential building with fireplaces and garderobes on each floor. To its south is a range with steps down to two barrel-vaulted basements and steps up to a large, once well-lit room, with the remains of a large fireplace in its west wall. Evidently the de Braoses lived in some comfort here.

There remains the chapel block on the east side, architecturally the high point of the castle. This was added in the early 14th century, and is usually attributed to Lady Alenora de Mowbray, wife of lord John de Mowbray who held the castle then. It blends in well with the rest of the castle, but its details suggest a much greater level of refinement. It is a three-storey, rectangular block entered through a doorway on the south side. On the ground floor are a large fireplace, narrow trefoil-headed splayed windows and a garderobe in the south-east corner. Above is a similar floor. But on the top floor was a large chapel, the great glory of which is its east window. This, and the other chapel windows, two on the north side and one on the south, retain their very fine tracery, the finest of the period of any window in south-east Wales. On the south wall is a well preserved *piscina*, which also retains some of its delicate tracery.

The chapel's use, alas, was short-lived, for by 1331 the lords of Gower lived elsewhere. A gradual decline set in, and by the 16th century the castle was ruined. It still has the power to stir the imagination, to conjure up de Braoses and de Mowbrays, and private devotions in the lovely chapel.

110
Weobley Castle, Llanrhidian, Gower
Medieval masonry castle
13th–15th century
OS 159   SS 478928   R1   Cadw

Take B4295 to Llanrhidian. Continue W, fork R at Oldwalls towards Llanmadoc. After 0.6ml (1km) turn R (signed to castle). Park on LHS. Entrance charge (pay at farm). Cadw standard hours

Thomas: Official Guide; Robinson: Cadw Guide

Weobley Castle is a small gem perched on the northern edge of the Gower plateau. The splendid view from it can have changed little since the medieval period – a steep drop below, and then the Llanrhidian marshes stretching way out towards the Loughor estuary. This is the only stone castle on the north side of the Gower, all the rest being on the south in the area of primary Norman control (see nos 109 and 111). The original castle of the Weobley area, of castle-ringwork and bailey type, may have been at nearby Cilifor or North Hill Tor. In the 13th century the seat of this sublordship moved to Weobley. By the time it is mentioned in records, in the early 14th century, the castle was almost certainly in the hands of the de la Bere family, who continued to hold it until the late 15th century.

Most of the castle was built in the late 13th century, by which time Edward I had largely removed the threat of Welsh uprisings. It was conceived, therefore, more as a comfortable manor house with a prudent amount of fortification, than as a full-blown castle. Where they survive, on the north and east sides, the outside walls are high and forbidding, with a wall-walk along the top. But arrowslits are conspicuous by their absence, and the two external towers are for stairs and garderobes, not for defence. The north gatehouse, too, is a simple arched entrance

Above: Weobley Castle from the east
Right: Weobley Castle

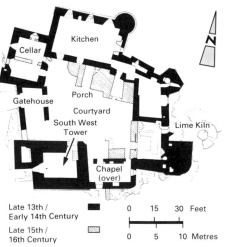

Late 13th /
Early 14th Century

Late 15th /
16th Century

0   15   30   Feet

0   5   10 Metres

with doors but no portcullis.

The castle is compact, with buildings ranged around a small courtyard. There is evidence that the enclosure was originally intended to include the flat area to the west, but this came to nothing. The visitor enters through the original gatehouse, of which only the front and back walls survive. In front was a small rock-cut ditch. To the right is the oldest part of the castle, the south-west tower, which could date from the mid-13th century or even earlier, and was possibly originally a small free-standing keep of two or three storeys, only the lowest part of which survives. Two enlarged arrowslits show that this building placed greater emphasis on defence than the rest of the castle. Against its west side is an early 14th-century garderobe.

Very little survives of the building next to the south-west tower on the south side of the castle. Its outer wall was the curtain wall, in which there was a postern doorway. The finding of parts of a finely carved early 14th-century *piscina* indicates that there was a chapel here, probably on the first floor.

To the east is the most complicated part of the castle. The curtain wall, with postern

doorway in it, dates from the late 15th century, when the whole of the east block was remodelled. Outside it are the foundations of further walls and a substantial corner tower, which were started in the late 13th century but were never completed. In the base of the tower is a large curving passage-drain for three latrine shafts. (The provision of numerous garderobes is a feature of the castle.) Beyond the tower are the footings of a limekiln presumed to be contemporary with the building of the castle.

Back in the courtyard, the hall lies to the north. It is now largely hidden behind a porch block added in the late 15th century by Sir Rhys ap Thomas. Sir Rhys was a powerful magnate, in great favour with Henry VII, and he altered the castle to reflect his elevated status. All the windows in the hall block are later alterations except the 14th-century trefoil-headed one, which was reused. The entrance is a simple archway, with a blocked window to the right. Inside the arrangements were all altered in the 16th century and later, as this part of the building was adapted as a farmhouse.

At the top of the steps a restored doorway leads into the hall, the finest and largest room in the castle. A wooden platform takes the visitor along the east side at original floor level. Below was the kitchen. The highlight of this room is the fine east window, which dates from the early 14th century. It has two lights with cusped heads, and still retains its mullion and transom. On the north wall is a large fireplace, and in the north-east corner is a doorway to the stair turret which gave access to the wall-walk at parapet level. At the very top the tower projects above this level, providing a fine look-out if needed.

The east range is reached from the kitchen. It was originally of two storeys, but in the late 15th-century remodelling the floor levels were altered to make three. The original first-floor chamber, with tall lancet window, was probably the guest chamber. It was built in the late 13th century, and was slightly altered in the early 14th century when the three-storey polygonal garderobe turret was added in the north-east corner. The highest garderobe was only accessible from the parapet wall-walk.

On the west side is the early 14th-century first-floor solar, with cellars below. Judging from the fireplace, which was modified in the late 15th century, the large windows on the north and east sides, and the private garderobe in the south-west corner, this was a comfortable and pleasant room. It now houses an exhibition, and has a modern floor

and roof, although the corbels for the original roof remain. The basement beneath was altered in the late 15th century by dividing it into two barrel-vaulted rooms.

Fragments of decorative stonework, the many garderobes and other details suggest that the de la Beres and after them Sir Rhys ap Thomas enjoyed comfortable and gracious living at Weobley. Its history from the 16th century onwards is more prosaic: part became a farmhouse, the rest fell into decay.

111
Pennard Castle, Southgate, Gower
Medieval masonry castle
12th–14th century
OS 159   SS 544885   U2

Take B4436 to Pennard, then minor road to Southgate. Leave car near right-angle bend at Golf Club, and take public footpath NW across golf course, roughly towards water tower. Near tower, fork L between a tee and a green. Castle a short distance. Take care crossing fairways

Pennard Castle's situation is dramatic and beautiful. It is perched on the eastern edge of the valley of the Pennard Pill, with a sheer drop below to the north and west. From it there is a sweeping view out towards Three Cliffs Bay, and across the valley to Penmaen Burrows. It was a perfect position for a castle, except for one thing which cannot have been foreseen when it was built: it was vulnerable to sand blow. By the end of the 14th century sand encroachment had led to its abandonment.

In the early 12th century Henry de Beaumont, first earl of Warwick, was granted the lordship of Gower, and it was probably he who built the ringwork castle here. It had a bank and ditch around it, and a primitive stone hall. On the opposite side of the valley, at Penmaen, was a very similar castle of the

Pennard Castle gatehouse

same date (see Appendix). The only traces of this early castle are the footings of the hall at the west end of the courtyard, which was probably added to the ringwork in the early 13th century. It was a rectangular building, divided into three rooms. The hall was the middle room, and had a central hearth and stone benches around its walls.

In the late 13th or early 14th century the castle was rebuilt in stone, using local limestone and reddish sandstone, and the present-day ruins are the remains of this castle. It was probably the work of the de Braoses, who held the castle for a while in the 13th century. In 1321 it passed to the de Mowbray family.

The castle is small and rather crudely built, with a curtain wall around a courtyard. It incorporated up-to-date elements such as the twin-towered gatehouse, but they were built in an amateurish way, with little understanding of their real purpose or construction. The circular trace of the curtain wall follows the line of the earlier ringwork bank except on the north side, where the ground falls steeply below. Here the wall is well preserved, standing to battlement height in places, and is particularly impressive from the outside. On the south and west it has almost completely gone. At the west end of

the north side it incorporates a small semicircular turret with a single arrowslit facing westwards. The gap to the east of it was probably a garderobe. A square tower, the base of which survives, was added to the outside of the west curtain wall. This appears to have been residential, with splayed windows on the west and south sides.

The only entrance was through the gatehouse on the east side, which consisted of an archway between two half-round towers with square inner sides. The northern side is best preserved; the southern side, except for part of the front wall, is very ruined. The entrance passage had a simple portcullis, but the grooves do not reach the ground. Further evidence of lack of understanding of military architecture by the builders are the ineffective arrowslits and two square holes of unknown purpose from the guardrooms to the passage.

A small settlement grew up around the castle, and to its east a solitary section of wall is all that is left of St Mary's church, abandoned in 1532. Castle, village and church were all overwhelmed by sand.

112
Grosmont Castle, Grosmont
Medieval masonry castle
11th century to 1360
OS 161   SO 405244   U2   Cadw

In Grosmont, on B4347 Pontrilas to Rockfield road. Access down pedestrian alleyway opposite Post Office. Guidebook from Post Office

Knight: Cadw Guide

The castles of Grosmont, White Castle (no. 113) and Skenfrith (no. 114) are known as the 'Three Castles' or 'Trilateral', and during all their active life they were held collectively. They lie within a few miles of each other on or near the English–Welsh border, and they were probably first built by the Norman earl William fitz Osbern (see also nos 98 and 99) to

Above and left: Grosmont Castle

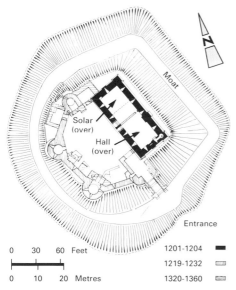

0   30   60   Feet

0   10   20   Metres

1201-1204 ■
1219-1232 ▧
1320-1360 ▨

uncertain, but all may have been castle-ringworks of earth and timber, possibly with free-standing stone keeps.

Perhaps the best way to start a tour of Grosmont Castle is to walk right round the outside. The steep-sided mound, with some of its stone revetment still in place on the north side, and the deep ditch are massive earthworks. The mound is an inverted D-shape, with the straight edge along the north-east side. This shape may have been necessary to accommodate an already-existing rectangular keep, but is equally likely to have been created before the building of the keep/hall. Above the straight side is the hall block, a simple rectangular building of uncertain original date. There are two possibilities: either it began life as a free-standing keep built in the late 11th or 12th century before the rest of the stone castle, and was subsequently improved for domestic use in the very early 13th century by Hubert de Burgh; or it was built from scratch by Hubert de Burgh in the very early 13th century.

Hubert de Burgh, royal justiciar, was a distinguished soldier who fought much in

secure his hold on the area and deter further Welsh attack. It is known from royal records that all three were in existence by 1161/2, when money was spent on repairs, and between 1177 and 1188 a certain Ralph of Grosmont was supervising work at all three. The form the castles took at this time is

France. He held the Three Castles twice, from 1201 to 1204 and from 1219 to 1232, when he fell from power, and during both periods he instigated great building works at Grosmont and Skenfrith.

The hall block is a two-storey building, with four narrow lancet windows on the ground floor, which would have been a storeroom, and three large round-headed windows on the first floor. This was originally divided into two – the southern, larger room being the hall, and the northern, smaller one the lord's private room or solar. In the east corner there is a broken spiral staircase. Access to the first floor was by external wooden stairs on the inner side.

A modern bridge spans the ditch in the same place as did the original one; below on the inner side is the 14th-century drawbridge pit. At the far end is the ruined gatehouse, originally a two-storey building. The faceted curtain wall and round towers at its angles date from 1219–32 and are best appreciated from the outside. Only the stub of the north tower survives, but the other two stand almost to their full height, as does the curtain wall on the west side. Not for the faint-hearted is a clamber up to the very exposed wall-walk on top, accessible from stairs in the south-west tower.

Inside the castle the hall on the right-hand side should be visited first. The ground-floor doorways and cross-wall were inserted in the 1219–32 building phase. Some white plaster and good-quality facing stone high up in the south-west corner give an idea of the 13th-century interior. Next look at the west tower, which is pure Hubert de Burgh. It is austere, built only for defence, with arrowslits the only openings in the walls. The south-west tower, on the other hand, although originally similar, was altered in the last building phase, between 1320 and 1360, to provide more comfortable living accommodation.

In 1266 the Three Castles were granted to Edward I's brother Edmund, earl of Lancaster. Their military role ceased towards the end of the century, when Edward subjugated Wales, and Grosmont became a favourite residence of the earls, later dukes of Lancaster. Between 1320 and 1360 it was remodelled to provide suitable accommodation for such noble occupants. The south-west tower was altered, and two new rectangular blocks were added on the north side.

The inside of the south-west tower is imposing: an enormous arched lobby was added and all the upper floors were rebuilt with windows, fireplaces and now-vanished garderobes. The only unaltered 13th-century parts are the windowless basement, typical of round towers of that period, and the arrowslits on the ground floor.

Of the two northern blocks, built outside the curtain wall on either side of the 13th-century round tower, very little survives, with one remarkable exception – the very fine and well preserved chimney. It is very tall, much of its ashlar facing stone remains in place and it is crowned by an elaborate Gothic chimneypot, a beautiful and rare survival from the medieval period.

It was at Grosmont that the Glyndŵr rebellion was dealt a mortal blow in 1405 by the future King Henry V, who routed the besiegers in a battle said to have cost 800 Welsh lives.

113
White Castle, Llantilio Crossenny
Medieval masonry castle
12th–13th century
OS 161   SO 379167   U1   Cadw

Take B4233 Abergavenny to Monmouth road. In Llantilio Crossenny, 6ml (9.6km) E of Abergavenny, turn N up minor road (signed to castle). Castle at top of hill on LHS. On Offa's Dyke long-distance footpath

Knight: Cadw Guide

White Castle, whose name may have arisen from the original white plaster coating of the walls, is the most romantic of the Three Castles (see also Grosmont, no. 112, and Skenfrith, no. 114). Its great round towers and high curtain wall give it the appearance of an archetypal castle. It occupies a fine commanding position on a hilltop, best appreciated by approaching it on foot from the west along the Offa's Dyke path. The true grandeur of this castle is really only apparent from this direction, and it is no accident that this would have been the direction of any Welsh attack.

Like Grosmont and Skenfrith it was probably originally an earthwork and timber castle of the early years after the Norman Conquest, built by William fitz Osbern to stamp his overlordship on the area. The great mound the castle stands on, its deep surrounding moat, which retains much of its stone revetment, and the crescent-shaped hornwork to the south may all have been part of this original castle.

Despite its apparent unity the castle is the result of two distinct building phases about a hundred years apart. To best appreciate this first go to the far end of the inner ward. Here are the immensely thick foundations of the earliest stone building of the castle, a small squarish keep dating from the first half of the 12th century. The repairs recorded in 1161/2 may have been to this. At the time the curtain wall would have been of timber.

The pear-shaped curtain wall was constructed next, probably starting in the 1180s. At this time the entrance to the castle was on the south side next to the keep, an arrangement similar to other 12th-century castles in south Wales (nos 102, 103, 104). The curtain wall had no towers, and like others of its period it was faceted. Except on the east side it stands almost to its full height, and parts of the wall-walk on top are visible. The south wall, behind the keep foundations, is of later date.

Hubert de Burgh appears not to have made any changes here in the early 13th century. The next great phase of fortification was undertaken by the Crown: in 1254 the Three Castles were granted to the Lord Edward, later Edward I, and it was probably he who remodelled the castle extensively in the 1260s. This was his first castle in Wales, the antecedent to all his magnificent castles in north Wales. To best appreciate his work go

White Castle

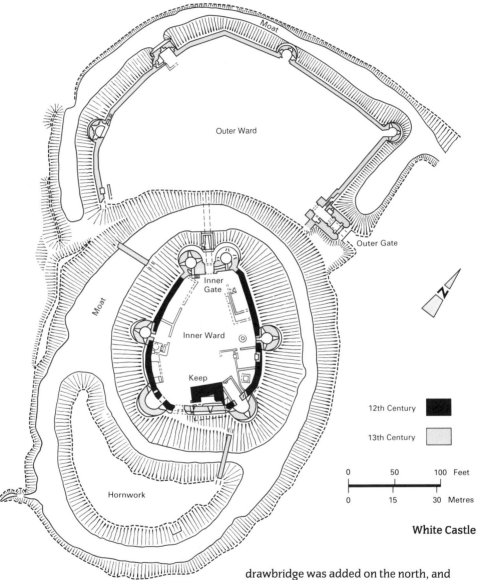

Moat

Outer Ward

Outer Gate

Inner Gate

Inner Ward

Moat

Keep

12th Century

13th Century

0		50		100	Feet
0		15		30	Metres

White Castle

Hornwork

back out across the moat and look at the inner ward from the outside. The old keep was demolished, and the castle was reorientated 180°. A strong gatehouse with two round towers, doors, portcullis and

drawbridge was added on the north, and round towers were built on to the angles of the curtain wall. Lastly the outer ward to the north, which may have already existed in timber with a ditch around it, was walled in stone, with towers at the angles and a small gatehouse on the south-east side. The castle now took on its present-day appearance.

All through its life the sole purpose of White Castle was military, and as a deterrent it succeeded admirably, for it was never attacked. It is austere and functional: only arrowslits pierce the tower walls, and the moat is exceptionally deep and steep-sided. The only civilian concession was a chapel, whose chancel was on the second floor of the south-east tower, and whose nave projected into the inner ward. Simple timber-framed buildings in this ward ranged along the east and west curtain walls, of which only the stone plinths remain. The kitchen, with its circular oven, was on the west; the hall, buttery and pantry on the east, with a well, a private apartment, possibly of the constable of the castle, and a deep latrine pit to the south.

Troops were probably garrisoned in the outer ward in timber buildings. The tower in the north-west corner is slightly different from the others and contained lodgings, possibly for the troop commander, on the upper floor and a garderobe in the projection on the left-hand side. In the south-west corner is a garderobe pit recessed in the curtain wall. The slot on its right-hand side was for wooden seats.

After Edward I's pacification of Wales the castle continued as an administrative centre, but by the 16th century it had fallen into decay.

114
Skenfrith Castle, Skenfrith
Medieval masonry castle
13th century
**OS 161   SO 457202   U1   Cadw/
National Trust**

*Take B4521 Abergavenny to Ross-on-Wye
road to Skenfrith; 10ml (16km) from both. Turn
N into village, castle on RHS. Guidebook from
Post Office opposite*

Craster 1967; Knight: Cadw Guide

Skenfrith is one of the Three Castles (see also Grosmont Castle, no. 112, and White Castle, no. 113) planted close together in north Gwent, probably by William fitz Osbern, in the early years of the 12th century. Nothing remains above ground of the first castle at Skenfrith which was levelled to make way for the 13th-century stone one. Remains of this earlier castle have been found during excavations and include a large defensive ditch and walling from a 12th-century keep. Except for the solid semicircular tower in the middle of the south-west side, which was added later in the 13th century, the present stone castle was built in one short period, between 1219 and 1232, by Hubert de Burgh. He undertook rebuilding of Grosmont Castle at the same time in his bid to become a great marcher lord.

The castle's position is a pleasant one on the Welsh bank of the river Monnow, but its great stretches of blank curtain wall give a sombre impression. These enclose a roughly rectangular area and except on the north side stand almost to their full height, with a well preserved wall-walk on top, which went up steps and round the towers at the corners. On the outside rectangular holes in the walls just below the top were for beams to carry wooden fighting galleries or hoards.

The castle is entered on the north side through a ragged gap in the curtain wall. It is thought that the original entrance here was just a plain archway, not a gatehouse. The dominant feature of the castle is the round tower which stands in the middle of the interior. This was the last part of Hubert de Burgh's castle to be completed, and represents a different military tactic from that employed, for example, at Grosmont, White Castle and Caldicot (no. 115). Similar towers of the period can be seen at Tretower and Bronllys, both in Powys; all were capable of independent defence. Unlike the corner towers, this evidently housed living accommodation. It has a battered base with a fine roll-moulded string course around the top. Wooden stairs originally led to the entrance at first-floor level on the north side,

Above and below: Skenfrith Castle

part of whose doorway survives. Spiral stairs on the west side then led to the upper floors. The ground floor was dimly lit by two arrowslits. The upper floors, the levels of which are visible inside where holes for floor beams pierce the wall, show signs of comfort, with a fireplace in the south side, larger windows, moulded corbels on the east side and an upper doorway which originally led to a garderobe.

Most of the remaining living quarters, including the hall, were ranged along the west curtain wall, and only survive to basement level. The hall would have been above, on what was originally the first floor; when the level of the courtyard was raised after the block was built the ground floor became a basement, with a long shallow flight of steps down to it. Some architectural details of

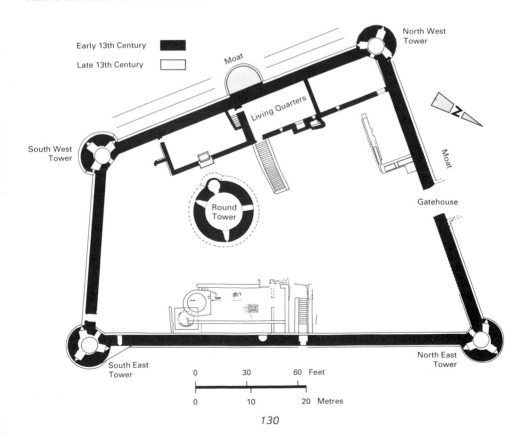

interest remain in these rooms – door jambs, a fine blocked fireplace and a window with its original iron bars and shutter hinges.

Further buildings have been found by excavation along the east side, but their foundations are now under the turf. Steps lead down to a water-gate on this side.

Like Grosmont and White Castle, Skenfrith was strategically important to the Normans as a bastion against Welsh incursion until 1283, when Edward I finally broke the Welsh resistance. Thereafter it remained with the earls, and later dukes of Lancaster, but appears not to have been lived in as Grosmont was. In the church is the fine tomb of the last governor of the Three Castles, John Morgan (d. 1557), steward of the Duchy of Lancaster.

115
Caldicot Castle, Caldicot
Medieval masonry castle
12th–14th century
OS 171   ST 487885   R1

Take B4245 to Caldicot (junction 22 or 23 off M4). In the village castle access opposite church (signposted). Entrance charge. Standard opening hours (interior in summer only)

Morgan and Wakeman 1854

Tucked away on low-lying ground near the Bristol Channel is this unexpectedly large and impressive castle. It has much in common with Cardiff Castle (no. 83); both have an early Norman motte, a later curtain wall and towers, and were restored in the late 19th century, here less flamboyantly than at Cardiff. The castle's life appears to have been a peaceful one, unscathed by Welsh rebellions. Only in the 1460s was it rendered untenable as a military stronghold by the breaching of the curtain wall on the east side by William Herbert of Raglan Castle (no. 122), on the orders of Edward IV. William was the Yorkist leader in Wales, and Caldicot was held at the time by the Duchy of Lancaster.

The castle was built in five phases, each of which is clearly distinguishable. In the north corner is the first phase, the high, steep-sided mound, surrounded by a ditch, which the later circular tower sits on. It is an early 12th-century Norman castle, possibly the work of Walter fitz Roger.

The next phase is represented by the stone keep itself. It was built on top of and into the motte, probably in the second quarter of the 13th century by Humphrey de Bohun V, called 'the Good'. The castle was to remain in the hands of the de Bohuns, hereditary constables of England, until it passed to the Crown in 1373. This great keep is immensely strong. Its squared stonework of reddish-yellow local gritstone is of very high quality, and the walls are 3m thick, with a battered base topped by a bold roll-moulded string course. In style it is similar to the contemporary keeps at Skenfrith (no. 114) and Tretower and Bronllys in Powys. The walls are plain except for cross arrowslits and some small windows on the upper floors. The lower windows were added in the 19th century. At the top is a crenellated parapet, partly blocked up. On the keep's west side is a small semicircular tower which is curious in that it is solid, except for a vaulted dungeon in its basement and a chamber in its upper part. The rows of holes near the top of the keep were to hold the timbers of a wooden fighting platform, or hoard. Inside Victorian restoration is immediately apparent, but the original layout still exists. There are four floors, and stairs in the thickness of the wall. The basement is lit only by an arrowslit. A stone bench lines the room, and a trefoil-headed doorway leads to a small vaulted dungeon or cesspit beneath the attached tower, reached only by a ladder. This unpleasant place is visible through a grille by the far wall. The ground floor was lit by four arrowslits, in the thickness of one of which is a well. Each floor has an original hooded fireplace and passage to a garderobe. The climb to the top is repaid by panoramic views.

The high, battlemented curtain wall and round towers at its angles were built in the mid-13th century, soon after the building of the keep. A large, roughly rectangular area was enclosed, incorporating the existing keep in the north-west corner, and blocking one of its arrowslits in the process. For the most part the wall is well preserved, in places to wall-walk and battlement level. All around the outside there was a deep, steep-sided moat, probably filled with water from the nearby Nedern brook. Blocked arches in the bottom of the keep's ditch suggest that water was let in to surround it.

The main entrance to the castle at this stage was through a simple arched gateway set in the side of the round tower in the middle of the west side. This is a curious arrangement not seen elsewhere in the area except at Pembroke Castle (Dyfed). The two-storey tower, which survives to hoard level, has a battered base, at the top of which is a string course which continues southwards to the south-west tower at a lower level. The entrance was protected by a gate, a portcullis and two murder holes above. Some original

details survive inside – remains of vaulting, a corner fireplace, a garderobe, some original cobbling and a door to the wall-walk.

The two-storey south-west tower is similar but without a string course, and survives to hoard level. Its inner wall would have been of timber. At this stage the long north and south curtain walls were probably punctuated by similar towers where the gatehouse and Woodstock Tower now stand. In the south-east corner is a larger tower which survives to battlement level, with arrowslits in the merlons and holes for a hoard. It appears to have contained the grandest apartments of the castle on the upper floor, which has a fine fireplace and a two-light window.

On the east side there is a modern entrance where the curtain wall was breached in the 1460s. The small octagonal turrets were garderobe towers for timber buildings, now gone, against the inside of the wall. The two-light mullioned and transomed window in the upper floor is a 14th-century insertion. The north curtain wall, completely blank on the outside, has an interesting inner face which shows that there were buildings, presumably

Caldicot Castle, aerial view from the north

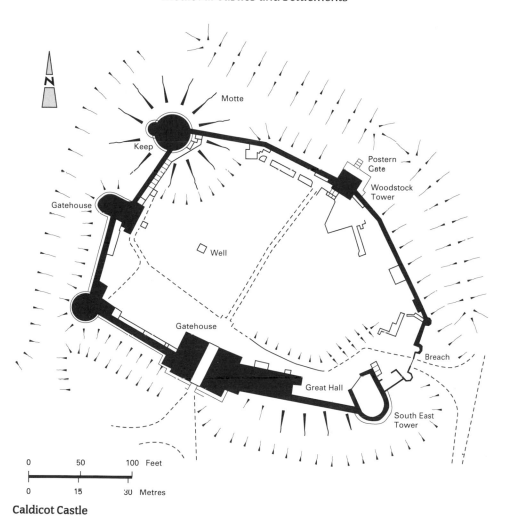

Caldicot Castle

of timber, against it: four large fireplaces, of a later medieval type, are built into the thickness of the wall.

The fourth phase of building was in the 1340s, when the great hall on the first floor against the south curtain wall was built. This was probably a timber building, and nothing remains except its three fine windows with Decorated tracery in the south curtain wall.

In 1373 the last male de Bohun died, leaving the castle to his two daughters, Mary and Eleanor. Mary married Edward III's grandson, who became Henry IV, and Eleanor married Thomas of Woodstock, duke of Gloucester, sixth and youngest son of Edward III. The castle thus passed into royal hands. More building works were set in hand; between 1384 and 1389 the Great Gateway on the south side and the Woodstock Tower on the north were built.

The Great Gateway through which the castle is now entered became the main entrance, and also housed the lord's apartments. It was much restored in the late 19th century, and the interior is entirely modern. It was approached by a drawbridge, and in the vaulted entrance passage were two portcullises, two gates and three murder holes above. The central section may have been intended to be higher and may never have been finished, which would explain why the top is not machicolated like the flanking towers, which are higher. The western one survives more or less intact. Despite their impressive appearance they were merely garderobe towers. At the level of the lord's apartments, on the first floor, each tower has a small, highly ornate window. The corbels supporting the machicolated arches are interesting in that they are carved into heads, each one different. One on the west tower is crowned and is said to resemble portraits of Edward II.

Opposite the Great Gateway is the semi-octagonal Woodstock Tower, built at the same time. It has a postern gate on its outer side in the right-hand jamb of which is a quatrefoil panel with the name 'Thomas' in it. A much worn stone carved with 'Alianore' which was originally opposite it is now under cover in the guardroom. These must refer to poor Thomas of Woodstock, who was murdered in 1397 in Calais by being smothered by a feather bed, and his wife Eleanor. There are three storeys, each with one room, a small Decorated window and a garderobe. The restored interior is plain, but the amazing bath jammed into one of the original garderobes is worth looking for. On the top the outward face has a fine machicolated battlement projected out on massive corbels. The wall-walk along the curtain wall continued through the tower in the thickness of its wall.

To the west of the castle is a large level area enclosed by a scarp along its north side and bank on its west side. This may have been an outer ward or bailey on which the medieval borough of Caldicot grew up.

The castle passed to the Duchy of Lancaster and was leased by various local families until the mid-19th century. In 1885 it was bought by J R Cobb who restored it and used it as a family home. Only in 1963 did the castle pass into public ownership.

116
Caerphilly Castle, Caerphilly
Medieval masonry castle
13th–14th century
OS 171   ST 155871   R1   Cadw

In centre of Caerphilly, 5ml (8km) N of Cardiff on A469. Car park to W of castle off Crescent Road. Entrance charge. Cadw standard hours

Rees 1971; Renn: Cadw Guide

Caerphilly Castle is one of the great medieval castles of western Europe. Several factors give it this pre-eminence – its immense size (1.2ha), making it the largest in Britain after Windsor, its large-scale use of water for defence and the fact that it is the first truly concentric castle in Britain (although this is somewhat spoilt by the buildings between the two curtain walls on the south side). At the time of its building, in the late 13th century, it was a revolutionary masterpiece of military planning.

One of Henry III's most powerful and ambitious barons, Gilbert de Clare, lord of Glamorgan, built this castle. His purpose was to secure the area and prevent lowland south Wales from falling into the hands of the Welsh leader Llywelyn the Last, who controlled most of mid- and north Wales. De Clare built other castles on the northern fringes of his territory for the same purpose, such as Castell Coch (no. 117) and, much later, Morlais Castle (no. 119). He had seized the upland district of Senghenydd, in which Caerphilly lies, from the Welsh in 1266 to act as a buffer against Llywelyn's southward ambitions. Llywelyn realised the threat and tried but failed to prevent the castle from being built; it was

Caerphilly Castle

begun on 11 April 1268, was attacked by Llywelyn in 1270, and was begun again in 1271. This time it was completed without hindrance. Its message was not lost on Llywelyn, who retreated northwards. Apart from the remodelling of the great hall and other domestic works in 1322–6 for Hugh le Despenser, no more alterations were carried out making it a very pure example of late 13th-century military architecture.

Caerphilly is unusual in being a late castle built on a virgin site. This allowed a unity of conception rare in medieval castles. It is a double-skinned parallelogram surrounded by large-scale water defences. This concentric arrangement, which derived from castles such as Dover (Kent) and Château Gaillard (France) and ultimately from Byzantium and

the Near East, was more flexible than earlier plans. It gave rapid access to any part of the castle by mural passages and wall-walks, towers and gatehouses could be independently held, attackers could be well covered and there was no possibility of mounting siege engines against the inner walls. The castle's cellular structure and strength is indicated by the presence of numerous portcullises.

The outer skin or ward is formed by a low battlemented curtain wall with large semi-circular projections in the corners and gatehouses in the middle of the east and west sides. Only a narrow strip separates this from the much stronger inner ward which has high curtain walls, circular corner towers and two large strong gatehouses corresponding with the outer ones. The great east gatehouse is the highest part of the castle and was its nucleus. As will be seen, it could be separately defended if necessary.

The south and north lakes around the castle formed an almost insuperable barrier to attackers. The dams themselves are a major achievement of medieval engineering. The southern, earliest one is a massive earth platform revetted in stone and strengthened on its lower side by eight great buttresses. To the right of the entrance to the castle is the northern dam, a narrower platform with a high outer wall with three great towers which are now unfortunately suffering from subsidence on the marshy ground. At its end is a strong postern gate and drawbridge. Outside the dams is a moat fed by sluices in the south dam.

The outer defences were completed by making a 1.2ha artificial island to the west of the castle, known as the hornwork. A trench had already been dug in the early stages of construction outside the west side of the castle; now another was dug further west and the area between was raised, levelled and revetted in stone to form the hornwork. The north-west side has two semicircular projections covering the drawbridge, the

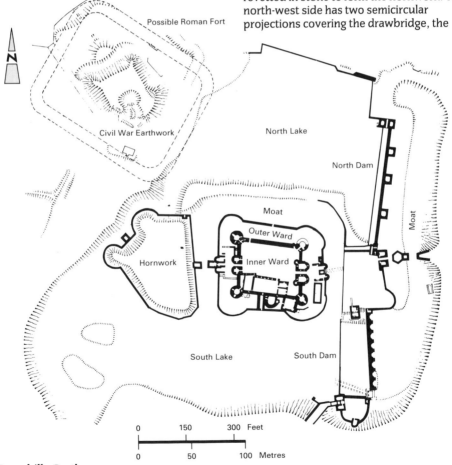

Caerphilly Castle

ruins of which can be seen between them.

The outer gatehouse on the east side is both the present and original entrance. Here the main characteristics of the castle as deterrent become apparent – its great strength, its severity, its lack of windows and lack of decoration. Inside the gatehouse is an exhibition about the castle, and stairs lead up to roof level, from which there is a panoramic view. Crossed rather than plain arrowslits in this gatehouse and in other buildings on the dams show that they are slightly later than the main castle. To the left is the platform of the south dam, the wider northern end of which may be partly natural, but the southern end of which is entirely artificial. Half-way along are the ruins of a mill, and at the south end are two towers and a rectangular gatehouse which gave access to the medieval borough.

Next is the outer ward or 'lists', entered via a bridge leading to its east gatehouse with twin D-shaped towers, only the restored outer walls of which remain. Its opposite number on the west is slightly better preserved. There the stone piers supporting the drawbridge leading to the hornwork can be seen, as can chimneys and fireplaces on two floors indicating comfortable living quarters. The false machicolation, poorer masonry and chimneys may indicate that this gatehouse was rebuilt at a later date. In the south-east corner is the base of a large rectangular building, possibly a granary. The south side is entirely blocked by a two-storey D-shaped kitchen tower, stores and servants' quarters. Below is a water-gate to the lake.

The inner ward is the most impressive part of the castle. The corner towers demonstrate varying degrees of preservation. The north-west tower is complete, and an exhibition on Welsh castles is housed there. Little remains of the north-east tower and the south-east tower is partly ruined. It stands 15m high and leans at an alarming angle, 10° out of true. The cause, whether subsidence or Civil War slighting, is unknown.

The imposing east gatehouse of the inner ward is the climax of any visit to the castle. It consists of twin D-shaped towers, a central passage with portcullises at both ends, and circular stair turrets on the inner corners. Like much of the inner ward it was ruinous by the 19th century, but was meticulously restored by the 4th marquis of Bute. The handsome and comfortable apartment on the second floor was probably that of the keeper, or constable of the castle. On the opposite side of the inner ward is a similar but smaller gatehouse. Whoever occupied the first floor lived in less comfort than the constable as the portcullis came up through the floor in the middle of the room.

On the south side of the inner ward are the great hall and state apartments. The large ground-floor hall, which was evidently a sumptuous building, was remodelled for Hugh le Despenser the Younger in 1322–6 and was restored by the 3rd marquis of Bute in the late 19th century. Originally the timber roof was lower, carried on the four carved corbels still in place in the south wall. Hugh le Despenser brought in the best craftsmen, who raised the roof and gave the four windows a Decorated ogee shape, rich mouldings, ornamented with pomegranate or ball-flower designs, and glass. The door was treated in the same way, and the whole building was faced with ashlar. The two doors at the east end led to a buttery and cellar, possibly with a small chapel over them. To the west were the state apartments, well-appointed rooms with fireplaces and a large traceried window on the first floor.

The castle's active history was an extremely short one. By 1283 Edward I had removed the threat of Welsh independence and the need for Caerphilly had gone. Minor Welsh attacks in 1294–5 and 1316 failed to make any impact. The last action that Caerphilly saw was in the war between Edward II and his queen, Isabella. Intent on destroying the power of her husband and his favourite Hugh le Despenser, Isabella besieged the castle from December 1326 to March 1327. But by this time Edward had fled and Hugh had been hanged. Thereafter the castle declined and fell into ruin. In the late 16th century Thomas

Lewis of The Van, just outside Caerphilly, was granted permission to use its stone to build his new house, thus accelerating its dilapidation. In the Civil War it was unusable and an earthwork redoubt was built instead to the north-west, the remains of which are still visible in trees beyond the north lake. By the 18th century the lakes were dry and houses had been built against the foot of the south dam. That the castle rose again from its sorry state is due to the visionary clearance and restoration work undertaken by the Bute family and the imaginative reflooding of the lakes by the state in the 1950s.

117
Castell Coch, Cardiff
Medieval masonry castle
13th and 19th century
OS 171   ST 131826   R1   Cadw

5ml (8km) N of centre of Cardiff. Take A470 Pontypridd road and turn off at 1st junction after M4. Double back to Tongwynlais. In Tongwynlais take 2nd L turn (signed to castle). Castle entrance is on LHS a short distance further on. Entrance charge. Cadw standard hours

Rousham: Cadw Guide

Perched on a steep rocky slope at the entrance to a narrow gorge, its round towers and conical roofs rising mysteriously out of the surrounding woodland, Castell Coch, the 'red castle', could hardly present a more romantic picture. One almost expects the river Loire or Rhine to be flowing by beneath it, not the humble Taff. Its appearance today is the result of the passionate desire of the 3rd marquis of Bute and his architect William Burges to recreate the medieval past as fully and accurately as possible. In the late 19th century they rebuilt this small 13th-century castle on its original foundations, using every available scrap of evidence to make it as authentic as possible. From the outside, at

Castell Coch, gatehouse and keep tower

least, it gives a good overall impression of a 13th-century castle, although the towers are probably too high and too uneven in height, and the pitched roofs and courtyard may be misleading. Inside all is architectural romanticism and flights of decorative fantasy, with only a few reminders of the original. (Burges died in 1881, before the interior was finished, and left only sketchy plans. The decoration was completed in less exuberant style than his masterpiece at Cardiff Castle.)

Here we are concerned with the medieval castle, which was built by that redoubtable castle-builder Gilbert de Clare, lord of Glamorgan, in the second half of the 13th century (see also nos 116 and 119). There may be an underlying 12th-century motte, but the earliest stone castle here dates from about 1266, when Gilbert was strengthening his northern boundary against the Welsh and attempting to eject Gruffydd ap Rhys from lower Senghenydd. He succeeded in 1267. Castell Coch, standing in a strategic position guarding the narrow Taff valley route into the hills, was well placed to help in these tasks. Its position was a strong one, with a steep slope below on the south, and was further strengthened with a deep ditch around it on the other sides.

The castle has a roughly circular plan, with three round flanking towers around an open courtyard, the gatehouse on the east side, and the hall between the two towers on the south side. The curving north-west side of the courtyard is a curtain wall with embrasures, standing on a massive splayed base.

The best way to start a tour of the castle is to walk anticlockwise round the outside. The

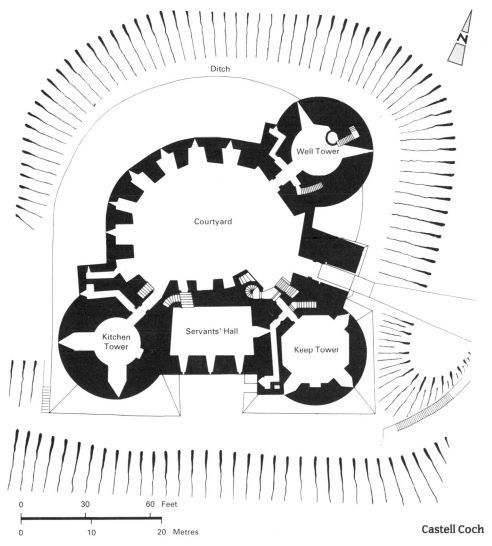

Ditch

Well Tower

Courtyard

Kitchen Tower

Servants' Hall

Keep Tower

| 0 | 30 | 60 | Feet |
| 0 | 10 | 20 | Metres |

Castell Coch

castle's great strength is immediately apparent, and the join between the medieval and 19th-century masonry is clearly visible. First, the gatehouse wall, with its drawbridge, portcullis and projecting wooden gallery, is mostly 19th-century. The lowest part of the wall is medieval, but above (from where the stone changes colour) is all restoration, the original wall here having been the most ruined part of the castle when Bute and Burges started work. However, all the details are correct for the period. The keep tower to the left is also all reconstruction. Next is the well tower, the bottom third of which is medieval. The walls here are 3m thick at the base. The massive curving courtyard wall has a clear join between medieval and 19th-century work at the top of its great splayed base, with the medieval wall extending on up the east end to include the three easternmost embrasures.

The south-west or kitchen tower is perhaps the most impressive part of the castle, with its massive pyramidal spurs anchoring it to the rock. It was also the least ruined part, the original stonework surviving to above the top of the spurs. A late 18th-century watercolour shows it standing even higher. On the south side the original masonry survives to above the lower windows. Above is the restored hall. Steep steps lead back to the entrance.

Inside the castle there are only a few original elements, of which the well in the well tower, although now capped with a 19th-century pump, is the least altered. The dungeon is an authentic but 19th-century touch, and the servants' hall, now the exhibition room, is an accurate reconstruction. The remainder is from another world, very different from that of the warlike Gilbert de Clare.

The 3rd marquis of Bute did not neglect the surroundings of the castle: he it was who planted the beech woods on the slopes all around and, to add what he thought was a true authentic touch, he planted a vineyard here in 1875, to produce home-grown wine for his table. Gilbert de Clare had other preoccupations.

118
Llantrisant Castle, Llantrisant
Medieval masonry castle
13th century
OS 170   ST 047834   U2

In centre of Llantrisant, E of church. Turn L off Swan Street in front of church. Castle to L

A dark, ivy-covered ruined tower is all that is left of one of the more important 13th-century castles of Glamorgan. It was built in about 1250 by Richard de Clare, lord of Glamorgan, to hold this hill district of Meisgyn which he had just wrested from its Welsh overlords. The castle's strategic and commanding position, guarding an important route from the upland to the lowland zone, is very apparent.

The castle stands on a flat-topped blunt spur on the edge of a steep drop to the south. Parts of the spur's stone revetment are still visible, and ditches separate it from the rest of the ridgetop on the east and west sides. The north side of a circular tower, once called the Raven (or Gigvran, in Welsh), is the main upstanding stonework of the castle. Details on a doorway half-way up it point to a mid 13th-century date, and also give an idea of the height of the curtain wall, the wall-walk of which was originally reached from this doorway. The curtain wall would have skirted the spur, but very little of its survives. On the south-west flank there is the much-overgrown base of a half-round projecting tower.

The open green to the north of the castle is the probable site of a bailey, but no traces of earthwork or masonry defences survive. The church to the west was originally an aisled Norman church before 19th-century rebuilding.

119

Morlais Castle, Merthyr Tydfil

Medieval masonry castle

13th century

OS 160   SO 048097   U2

1ml (1.6km) N of Merthyr Tydfil. Take minor road N from Merthyr Tydfil towards Vaynor. Take 1st track on RHS below old quarries. At end of track castle above quarries on RHS

Robinson 1983; Kenyon 1985

Although not much is left standing of Morlais Castle the climb up to it is rewarded by panoramic view of the hills all around. The castle's dramatic hilltop situation is somewhat heightened by the sheer drop on its west side to a huge disused quarry.

This is one of Gilbert de Clare's castles (see also nos 116 and 117), with which he conducted his power struggles against the Welsh and neighbouring marcher lords. He built it some time in the early 1290s. Its siting, on disputed territory between the lordship of Glamorgan and the lordship of Brecon, was contentious and provocative, and Humphrey de Bohun, lord of Brecon, did not let it pass.

By 1290 open warfare had broken out, speedily ended by Edward I, who clapped them both in the Tower of London for a short while.

The castle remains consist essentially of a collapsed curtain wall around the oval-shaped hilltop, with a number of ruinous angle-towers, an inner ward and keep at the narrow north end, and the foundations of several buildings. A quarry has eaten into the west side so that little remains of the curtain wall there. On the other sides the hilltop is surrounded by an impressive rock-cut ditch with causeways across it in the south-west corner and on the east. From this causeway there is a good view of the long east curtain wall, mostly collapsed but standing in places up to 3m high. The only surviving entrance is a narrow ragged gap in the wall diagonally to the right. To its right is a collapsed drum tower. Six round towers can be made out around the curtain wall, three on the east side, one on the west and one each at the north and south ends.

Outlines of rectangular buildings against the curtain wall to the left of the entrance, and the outline of a cross-wall cutting off the northern end of the castle are visible. In the middle is a large, square, rock-cut hole whose purpose is obscure; the most likely

Morlais Castle, the keep at the north end

explanation is that it was a water cistern. The inner ward at the north end contains further building outlines; the rectangular building along the west curtain wall could have been the hall, with ancillary rooms and an oven in its south-west corner, and the apsidal building on the cross-wall could have been a chapel or possibly a solar. At the northern apex of the castle stand the ruins of a large round tower, which was probably the keep. Although now little more than a heap of stones, a 1741 engraving by Samuel and Nathaniel Buck shows that this was once a substantial tower, then already ruinous, but standing in part to first-floor level.

The most complete feature of the castle is the undercroft of the south-east tower. The tower is now reduced to a stony grass-covered knoll, but the gloomy undercroft with its central pillar and twelve vaulting ribs, entered through a narrow arched doorway on the north side, has astonishingly survived intact and is now protected by a concrete capping. The ceiling is complete, and the whole effect is one of graceful simplicity.

120
Barry Castle, Barry
Medieval masonry castle
14th century
OS 171   ST 101672   U1

Take A4055 into Barry. Where road swings L to cross causeway to Barry Island continue straight on along Romilly Park Road. Follow road around park, leaving the stones to the R, bear L (N) to T-junction. Turn L. Castle on RHS before road forks

This small, two-storey gatehouse and the adjacent walls of a hall, now pleasantly landscaped and restored, are all that remain of the seat of the de Barry family. The castle was really little more than a small fortified manor house, built in the 13th and 14th centuries to replace an earlier earthwork castle of which there is now no trace.

Barry Castle

By the late 13th century the castle had two stone buildings on the east and west sides of a courtyard, but nothing now remains of these above ground. Early in the 14th century the castle was strengthened by the addition of a large hall and gatehouse on its south side, and it is the ruins of these that can be seen today.

The gatehouse passage is arched, with a portcullis groove on the east side. As well as a portcullis it had a drawbridge and double doors. A small room above, whose outer wall and arched window survive, held the portcullis windlass and also possibly a chapel. Behind the gate passage is a rectangular room with a blocked staircase in the south-east corner and an arrowslit in the east wall. The walls of the hall block to the west are much lower, with a low arched doorway and an arrowslit on the north side. The hall itself was on the first floor, and was heated by a fireplace on the north wall. There was a narrow mural stair in the south-east corner on to a wall-walk on the curtain wall, and a door, the bottom part of which is visible, in the east wall leading to the portcullis chamber/chapel. There is evidence that the hall was roofed with Cornish slate, and had green glazed ridge tiles.

Also in Barry are St Barruc's chapel on Barry Island (no. 132) and Knap Roman site at Cold Knap (no. 71).

121
Newport Castle, Newport
Medieval masonry castle
14th–15th century
OS 171   ST 312884   U1   Cadw

In centre of Newport on W side of bridge over river Usk by railway station. No direct access: view from pavement or road

The demands of modern transport have almost squeezed this castle out of existence: most lies under roads, and only the east side survives, sandwiched between a road and a railway bridge. However, what little remains is not without interest, and the best place from which to get an impression of its original grandeur is half-way across the adjacent bridge, from where its position right on the bank of the river Usk can best be appreciated. The projecting central tower with its water-gate or dock beneath is the dominant feature. Flanking it are two octagonal towers with prominent spur buttresses. These mark the north and south ends of the castle, from which a curtain wall ran westwards enclosing a roughly rectangular area. Outside the curtain wall was a deep moat which filled with sea water at high tide.

The castle was built between 1327 and 1386 by Hugh d'Audele or his son-in-law Ralph, earl of Stafford. It replaced an earlier motte-and-bailey castle on Stow Hill, near the

cathedral. Newport was the headquarters of the Norman lordship of Wentloog or Gwynlliog, which had been within the lordship of Glamorgan until 1314. The new stone castle reflected Wentloog's enhanced status as a separate lordship. The castle was of the usual medieval type with a curtain wall enclosing a courtyard or ward. Towers punctuated its sides and there would have been at least one entrance gatehouse.

The next building phase was in the second quarter of the 15th century when the castle was strengthened and embellished for Humphrey Stafford, who became the first duke of Buckingham. The most important of these alterations were the raising of the north curtain wall and the heightening and modernising of the south tower. After 1521, when the 3rd duke of Buckingham was beheaded, the castle was neglected, and by the 18th century was mostly ruinous. During the 19th century parts were used as a brewery and the curtain wall was gradually demolished. What remains of the castle has been restored in places, but much of the original stonework of mottled pink Old Red Sandstone and white Dundry stone survives.

Starting at the north (railway) end and working southwards, first is the north tower, a two-storey semi-octagonal building which contained plain but comfortable rooms. To the west of it was a garderobe, now gone, next to which is thought to have been an entrance gate. Next to the north tower are the remains of the hall. This was at first-floor level, and had two large arched windows overlooking the river, with a fireplace between them. The next window, which is similar, belonged to an ante-room of unknown purpose.

In the middle is the great central tower which originally extended further westwards. From the west it is possible to make out all its principal features – the water-gate beneath, which was closed by a portcullis, the room above with its fine ribbed vaulting, a spiral staircase housed in a much restored octagonal turret in the north-west corner, and the stub of an upper storey. The main room

Newport Castle, east side

would probably have been the lord's audience chamber, and the room above a chapel. In Humphrey Stafford's day (1436–47) the west side was rebuilt, and its vaulting and arch were inserted.

To the south of the central tower was a long narrow room dating from this 15th-century rebuilding, and next to it a wall gallery, whose small windows are visible, leading to the south tower. Originally the tower could only be entered this way; the door on the south side is a later insertion. The lord's apartments were in this tower, which was originally two storeys high but was heightened to three by Humphrey Stafford. The quality of the Decorated windows, the fireplaces and the carved corbels on the upper floor indicate sophistication and comfort.

Newport Castle had an active life of only about 200 years, and during very little of this time was it actually occupied by its lord. For a brief time at the beginning of the 16th century Jasper Tudor, Henry VII's uncle, lived here. It played no significant part in national politics, and its main function was the day-to-day administration of the lordship of Wentloog.

122
Raglan Castle, Raglan
Medieval masonry castle
15th–17th century
OS 161   SO 415083   R1   Cadw

Raglan is 7ml (11km) SW of Monmouth and can be reached on the A40 from Abergavenny and Monmouth or A449 from Newport. 0.5ml (0.8km) N of village. Small access road off eastbound carriageway of A40 (signposted). Entrance charge. Cadw standard hours

Taylor 1950: Official Guide; Kenyon 1988: Cadw Guide

Raglan Castle is one of Britain's most magnificent late medieval castles and was, according to a 17th-century description, 'when in its splendour, one of the fairest

buildings in England'. It is now one of the country's fairest ruins. Situated on a prominent rise in the rolling countryside of mid-Gwent, it still dominates the surrounding area. It had an active lifespan of just over 200 years, and ironically was only used in a military capacity right at the end of its life in the 17th-century Civil War. Despite its appearance, and unlike earlier medieval castles, it was never primarily a military stronghold.

In 1432 the soldier of fortune Sir William ap Thomas bought the manor of Raglan, demolished most of the existing manor house of the Bluet family, and in the next 10 years built himself a fortress-palace. He built the Great Tower, the South Gate and the hall range, in which only fragments of his work now remain, and the Fountain Court was enclosed by a curtain wall (but there is a possibility that this was part of the original Bluet manor) which was completely demolished in the next building phase. Sir William was building to impress, to demonstrate his new-found wealth and rank, and his Great Tower, known as the Yellow Tower (Tŵr Melyn) of Gwent, was the ultimate status symbol.

William died in 1445 and his equally ambitious son, Sir William Herbert, the most prominent Yorkist supporter of Edward IV in Wales, continued the building programme until his execution in 1469 with continuity of style and concept. Sir William's great wealth was lavished on Raglan, and most of the remaining castle is his work. All the 15th-century buildings are characterised by very high quality stonework, with ashlared walls of pale yellow sandstone from Redbrook in the Wye valley. Some of the earliest brickwork in Wales is visible in the later 15th-century parts; it was used extensively in vaulting, in the backs of fireplaces, over windows and in awkward corners. William Herbert arranged his palace around two courts, now called the Pitched Stone Court and the Fountain Court. He moved the entrance to the great gatehouse (the present entrance), added the chapel on the west side of the hall and made some changes to the Great Tower.

The palace was now essentially complete, and there were no further additions until 1549, when William, 3rd earl of Worcester, inherited it. William, a cultured man and prominent courtier, instituted great changes while respecting the existing layout and style.

His building work is characterised by a redder sandstone and rubble rather than ashlar walling. He rebuilt the east side of the hall, lengthened the hall range and added that quintessentially Elizabethan room, a long gallery, which ran the length of the range, above the chapel. The north-west and

Raglan Castle gatehouse

north-east sides of the Pitched Stone Court were rebuilt, and a fountain called the White Horse was added in the middle of the Fountain Court. William built garden terraces to give his palace appropriately grand, almost Italianate gardens, enhanced by a large lake in the valley below to the north-west.

Edward, 4th earl of Worcester, succeeded William in 1589. He too was a cultured and brilliant man, and held high office at the courts of both Elizabeth I and James I. His additions of the White Gate, the moat walk around the Great Tower and the unusual 'water parterre' at the head of the lake gave the castle even more of a Renaissance air.

The disaster of the siege and surrender of Raglan in the Civil War, in 1646, dominates the last phase of its existence. The 1st marquis of Worcester, who succeeded in 1628, paid a heavy price for his strong support for the king. He made few alterations

to the buildings, beginning but never finishing an outer brick gate, the 'Red' gate, now buried under the car park, and throwing up some earthen defences to the east and south of the castle against the Parliamentary besiegers. But heavy pounding from mortars and overwhelming numbers forced a surrender, and on 19 August 1646 Raglan was abandoned, never to be lived in again.

Before beginning a tour of the castle it is worth noting some general points about the buildings. First, there is a hexagonal theme running throughout the castle. All the large towers and the two sides of the White Gate are hexagonal or semi-hexagonal. The idea of a polygonal keep originated in France, as did further details such as machicolations around the tops of towers. These survive on the gatehouse and the Closet Towers, and the Kitchen Tower and Great Tower would also have had them. The many gunports

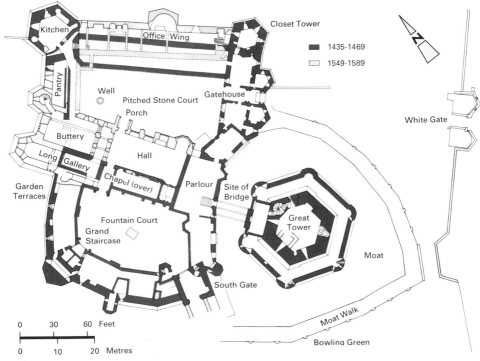

Raglan Castle

throughout the castle are another prominent feature. On the outside they are symmetrically placed in horizontal rows in the lower parts of the walls, but on the inside some are in absurd positions, like the bases of fireplaces and the backs of latrines. Their purpose, therefore, would seem to have been more decorative than defensive. Notice the profusion of fireplaces, and finally the many garderobes and where they drain into – some straight into the moat.

The outer entrance to the castle is through the 4th earl's White Gate, two ruined pavilions either side of a gateway. Two scallop-headed niches on the right-hand side give some idea of their original sophistication. In front is the great four-storey gatehouse, before which is a 16th-century bridge. To the right is the impressive, almost complete Closet Tower which housed garderobes and private rooms. The dark basement may have been a prison. On the first floor of the gatehouse wing was a large room, divided in two in the 16th century, which must have been one of the finest rooms in the castle, with six large windows facing the court. The attic storey above, added in the 16th century, rather spoils the original proportions. In the south-west corner is an odd skewed window indicating subsidence problems.

The Pitched Stone Court still has its original 16th-century cobbling, laid down on the 15th-century surface. To the right is all that remains of the 16th-century office wing, which housed service rooms and which was severely damaged by mortar fire in 1646. The 15th-century office wing lay slightly inside it.

In the north corner is the Kitchen Tower, with a cool room in the basement, a kitchen with two large double-flued fireplaces and a drain on the ground floor, and two living rooms, now floorless, above. To the west of this tower is all that remains of the 16th-century pantry block and passage to the hall (now an open path).

Along the south-west side of the Pitched Stone Court is the largest and most important building in the castle, the hall. Its north-east side was remodelled by the 3rd earl in the

16th century to include the three-storey porch entrance and large mullioned and transomed Tudor windows, including the huge oriel window at the dais, or high-table end. The cusped heads of the windows match the earlier 15th-century windows in a nice touch of continuity of style. Inside, the hall is completely bare, but the walls stand to their full height and at their tops are the carved corbels on which the 16th-century hammerbeam oak roof rested. On the north-east wall is a huge fireplace, and above the dais end is a worn plaque bearing the 3rd earl's coat of arms. Originally there was a doorway at this end into the parlour, which had the lord's private dining room above it. A doorway in the south corner leads down to the cellars. At the lower end of the hall is a serving hatch flanked by two doors. These lead into a passage and then the buttery, with living rooms above. This part was remodelled and extended north-westwards in the 16th century, and the top floor contains two fine Tudor fireplaces.

Opposite the storeyed porch was a 15th-century porch of which only the foundations and the base of a door jamb survive. To the left was the chapel, now gone. The curving bite out of the wall is all that remains of 16th-century stairs to the long gallery above. At its north-west end this projected right out beyond the original outer wall of the castle, and ended in three great windows from which there would have been magnificent views out over the gardens, lake, deer park and the Black Mountains beyond. The stonework of these windows and the right-hand side of an ornate fireplace are all that survive of this once magnificent long gallery.

In the Fountain Court only the base of the White Horse fountain, said to have run 'both day and night', survives. Around the court were two-storey living apartments, most of whose inner walls have completely gone. Two wings flanked the grand staircase, now replaced by a modern wooden stair. Windows to the outside were small and simple, but to the inside were much larger and finer, as can be seen from the window over the grand stair.

In the south corner of the Fountain Court is the South Gate, the main entrance to William ap Thomas' castle. It is plain, originally three-storey, and has an off-centre archway with one small window on the outside. Its battered base is of rougher construction, which suggests that it has even earlier foundations. When the great gatehouse was built it became redundant; William Herbert removed its fan vaulting, blocked the entrances and turned it into a room, and in the 16th century it was unblocked to provide access to the bowling green. To its north-east is a garderobe turret squeezed in at an odd angle, and further apartments, of which very little survives. Below are extensive cellars vaulted in brick.

Between the hall and the moat are the state apartments, the parlour, dining room and on the first floor beyond, the lord's bedroom. These rooms are now reduced to a few fragments of walling, but enough remains of some of their windows to give an idea of their former sumptuousness. The parlour and dining room had oriel windows overlooking the moat, and part of the left-hand side of the dining room window survives. The bedroom has a very fine window, elaborately carved on the underside of the top, and with heraldic motifs over it on the outside. These feature shields and a *bascule* or drawbridge counterpoise, a motif no doubt taken from the actual one on the Great Tower opposite.

The moated Great Tower, William ap Thomas's masterpiece, was capable of independent defence, built to withstand gunpowder, and was modelled on similar contemporary French towers. In this country it was innovatory and rare. It was originally five storeys high, topped with machicolated battlements. The top storey has gone, but even without it the tower is still an impressive height. It was reached by a fixed wooden bridge which rested on stone piers, and two drawbridges of the French *bascule* type. Their counterbalance beams fitted into the vertical grooves on the face of the tower when the bridges were raised. This arrangement was soon replaced by William Herbert with a two-decker 'sumptuous arched bridge' which

crossed to a building, now gone, in front of the tower.

At basement level, there are unusual combined gunports and cross arrowslits in the middle of each side, with a well in the embrasure of one of them. The tower had a single room and a garderobe on each floor. On the first floor was the great chamber, lit by small single-light windows, while above were bedrooms with larger windows. The top of the tower is only for those with a good head for heights. The lack of a top storey is due to slighting by Parliamentarians after the siege of 1646. Around the base of the tower William Herbert added a decorative low hexagonal 'apron' wall with six small corner turrets, one of which houses a garderobe and another of which has a postern door to the moat.

To begin a tour of the gardens start at the South Gate and walk out on to the bowling green, where Charles I was entertained to a game of bowls in 1645. Steps lead down to a squarish, flat area with a raised terrace around two sides of it which was undoubtedly laid out as a formal garden. In its south-west corner are the foundations of a brick summerhouse. To its south are steps down to a further large garden terrace which is now a field. To the north-west of the castle are long garden terraces, originally revetted in stone, below which was the lake or 'great Poole'. At its head the 4th earl added a formal water garden or 'water parterre' laid out in diamond-shaped channels, islands and walks. This can just be made out (the best view is from the Kitchen Tower windows) in the valley floor to the north of the castle as boggy, iris-filled ditches and low mounds and banks. Back at the South Gate, the moat walk can be reached under the bridge to the bowling green. This was a touch of great Renaissance sophistication, also added by the 4th earl. According to a 17th-century description it was 'a pleasant walk set forth with several figures of the Roman emperors in arches of divers varieties of shell work'. The 15 brick niches survive, with some of their painted plaster and shellwork still intact, but the Roman emperors disappeared in the Civil War.

8

The Medieval Period: Ecclesiastical and Miscellaneous Sites

In parallel with the development of castles in south-east Wales during the medieval period was the development of the monasteries, which were the spiritual arm of the Norman military conquest. They could be seen as the bishops in the chess game analogy suggested in chapter 7. The ruins of some of them are among the finest monuments in the area. Founding a monastery and endowing it with land was a traditional act of piety for Norman knights. Within a short time William fitz Osbern had founded Chepstow Priory; Robert, earl of Gloucester, Margam Abbey; Maurice de Londres, Ewenny Priory; Walter fitz Richard, Tintern Abbey and Richard de Granville, Neath Abbey. Some of the earliest ecclesiastical Norman stonework in the area is at Ewenny Priory (no. 127), where the church shows typical Norman severity and simplicity, with only a little geometrical decoration to relieve the blank walls.

The most spectacular and beautiful monastic remains are almost all of houses of the Cistercian order, which quickly became the most successful of the monastic orders in Wales. Tintern (no. 123), Neath (no. 124) and Margam (no. 125) were all Cistercian abbeys, placed in remote, well-watered spots, well away from earthly distractions. Although their surroundings have been altered, and in the case of Neath spoilt, it is still possible, especially at Tintern, to imagine the original beauty and tranquillity of their locations. However, some were uncomfortably close to the disaffected Welsh, and the monasteries in the west of the area and Llanthony Priory up in the Black Mountains suffered periodically from Welsh raids. The Benedictines of Ewenny Priory felt the need for a show front of great strength to deter attackers.

For the Cistercians remoteness of site was matched by simplicity of living, at least to begin with, and by severity and lack of ornament in building, well demonstrated by the lay brothers' range at Neath Abbey. Later, buildings would become more ornamented, culminating in the great cruciform churches of Neath and Tintern, with their huge traceried windows, originally filled with stained glass. Cistercian abbeys were laid out to a standard plan, and those in south-east Wales are no exception. The cloisters were the nucleus around which all the buildings ranged – the church to the north, the kitchen and refectories to the south, the entrance and lay brothers' ranges to the west and the chapter house, with the monks' dormitory over it, to the east. Outlying buildings such as latrines, the abbot's house and the infirmary, were usually to the south and east. The whole would be enclosed in a precinct wall, beyond which there might be further buildings, such as guesthouses and agricultural buildings, in an outer precinct. The layout of other orders' monasteries differed little from this basic plan, the main difference being that only the Cistercians had to cater for the needs of lay brothers (or *conversi*).

Extensive tracts of land were given to the monasteries, and the Cistercians, who used lay brothers for much of their manual work, became major agriculturalists and aggressive entrepreneurs, running huge flocks of sheep, shipping, docks and even mines. The Cistercians used a system of outlying granges to farm their land. These were enclosures containing farm buildings including a large storage barn, ponds, a dovecote, sometimes a chapel and other buildings. There are 54 granges alone in Glamorgan, 28 of which belonged to Margam, 17 to Neath. The most visible parts of their very fragmentary remains are usually the great barns and dovecotes (for example Monknash Grange, no. 128). Most of the building remains of these granges date from the 13th century, but apart from a few exceptional survivals and some stumps of walls little can be seen of them.

By the end of the 13th century the monasteries had amassed great wealth, but the 14th century saw a downturn in their fortunes, with Welsh raids on their property, plague and other calamities, such as sand encroachment on Margam

19th-century engraving of Neath Abbey

lands. Despite a brief revival in the mid-15th century, inexorable decline set in, and when the monasteries were dissolved in the 1530s there were very few monks left. Some abbeys, like Neath and Margam, were partially converted into houses for leading families of the area; the rest were left to decay. It was not until the late 18th century that travellers in search of the romantic and picturesque rediscovered them.

Although the monasteries are the main ecclesiastical monuments in the area, there are others not connected with them. Above Llandaff Cathedral, Cardiff, stands the stump of a 13th-century bell tower (no. 131), and next to it the ruins of the Old Bishop's Palace (no. 130), in appearance more a typical 13th-century military stronghold than a bishop's residence. The churchyard crosses found in many parish churchyards, usually on the south side of the church, date from the 15th century, and were preaching crosses. They took a standard form of tapering steps (usually square), a cubical base, a narrow column (often octagonal) and a lantern head with carved biblical figures and scenes on each of its four sides. Very few of these crosses remain in their entirety, and only a handful still have their original lantern heads (see nos 134, 135, 136). Many have been heavily restored. There are also a few ruined late medieval chapels in the area, for instance at Margam (see Appendix), Merthyr Mawr (see Appendix), and the stump of one on the top of the Skirrid mountain (no. 133).

There are a few miscellaneous sites included here also which give further insight into the medieval world – parts of two town walls (nos 144 and 145), a very eccentric dovecote (no. 146), a famous fortified bridge (no. 147), a healing well (no. 148) and two noble houses (nos 149 and 150) which began life in the medieval period but whose principal remains are Tudor.

123
Tintern Abbey, Tintern
Medieval monastic site
12th–15th century
OS 162   SO 534000   R1   Cadw

11ml (18km) S of Monmouth, 5ml (8km) N of Chepstow, on A466, in Tintern village. Entrance charge. Cadw standard hours

Robinson: Cadw Guide

The Cistercian abbey of Tintern is one of the great monastic ruins of Wales. It was only the second Cistercian foundation in Britain, and

the first in Wales, and was founded on 9 May 1131 by Walter de Clare, lord of Chepstow. It soon prospered, thanks to endowments of land in Gwent and Gloucestershire, and buildings were added and updated in every century until its dissolution in 1536. However, it was never very large or important, and its history was relatively uneventful. Its position well away from the Welsh heartland meant that unlike Margam, Neath and Llanthony it suffered little in the periodic Welsh uprisings of the medieval period.

Tintern was always closely associated with the lords of Chepstow, who were often generous benefactors. The most generous was Roger Bigod III, grandson of William

Marshal's daughter Maud; his monumental undertaking was the rebuilding of the church in the late 13th century. In gratitude the abbey put his coat of arms in the glass of its east window. It is the ruins of Roger's church which dominate the site today.

The abbey buildings were arranged in a standard Cistercian plan, except that the cloisters and all its ancillary buildings were to the north of the church rather than the south, which was more usual. Pragmatic considerations like the drains may have led to this reversal. The present-day remains are an amalgam of several phases of building spanning 400 years, but throughout the basic arrangement remained the same.

Of the first buildings, which date from the 12th century, very little remains above ground. A few sections of walling are incorporated into later buildings, and the two recessed cupboards for books on the east of the cloisters are of this period. The church was smaller than the 13th-century one, and lay slightly to the north. Its cruciform plan is laid out in gravel paths and stone edgings within the later church. In the late 12th century the first-floor monks' dormitory, which ran northwards from the north transept of the church, was extended; its northern end and the latrines over the drain to its east are of this phase.

During the 13th century the abbey was more or less completely rebuilt, starting in about 1220 with the cloisters and domestic ranges around them, and finishing with the great church. The entrance to the precinct was on the west side of the cloisters, through the unassuming late 13th-century porch and outer parlour. (The modern entrance to the abbey is well to the north.) Above was a small lodging, possibly for the cellarer. To the north was a cellar and the lay brothers' range of refectory and dormitory, which was extended in the late 13th century.

Along the north side of the cloisters are ranged, in clockwise order, the kitchen, the monks' refectory and the warming room. The kitchen was conveniently sited between the two dining rooms, with hatches through to

both. The abbey's main drain can be seen running under this range; the system was complex, and in the novices' lodging there is a sluice where the drain could be dammed, raising the water either to provide a head for flushing out the latrines just to the east, or to let water into the higher drain leading off to the abbot's lodgings. The monks' dining hall, or frater, was entered from the cloisters; recesses by the door held bowls for washing and towels. It was a fine room with simple traceried windows along the east side. In the west wall is a small stair which originally led to a pulpit from which a monk could read aloud during meals. To the east was the pantry, next to which are further recesses for washing and storing plates and spoons. The warming house, which retains its simple rib vaulting, had a central fire, and must have provided very welcome warmth in what appears otherwise to have been a chilly environment.

The cloisters themselves were originally covered walks with pent roofs. That nearest the church was for study, supervised by a prior sitting in the canopied seat in the middle. Along the east side were the novices' lodgings, a passage, a parlour, the chapter house, book room and sacristy, with the monks' dormitory running over the whole range. Enough detail survives to show that the quality of stone carving was high; the rectangular chapter house had a finely carved entrance, rib vaulting and probably three east windows, and the 14th-century entrance to the book room is also richly carved.

Immediately to the east of the latrines is the stub of a two-roomed early 13th-century building which may have been the abbot's private lodgings. Further to the north-east is a ruined rectangular building of the same date which may originally have been for visiting abbots. In the 14th century it became part of the resident abbot's lodgings. To its south are the remains of an open-aisled hall, an infirmary built later in the 13th century.

Tintern's crowning glory, its great church, was built between 1269 and 1301. It stands today much as it did then, apart from its lack of roof, window glass and internal divisions.

Tintern Abbey, looking west from the presbytery

Although not nearly as long as the great Yorkshire Cistercian abbey churches at Fountains and Rievaulx, its completeness makes it impressive. It has a simple cruciform plan, with an aisled nave, transepts each with two chapels, and a square-ended aisled chancel. Cistercian rule and liturgy dictated the internal divisions, which have disappeared; the aisles were all walled off, and three cross-walls divided the body of the church into two main sections – the nave, reserved for the lay brothers, and the choir and presbytery at the east end for the choir monks. Stubs of the aisle walls can be seen against the piers. Aesthetically today's simplicity may appear more pleasing than the original clutter; this was certainly the motive for the Victorian removal of the main cross-wall or *pulpitum*. The internal wall surfaces are articulated into bays divided by clustered columns, above which are triple vaulting shafts which rise up to the springing of the rib vaulting, none of which remains. Some of the great bosses from the vaulting, carved with oak leaves and other foliage, lie upside-down in the chancel.

The fine west end is divided into three stages, with twin doorways and traceried arches in the lowest, a great seven-light window in the middle, and a smaller arched window, which has lost its tracery, at the top. This end, and the western part of the south side, may have been finished after Roger Bigod III's death in 1306. The delicate tracery of the main window, complete except for the circle at the top, is particularly fine seen from inside the church. By contrast, at the east end the great window, which took up most of the wall, is just a gaping hole. All that is left is the slender central mullion and circular window above. Daylight floods in, bringing the church into intimate contact with the woods beyond. The south transept window has likewise lost all its tracery, but that in the north survives and shows a curious feature: in order to maintain symmetry with the south transept it had to be carried on below the level of the monks' dormitory roof as panelling. Below it, slightly to the left, is the door which led to the dormitory, through which the monks would enter the church for night-time services. There were several other entrances into the church – the narrow diagonal passage in the north-west corner used by the lay brothers, the west doors and the great processional

doorway from the cloisters in the angle of the nave and north transept, a 14th-century embellishment which added a touch of splendour with its scalloped arch and richly carved surround.

The graves in the church are few, but not without interest. The only one in its original position is that sunk into the ground under the north arch of the crossing, which would have lain in the south transept of the 12th-century church. The inscription reads (translated) 'Here lies Nicholas of Llandaff'. In the south aisle is a grave slab with one large and two small fish incised on it, and an inscription which reads (translated) 'Here lies

Tintern Abbey

Dovecote

Entrance

Abbot's Hall

Abbot's Private Chamber

Lay Brothers' Dining Hall (Dormitory over)

Monks' Dining Hall

Novices' Lodging Dormitory (over)

Latrine

Infirmary Cloister

Kitchen

Infirmary Hall

Original Entrance

Cloister

Chapter House

Sacristy

Passage

North Transept

N a v e

Choir   Presbytery

South Transept

12th / Early 13th Century
Late 13th / Early 14th Century
Late 14th / 15th Century

| 0 | 50 | 100 Feet |
| 0 | 15 | 30 Metres |

William Wellsted'. Buried somewhere in the church are several lords of Chepstow and their relations, including Walter and Anselm Marshal (d. 1246), sons of William Marshal, Isabella (d. 1220), his wife, and Matilda (d. 1248), his daughter, who was carried into the choir by her four knight sons. William Herbert of Raglan Castle (no. 122) was buried here after his execution in 1469.

After the building of the church there was little major new building work. In the 14th century the austerity of Cistercian rule seems to have deserted the abbot, who had his lodgings greatly extended with the addition of a large hall to the west of his existing rooms, and a small chapel over them. All that can be seen of the hall, which was on the first floor, are the stubs of the ground floor storerooms and cellars. Also in the 14th century a covered passage was built from the infirmary to the church, and a small cloister made for the lay brothers south of the entrance. In the late 15th century the infirmary was made more comfortable and private with the insertion of walls in the aisles to form private rooms, each with its own privy and fireplace. To the north a new kitchen was built, identified today by its large fireplace and broken lintel stone. A start was made in the same period on rebuilding the cloisters, possibly with a view to vaulting them in stone, but little progress had been made by the time of the Dissolution.

The main abbey buildings were contained within a walled precinct of 11ha within which there were many other secular buildings. The remains of some, including the guesthouse, have been exposed to the west of the church, between the car park and the main road. The arch of the water-gate leading to wharves and a ferry over the river remains next to the Anchor Hotel, and the gatehouse chapel, clearly visible above the main road, has been converted into a private house. Sections of the precinct wall remain on the west and south, parts in a ruinous state, parts incorporated into garden walls.

When it became fashionable to visit the wilder parts of the country in the late 18th century the Wye valley became renowned for its picturesque qualities, and Tintern Abbey, then swathed in ivy, was rediscovered and visited by many famous seekers after the romantic and picturesque, including the painter J M W Turner and the poet William Wordsworth. But for one of these visitors, William Gilpin, it was not quite picturesque enough, and he advocated 'a mallet judiciously used' to render it less regular. Luckily his advice was not taken up, and since the early 20th century every effort has been made to keep standing one of the finest and most complete abbey churches in Wales.

124
Neath Abbey, Neath
Medieval monastic site and Tudor manor house
12th–16th century
OS 170   SS 738974   R1/U1   Cadw

On W side of Neath. Take A4230 Neath to Skewen road and turn S down Monastery Road to W of roundabout at end of dual carriageway into Neath. Gatehouse on N side of A4230 just W of Monastery Road turn. Entrance charge. Cadw standard hours

Butler: Official Guide

The ruins of Neath Abbey rank with those of Tintern (no. 123) and Llanthony Priory (no. 126) as the most important monastic remains in south-east Wales. Here the visitor is confronted by two very different ruins. To the north is the abbey itself, and to the south is the 16th-century house built after the Dissolution.

The abbey was founded in 1130 by a Norman knight, Sir Richard de Granville, who established a tenuous hold on the area west of Neath in Henry I's reign. He gave about 3,200ha of this land to the abbey of Savigny in France, which sent over an abbot and 12 monks. In 1147 the abbey became Cistercian, when the Savignac order merged with the Cistercian. It is hard to believe today that the

Neath Abbey living quarters

site the French monks chose for their abbey gave them rural solitude in a well-wooded, well-watered spot. More land was given, and the abbey prospered despite harrying by the Welsh, and quarrels with the nearby abbey of Margam (no. 125). By the end of the 13th century Neath was the second wealthiest abbey in Wales after Margam, with 40–50 monks and an even larger number of lay brothers who laboured on the abbey's extensive estates, in its coal mines and even on its ships, one of which was called the 'Hulc'. The abbey itself reflected this wealth, and great building programmes were set in hand.

The abbey was laid out to the standard Cistercian plan. On the west side of the cloisters is the oldest remaining part of the abbey, the lay brothers' range, built in the second half of the 12th century. This plain building, standing almost to roof height, is an excellent example of the simplicity and austerity of early Cistercian architecture. As elsewhere in the abbey the pale Sutton stone, used for quoins and window dressings, makes a lovely contrast with the dark local sandstone of the walls. The windows are simple lancets, and are particularly fine in the south gable end. The refectory was at the south end; the three octagonal pillar bases in the middle held piers which supported its rib-vaulted ceiling. To the north is the entrance to the abbey, with a 14th-century porch on the outside. The next room, where the springing of the vaulted ceiling can be seen, was the common room, and to the north are two narrow barrel-vaulted storerooms. Above was the dormitory. On the cloister side of the range was a narrow alley, separated from the cloisters by a wall, which enabled the lay brothers to enter the church without disturbing the choir monks. It is marked by the footing of a wall and a slightly lower level.

The next building phase was in the mid-13th century with the addition of claustral buildings on the east and south sides of the cloisters. Around the cloisters was an arcaded covered walk, now gone. On the south side the kitchen, refectory and warming house are represented by extremely fragmentary remains. Of interest are the drain at the south side of the kitchen (the westernmost building), the elaborately moulded base of the doorway into the refectory (in the middle) and the footings and moulded hand rail of the day

Neath Abbey

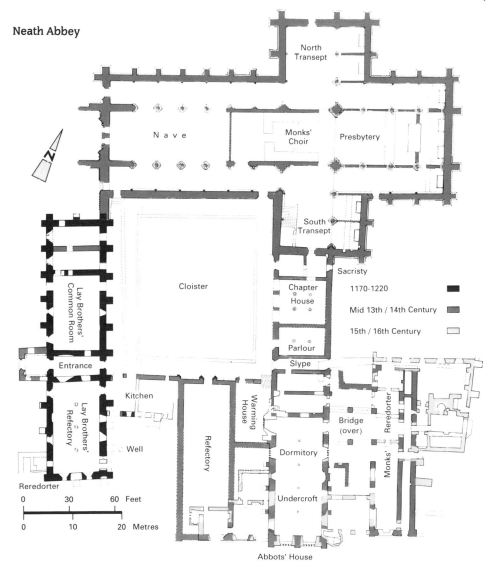

North Transept

Nave

Monks' Choir

Presbytery

South Transept

Sacristy

Cloister

Chapter House

1170-1220

Mid 13th / 14th Century

15th / 16th Century

Lay Brothers' Common Room

Parlour

Slype

Entrance

Kitchen

Warming House

Reredorter

Lay Brothers' Refectory

Well

Refectory

Bridge (over)

Monks' Reredorter

Dormitory

Reredorter

Undercroft

0   30   60 Feet

0   10   20 Metres

Abbots' House

stairs up to the monks' dormitory on the east wall of the warming house (the easternmost building). It is worth noting that the south wall of the refectory was the outer wall of the wing of the Tudor house directly to the south.

On the east side of the cloister the buildings have not fared much better; much was probably demolished when the Tudor house was built. Nearest the church are the footings of the walls of the book room and sacristy. To the south was the chapter house, with only the base of two round columns remaining. To its south was a parlour, also gone.

Part of the abbey was incorporated into the Tudor house and some of this survives remarkably intact. At the south end of the cloisters is a passageway, or slype, which still has its original paved floor and moulded stone doorway. To its south are two narrow rooms, also abbey survivals, the first still with its original doorway and window above. But the most remarkable survival is the dormitory undercroft. This cool and peaceful large room is more or less unaltered since it was built in the mid-13th century. It was probably for the novices, and when incorporated into the Tudor house became the servants' hall. Above, from the south wall to the church lay the monks' dormitory, part demolished and part altered in the Tudor rebuilding. The undercroft's details are similar to those of the chapter house at Llandaff Cathedral, built in 1260. Four slender circular columns support the rib-vaulted ceiling. The original tall lancet windows have been replaced by Tudor ones, and some openings have been blocked up. Miscellaneous bits and pieces from the abbey have been gathered together here – some roof bosses from the church, fragments of moulded stone, a grave slab in three pieces from a site nearby and some encaustic tile flooring found in the church.

To the west is another survival from the abbey, the bridge which led from the monks' dormitory to their privy or reredorter. It has fine square pillars and rib vaulting, and became part of the long gallery of the Tudor house. The long, narrow reredorter, which ran parallel to the dormitory, was also incorporated, but only the springing of the vaulting on the west side of its undercroft survives. Alongside it, to the west, is its drain, with rather noisome water in it.

The next stage was the construction of the church between 1280 and 1330. There would undoubtedly have been a 12th-century church, but it was demolished to make way for this new one, which is in many ways comparable to the great church at Tintern Abbey (no. 123), built at about the same time. Both were large, cruciform in plan, with an aisled nave. Both had two-stage elevations of nave and clerestory, and both had moved away from earlier austerity towards something more decorative. Internal layout was dictated by the rules and liturgy of the order. On the south side were two entrances from the cloisters, the western one for the lay brothers, who used the western part of the nave for their services, and the eastern one, which has some very rich moulding on the outside, for the choir monks. The walled-off part of the nave and crossing was used by the choir monks, and the site of the high altar is visible on a stone plinth. Smaller altars were ranged along the east wall, and each transept had two chapels on its east side.

The remains of the church are sadly fragmentary. The west end is the most complete part, but even here only two tall buttresses and part of the wall survive on either side of the gaping hole where once a great window would have been. Small parts of blind tracery remain on either side. In front are the broken stubs of a large porch or narthex. All that remain of the pillars of the nave are their great bases. On the side walls are fragments of attached columns and ragged window openings on the north. The south transept has some interesting details – against its west wall are the base of the steps and moulded hand rail of the night stair to the monks' dormitory, and in its south wall is a well preserved base of an attached column, a small alcove cupboard and washing basin or *piscina*. Two large pillars, once supporting the crossing, have been reduced to ragged irregular stumps. The east end, the presbytery and the ambulatory around it are very incomplete, with the east wall completely gone.

There are a few clues to the church's original sumptuousness. Excavations revealed large areas of encaustic tile pavement, decorated with benefactors' coats of arms and patterns of tracery and birds, and some painted wall plaster survives in the doorway to the sacristy in the south transept.

The building of the church was the high point in the abbey's history. Thereafter trouble and decline set in, with only a partial revival in the mid-15th century under the aegis of the great Abbot Thomas of Margam Abbey. The abbey flourished, but at a reduced level; culture and learning returned, and just before its dissolution in 1539, under another great abbot, Leyshon Thomas, it was the foremost Welsh Cistercian house, called by John Leland 'the fairest abbey of all Wales'.

In about 1500 the abbot carved a private house for himself out of the south end of the refectory and monks' dormitory. It is very difficult to make out now as it was overlain by the later house built in the second half of the 16th century either by Sir Richard Williams, who purchased the property in 1542, or his son Henry. This rebuilding is clearly distinguishable by its distinctive Tudor mullioned windows. The outer walls of a large part of this Tudor house still stand to first-floor level. The main entrance was on the south side, and the basic plan of the house was H-shaped, with the bridge in the centre. The monastic ground floor was largely unaltered, but the first floor was greatly changed and turned into the principal rooms, including a long gallery running east–west over the abbey bridge. This had a great oriel window, now a gaping hole, at its west end. An entirely new wing was added in the north-east corner, the gable ends of which still stand to their full height, although the rest is ruinous.

The buildings suffered the indignity of being used for copper smelting and then ironworks during the 18th century, with forges in the lay brothers' range. Decay continued throughout the 19th century, and it was not until the 20th century that the ruins were rediscovered.

An outlier to the main abbey site, but certainly part of the abbey precinct, is the 12th-century gatehouse whose ruins lie next to the main road to the north. The gateway itself was orientated east–west, and lay more or less where part of the modern road is. What remains above ground is its north side, which consists of two rooms, with arches flanking the gate-passage. The springing of both arches of the gateway is still visible.

125

Margam Abbey, Margam
Medieval monastic site
12th–13th century
OS 170   SS 802863   R1/U1

1m (1.6km) SE of Margam, off A48. Leave M4 at junction 38 and take A48 SE for short distance. Turn L into Margam Country Park. Abbey ruins and church behind Orangery. Entrance charge to Country Park

Evans: Guidebook

Only part of the church, the ruined chapter house and a few fragments of neighbouring buildings survive of this once great and wealthy abbey. After the Dissolution the nave of the abbey church, which was dedicated, as are all Cistercian churches, to St Mary, became the parish church, and it remains so. It is one of only three Cistercian churches still in use in Britain, and the only one in use in Wales. The rest of the remains now lie in the Margam Country Park.

In 1147, in the last year of his life, Robert the Consul, lord of Glamorgan, founded a Cistercian monastery at Margam. There may well have been an earlier church here, as witnessed by the early Christian stones found in Margam (no. 73), but of this there is no trace. Monks were sent from Waverley, in Surrey, to establish the abbey, and Robert endowed it well with 7,200ha between the

Margam Abbey chapter house

Afan and Kenfig rivers. By the Dissolution gifts from other local magnates had swollen this to about 20,000ha.

The great abbey church, cruciform in shape and longer than the churches of Tintern Abbey (no. 123) and Neath Abbey (no. 124), was begun in the 12th century, at its western end. The remains of this phase – part of the west end and some piers and arches of the nave – are in the parish church, which was heavily restored and altered in the 19th century. On the west front the fine deeply recessed door and three windows above are of this phase, and Romanesque in style. Of the same phase are the rectangular piers and plain semicircular arches of the nave. The rest of the abbey church, which dates from about 1200, lies to the east, and is much ruined. The most complete part is the south transept. In its east wall are two windows with very early Decorated quatrefoil tracery at their heads. There is a *piscina* with an octagonal bowl on the south wall. Part of the north and south walls of the choir remain, with an early Decorated window and a fine small doorway

with moulded decoration on the south side. This may have been the abbot's private entrance to the church. At the east end of the nave, on the south side, is a large double doorway (the western half is blocked) ornamented with moulding and trefoil patterns. The rest of the church has gone, with huge pier bases marking the site of the crossing and choir.

The layout of the abbey was probably the standard Cistercian one, with the cloisters and ancillary buildings to the south of the nave of the church. These have completely disappeared, and the only hint of their existence is the double doorway which would have led to the cloisters, and the remains of the vestibule on what would have been their east side. This vestibule is the rib-vaulted double-aisled passage to the west of the chapter house. Only its ground floor remains; over it would have been the monks' dormitory, which would have continued southwards. On its east side are three openings. The central one, with a pointed arch in pure Early English style, was the doorway into the chapter house. It is flanked by two plain lancet windows.

The chapter house, built in about 1200, is the crowning glory of the abbey remains. Until 1799, when it was badly damaged in a storm, it stood intact, and although ruined now it is still impressive in its dignified simplicity and purity of design. The chapter house of the 13th century was a peculiarly English phenomenon, and was often architecturally outstanding. Cistercian chapter houses were usually rectangular but this one was made 12-sided without and circular within. The smooth ashlar masonry that once covered the outside remains only around the windows and on the external flat buttresses. In the centre is a delicate clustered column of shafts crowned by a foliage capital, from which spring the bases of 24 moulded vaulting ribs. The chapter house's nine tall lancet windows are plainer than its interior and appear earlier in style. However, the mouldings of the window on the east side are slightly more elaborate, and below it is a square opening of unknown purpose with a quatrefoil light and a circular and richly moulded exterior.

To the south of the chapter house are the ruins of another building which may have been the infirmary. Part of the ground floor is all that remains. It has large arched openings on the north and south sides, and a rib-vaulted ceiling. The only other visible remain of this important monastery is the gable end of the mill on the western side of the lake to the north-west.

Margam Abbey flourished for about 200 years. Its secular activities were extensive; it had large tracts of land, huge flocks of sheep, mills, fisheries and coal mines. Among the precious books in its possession was the copy of the Domesday Book now in the British Museum. But Welsh uprisings and the encroachment of sand on the coast led to insecurity and decline, and by 1536 there were only nine monks left. After the abbey's dissolution Sir Rice Mansel of Oxwich Castle (no. 150) bought it and converted the buildings into his principal residence.

126
Llanthony Priory, Llanfihangel Crucorney

Medieval monastic site

12th–14th century

OS 161   SO 289278   U2   Cadw

10ml (16km) N of Abergavenny. Turn off A465 Abergavenny to Hereford road at Llanfihangel Crucorney, and take B4423 to priory. Signposted

Craster: Official Guide

Llanthony Priory was one of the earliest houses of Augustinian canons to be founded in Britain, and is one of only a handful in Wales. It is chiefly famous today for its wild and beautiful setting, far up the Vale of Ewyas in the Black Mountains. It was the priory's remoteness in the Welsh hills which was its undoing, however, making it vulnerable to attack. Giraldus Cambrensis described it, in the late 12th century, as being 'fixed amongst a barbarous people'.

William de Lacy, a knight in the service of Hugh de Lacy, is said to have chosen the spot while out hunting, when he sheltered in a chapel there dedicated to St David. Very quickly a church was established, dedicated to John the Baptist, and it was reorganised as a priory in about 1118. Hugh de Lacy, who had assumed the patronage, endowed it with land, and it soon became famous, enjoyed royal patronage and received many visitors. There were 40 canons in residence, but in about 1135 the 'barbarous people' forced a retreat to Hereford and Gloucester. Of this first priory nothing remains. Peace and renewed endowment by the de Lacy family from about 1175 brought canons back from Gloucester and ushered in the great rebuilding phase. It is the remains of this phase that can be seen today.

The priory's church, built between 1180 and 1230, was one of the great medieval buildings of Wales. Its plan was the standard cruciform one, with a massive crossing tower and two smaller towers at the west end. In style it is transitional, with a mixture of Norman round-headed arches and Gothic pointed ones. From the preponderance of round-headed arches at the east end and in the crossing it is surmised that building began here in the late 12th century and progressed westwards. The size and remaining details of the church show that the builders were both wealthy and sophisticated. Eighteenth-century travellers in search of the picturesque were lucky enough to see the east and west window tracery still in place, and in 1803 Sir Richard Colt Hoare actually witnessed the great west window fall. It had three tall lancets to the present height of the towers, and above that three smaller ones. All that remains now are the sill and jambs. The huge east window, replaced in the 14th century, probably had three tall lancets as well, and is now just a gaping hole.

The crossing tower, whose west and south sides survive, originally had one more level. The round-headed windows belong to a passage in the wall, and the doorway above on the west side led into the roof space of the nave. Recent excavation has produced evidence that there was a clock in the tower, probably of the late 14th century, and of a very early primitive and rare kind. It had no dials, but would have struck the hour.

The north transept is more ruined than the south, whose south wall with its large window openings remains intact. Opening off the transepts, on their east sides, were chapels, now reduced to footings only, which were altered in the 14th century when the large arch was inserted in the south transept, and the north transept and its chapels were converted to domestic use.

The main feature of the nave is the arcade of the north aisle. All eight bays survive, with a partly ruined triforium over them of paired lancet windows in round-headed openings. These would have been inside the church; above were the clerestory windows, now gone, which would have given light from outside. The positions of the exterior walls of the nave can be made out on the south side

Llanthony Priory, north side of church nave

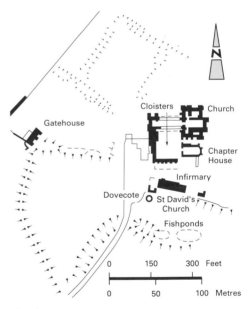

Llanthony Priory

by extending the broken edge at the east end, and on the north by following the drop in level. The roof-line can be clearly seen on the west wall of the crossing tower.

The exterior of the west end of the church is perhaps its finest part, and gives the best idea of its original appearance. The main impression is of lightness and elegance. The larger, simple arched openings of the ground floor provide the necessary weight to carry the round-headed arches and tall, thin blind lancets above. The whole is held together by the string courses and is perfectly balanced, even without its top storey and great window. In each angle were spiral stairs, lit by slits. There is no sign that there ever was a floor in the north-west tower; the south-west one was converted into a shooting box in the 18th century.

Little remains of the claustral buildings of the priory, and some have been much altered by conversion to a house and later hotel, a parish church and farm buildings. What remains there are date from the first quarter of the 13th century. To the south of the nave, where there is now an open lawn, were the cloisters. On their east side is a narrow corridor or slype, which led to the cemetery. It retains its fine archway with foliated capitals and its rib-vaulted ceiling. To the south are the remains of the chapter house. It has a semi-hexagonal east end, which is unusual. What little detail remains shows that it would have been a fine, elegantly vaulted room with a wide entrance on the west side and blank arcading and stone seating around the walls. On the south side of the cloisters was the refectory. Only its north wall survives, with the stumps of vaulting on its south side showing where the basement was. Half the west side of the cloisters is now taken up with the Abbey Hotel. Of the original range, the first floor of which was probably the monks' dormitory, only the vaulted outer parlour at the north end, and three vaulted basements to its south, which were probably originally one large cellar, survive.

Across the road is the parish church of St David, a 13th-century building which may have been the infirmary. To its south, reached by a little path off the road, is the circular base of the priory's dovecote.

This cluster of buildings formed the core of the priory, but it stood in the centre of a great precinct of about 16ha within which were farm buildings, fishponds and small enclosures. The precinct may originally have been surrounded by a high wall, parts of which remain on the west side. Its bounds are now a bank, ditch, ravine and road. Large yew trees mark its south and west corners. In the west corner, next to the road, is the 14th-century gatehouse, now used as a barn, with a large blocked arched entrance.

After the great rebuilding the fortunes of the abbey continued to see-saw, with most of the monks eventually retreating to Gloucester, especially after the devastation caused by Owain Glyndŵr's rebellion at the beginning of the 15th century. By 1504 there were only four canons left. After the Dissolution the site was sold for £160, and was left to decay. A late and rather bizarre chapter in the priory's history was its occupancy from 1807 to 1815 by the poet Walter Savage Landor, who was attracted by its wild romantic setting: 'Nature I loved and, next to Nature, Art . . .'. He wanted to restore it but never succeeded, and his wild extravagance coupled with an unbusiness-like approach to running the estate led to ruin. Of the many trees he planted in the valley few have survived, but his beeches, larches and Spanish chestnuts above the priory do enhance the setting of this most romantic of ruins.

127
Ewenny Priory, Ewenny
Medieval monastic site
12th–13th century
OS 170   SS 912778   U1   Cadw

1ml (1.6km) S of Bridgend. In Ewenny just S of bridge over river turn E off B4524 down minor road (signposted). Continue to end of road, park on LHS

Radford: Official Guide; Thurlby 1988

Ewenny Priory's Romanesque church of St Michael and precinct walls, towers and

Ewenny Priory, presbytery

gatehouses are all that remain of this outpost of Norman culture, but they are of great interest. All the claustral buildings, the cloisters, chapter house and living quarters of the monks have long since disappeared, swallowed up in or destroyed by the later house and other buildings within the original precinct.

The priory is linked to the early Norman settlement in the area, and in particular to the de Londres family of Ogmore Castle (no. 103) nearby. The present church was built on the site of an earlier one by William de Londres between 1116 and 1126. In about 1141 William's son Maurice founded a Benedictine monastic community here for a prior and 12 monks. St Peter's Abbey, Gloucester (now the cathedral), to which the church already belonged, was to be the parent abbey, and the church shows many stylistic similarities to the Romanesque part of Gloucester cathedral. Always an ecclesiastical backwater, alien, and never large or wealthy like the great Cistercian houses, Ewenny Priory had an uneventful

history, and in 1534 only three monks remained.

The church is a remarkable survival from the early 12th century. In style it is pure Romanesque, with round arches, barrel vaults and simple geometric decoration. The effect is sombre and austere. The masonry is rubble, with ashlar used only for the east wall of the presbytery, piers, arches, window surrounds and other decorative parts. The cruciform plan of the church is also typically Romanesque, with a nave, an arcaded north aisle, a simple rectangular presbytery at the east end, transepts with two side chapels off each on the east side, and a central crossing tower, whose warlike battlements were added later. Inside, the church is divided in two by a screen wall at the east of the nave; the west end was always used as a parish church, and still is. The round piers of the north aisle and the round arch of the central crossing are the visible remains of the 12th-century masonry in this part of the church.

The presbytery and transepts, the north one of which is ruined, are entered by a separate door on the north side. Disused since 1540, this is a cavernous, dark and empty place. But it is pure Norman: the great round arches of the ceiling, the chevron moulding, the round-arched windows in the east wall and south transept, the round-arched triforium high in the west wall of the south transept, and the fine decoration in 'billets' on one of the arches in the opposite wall are all elements of Norman Romanesque architectural style. To the east of the transepts were side chapels, now gone. The ceiling of the presbytery is interesting in that it is barrel-vaulted except for the easternmost bay, which has diagonal ribs. There is no structural reason for introducing rib vaulting here, and the main reason must have been aesthetic and symbolic – to express in the building style the presence of the altar beneath.

The contents of the church are few. The stone altar slab is massive and original. The wooden screen dates partly from the 14th century, and may have been taken from the

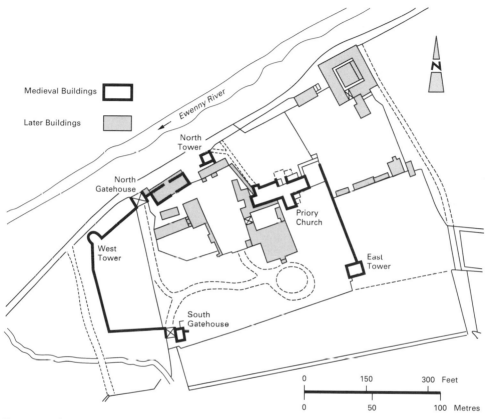

Ewenny Priory

west end of the priory church. Ranged around the walls are parts of tomb slabs, some early Christian, some medieval. In the south transept are the monuments of the founder, Maurice de Londres, of an unknown 13th-century knight and of Edward and John Carne, members of the family to which the priory was granted after its dissolution.

There are clues in the south wall of the church as to the existence of claustral buildings: blocked doorways in the nave and south transept which would have led to the cloisters, and a blocked door high up in the south-west corner of the transept which would have led to the monks' dormitory. It is

not hard, in the gloomy church, to people it with black-habited monks singing Compline in total darkness, or moving silently down the night-stair at four in the morning for Matins.

The precinct walls are something of an enigma. Why did such a small and unimportant priory feel the need massively to defend itself? And why, if the walls were for defence, is the east wall so much lower and smaller? Even though there were periodic Welsh uprisings in the area it was the only monastery to have had such strong defences. It may have been just a facade, a show of strength built only to impress, but if so it was a very solid and serious one.

The walls enclose a large area to the south and west of the church. From near the east end of the church a low wall runs southward to a rectangular tower. This is thought to be the oldest part, dating from soon after 1141. It was originally linked to the church, which in turn was linked to a wall, now destroyed, which ran along the north side of the precinct to the large gatehouse. The square tower north-west of the church has a nice trefoil-headed window on its east side which would date it to around 1300. It stands to first-floor level, and presumably was originally battlemented.

The north and south gatehouses were built at the end of the 12th century, and were remodelled and extended outwards in about 1300. The north gatehouse is austere and impressive. On the outside it has heavily spurred bases, and in the entrance passage portcullis slots and two murder holes. The south gatehouse, remodelled after the medieval period, is smaller, with a long vaulted passage, portcullis slot and murder holes. The battlemented walls at the west end, built in the 13th century soon after the gatehouses, stand to their original height. A wall-walk runs behind the battlements, and in the west corner is a sturdy round tower. The cross-wall between the gatehouses is a later addition. The original form of the wall along the south side of the precinct is unknown as it was demolished in the early 19th century to open up the view from the house.

128
Monknash Grange, Monknash
Medieval monastic site
12th–13th century
OS 170   SS 918707   U2/R2

Take B4265 from Llantwit Major towards Wick. In 2ml (3.2km) turn L to Marcross. In Marcross turn R to Monknash. Site in field on LHS, opposite lane on RHS. Public footpaths across site

Lands around Monknash were given to Neath Abbey (no. 124) in the 12th century, early on in its life. They were formed into one of the largest monastic farms in Glamorgan, and Monknash grange was established to run it. Its present-day remains, dating from the 12th and 13th centuries, are the most impressive of their kind in south-east Wales.

The grange occupies an area of about 8ha in several pasture fields on the west side of Monknash, bounded by roads on the north-east and south-east and a bank on the north-west and south-west. Within this area banks, ditches, levelled areas and ruined stone buildings bear witness to the farming activities of the lay brothers of Neath Abbey.

The main entrance is thought to have been in the middle of the north-east side where the Old Smithy is now. From here a hollow way runs into the site. In the middle, on the south side of the Nash brook which crosses the grange, are various ruined buildings, some reduced to mere turf-covered humps, some with walls still standing. Their exact original purposes are obscure, but they were all farm buildings. The best preserved, and one whose purpose is not obscure, is the dovecote. It is circular, built of mortared rubble, and stands

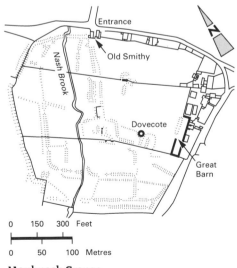

0   150   300 Feet
0   50   100 Metres

Monknash Grange

almost to its full height; only the corbelled roof is missing. The doorway is on the north-west side, and inside there are a few remaining nesting boxes. All over the enclosure there are low banks, scarps, ditches and levelled areas, which probably delineate small fields, tracks and, near the brook, fishponds.

The most impressive building of the grange, and the one which most clearly demonstrates the large scale of the monks' agricultural operation here, is its great barn, which stands on the south-east side parallel to the lane. It is 64m long, rivalling some of the largest English monastic barns. Its south-east wall stands almost to its full height, and the north-east gable end, much overgrown with ivy, is more or less complete. The other gable end is much ruined, and the long north-west wall is almost completely gone, partly reduced to a turf-covered mound. On the south-east side are two large entrances with porches, the more northerly one much cluttered up and ruined, and the southerly one built into a house.

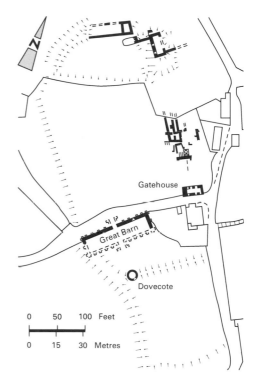

Grange of Abbot's Llantwit

129
Grange of Abbot's Llantwit, Llantwit Major
Medieval monastic site
12th–13th century
OS 170   SS 965687   U2/R2

Take B4265 to Llantwit Major. Site is W of church either side of lane to Old Vicarage. Public footpath across field to S. No access to field to N

Rodger 1915; Nash-Williams 1952a

Tewkesbury Abbey owned much property in Glamorgan, and early on, probably in the 12th century, was given land at Llantwit Major. The grange was its local farming base, where the great barn, dovecote and other farm buildings were located. Now, although mostly reduced to bumps and hollows in the fields, the grange has one outstanding feature which makes a visit worthwhile – the dovecote. This stands in the field to the south of the lane, and is complete. (Monknash, no. 128, has a similar but incomplete one.) It is well built of coursed local limestone, circular, with a corbelled roof finished off at the top with a shallow lantern. The entrance is on the south-east side, and inside are tier upon tier of stone-lined square nesting niches. Like the other building remains on the site it dates from the 13th century. It stands in the southern part of the 1.6ha enclosure which formed the grange. The northern part is in two fields to the north of the lane, misleadingly called Bishop's Palace Field and Monastery Field. Excavations here in 1912–14 and 1937 revealed the remains of various buildings, including animal sheds, stores and a cellar, but all that can be

Grange of Abbot's Llantwit, dovecote with gatehouse behind it

130
Old Bishop's Palace, Llandaff, Cardiff
Medieval ecclesiastical site
13th century
OS 170   ST 156780   U1

Take A4119 from centre of Cardiff to Llandaff. Turn R (signed to cathedral) after lights, and park on The Green. Palace to R, on corner

seen now are uneven hollows, with only one small low stretch of walling showing. The whole area was surrounded by a bank revetted with a stone wall on the outside, parts of which are visible in the fields as a low bank or scarp.

The 13th-century gatehouse of the grange stands complete at the east end of the lane. The entrance passage is blocked and the building converted to other uses (not open to the public). It is a two-storey simple building with external stairs to the upper floor. The blocked entrance is clearly visible from the lane, with a small doorway next to it still in use.

The grange's great barn stood along the south side of the lane, west of the gatehouse. It was intact until 1836, and roofless until about 1872, but all that can be seen now are the lowest parts of the long north-west side and north-east end wall, both of which have been incorporated into field boundaries. A gap in the middle of the north-west side indicates a main entrance, which originally had a porch, and was matched by a similar entrance on the south-east side. There is a further smaller entrance towards the east end.

William de Braose, bishop of Llandaff from 1266 to 1287, was probably responsible for this palace. He also built the fine Lady Chapel of the cathedral, and his magnificent tomb is on its north side. The palace remained the bishop's residence and seat of administration until attacked and damaged during the Glyndŵr rebellion in 1404. Thereafter only the gatehouse was habitable, but this appears to have been kept in use, as a first-floor window on the west side was refashioned in the Tudor period.

Although called a palace, this stronghold was built no differently from a small castle of the time, with a strong curtain wall, gatehouse, towers and internal buildings. The visitor enters through the original entrance, the gatehouse, which is the best preserved part of the palace. It stands to first-floor level, with a deep vaulted entrance passage with portcullis groove and door jambs in the middle. Its contrasting white and orangey-red stones give a lovely mottled effect. The room on the right, with an angled arrowslit, was the guard chamber. On the left was a vaulted room entered from the courtyard.

Inside, the four-sided rhomboidal courtyard has been turned into a pleasant public garden, with planting of interest all the year round. The curtain wall, restored in places, can best be seen on the west side where it survives to its full height. It was built soon after the gatehouse. At the north end of the east side are the fragmentary remains of the great hall; a stretch of thick wall and two large first-floor window openings are all that is left

Old Bishop's Palace, Llandaff

of it. Beyond is a steep drop to the river Taff.

The two towers in the east and south corners appear to be contemporary with the curtain wall. That on the east is small and circular, that on the south larger and square. The latter contained a number of chambers on several floors, but the remains are fragmentary; a flagstone stair ends abruptly in mid-air, and a spiral stair now leading nowhere ascends within the wall in the corner at first-floor level.

131
Llandaff Cathedral Bell Tower, Llandaff, Cardiff
Medieval ecclesiastical site
13th century
OS 171   ST 155781   U1

Take A4119 from centre of Cardiff to Llandaff. Turn R (signed to cathedral) after lights, and park on The Green. Site next to The Green

The ruined 13th-century bell tower or belfry of the cathedral stands on high ground above it. It is contemporary with the later phase of the Norman cathedral, begun in 1120 by Bishop Urban and continued for well over a hundred years. The tower is now railed off and forms part of the Llandaff War Memorial.

It was a square stone building, solidly built with thick walls, parts of which stand up to 4m high. There are large gaps on the north, east and west sides, and most of the facing stone has gone. The south side, which has a ragged door opening and a lancet window, is slightly better preserved, and retains some of its facing stone on the outside.

132
St Barruc's Chapel, Barry Island
Medieval chapel
12th–14th century
OS 171   ST 119667   U1

Take A4055 from Barry to Barry Island. Bear
right and follow Friars Road around to E end of
island. Chapel behind wire fence between road
and cliff edge

Fox 1936; Knight 1976–8

There are only scant remains of this simple
chapel, which was a focus of pilgrimage in the
medieval period. In 1540 Leland described it
as 'a fair little chapel where much pilgrimage
was used', and both he and Giraldus
Cambrensis say it was dedicated to St Barruc,
an early Christian saint of Irish origin. Giraldus
claims that when the chapel was built
Barruc's remains, which were evidently
already somewhere on the site, perhaps in a
grave-shrine in the cemetery, were
transferred to a shrine in the church.

The site was excavated in 1894–5 and again
in 1967–8. These excavations found that the
first church, built in the 12th century,
probably in about 1140, consisted of a nave
and chancel. The small chancel had an
unusual apsidal east end. The chapel was
entirely rebuilt in the late 13th century or
early 14th century, and the apsidal chancel
was replaced by a square-ended one lit by a
trefoil-headed lancet window at its east end.
There was further rebuilding in the chancel
necessitated by instability, and later a timber-
framed south porch and a priest's house were
added.

Little survives of the chapel and house, but
the excavations provided more information.
The walls of the chapel were of large coursed
blocks of limestone, and traces of wall
paintings were found by the earlier
excavators. Part of a stone relic container was
found built into the chancel floor, no longer in
its original context. It consisted of a portion of
half a rectangular stone box which would
have been placed within a larger shrine. This
box may have held the bones or other relics of
St Barruc. The shrine itself may have been
situated on the south side of the chancel,
where evidence was found for the removal of
a substantial structure during the 14th-
century rebuilding.

Remains of the altar were found at the east

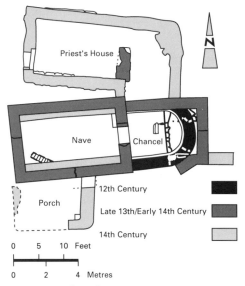

St Barruc's Chapel

end of the nave. Other finds included some
blue Cornish roofing slates. These are known
at other sites in south-east Wales during the
medieval period, for instance at Barry Castle
(no. 120), and are evidence of trade across the
Bristol Channel.

The priest's house was built over part of the
cemetery to the north of the chapel. It
consisted of a rectangular hall with a smaller
chamber to the east. The entrance was at the
south end of the west side.

Around the chapel was an extensive
cemetery, which continued in use into the late
medieval period. It was too large for the local
community, and can only be explained by the
desire of a wider population to be buried near
the shrine of St Barruc.

133
St Michael's Chapel, Ysgyryd Fawr, Abergavenny
Medieval chapel
Late medieval

OS 161   SO 331182   U4   National Trust

Take A465 Abergavenny to Hereford road, turn R on to B4521 Skenfrith road E of Abergavenny. After 1.5ml (2.5km) park on LHS. Signposted path. Steep uphill walk to chapel on summit

The panoramic view from the summit of the Skirrid mountain, or Ysgyryd Fawr, is ample reward for the effort of the climb up to it. But after admiring the view, spare a few minutes for the lumps and bumps at your feet, for these are all that remain of St Michael's chapel or oratory. Its only entrance is on the south side of the Trig. Point at the summit, and is now reduced to the stumps of chamfered door jambs. The simple rectangular chapel stood between here and the Trig. Point, its outline marked by low discontinuous banks. It stood within a contemporary or possibly prehistoric, almond-shaped earthwork, visible as low banks and ditches to the north, south and west.

The history of the chapel is obscure, but it stood where three parishes meet. In 1680, when Catholics were being persecuted, it is said that more than a hundred worshippers struggled up the hill for Mass.

134
St Donat's Churchyard Cross, St Donat's
Medieval cross
15th century
OS 170   SS 934680   U1

Take minor road W from Llantwit Major to St Donat's. Sign to church at entrance to Atlantic College. Cross in churchyard, S of church

This is one of the best preserved of the 15th-century churchyard crosses in south-east Wales, with all but its very top surviving. Its form is typical of those in this area: it has a

St Donat's churchyard cross

squarish base standing on steps, a tall octagonal shaft, here with a decorated foliate capital, and is surmounted by an elaborate carved lantern head. Although much weathered, the figures on the head can be made out in their canopied arches: on the west is the crucifixion, with St Mary and St John, and on the east Mary holding the infant Jesus.

135
Cross in St Mary's Churchyard, St Mary Hill
Medieval cross
15th century
OS 170   SS 958793   U1

1.5ml (2.5km) E of Coychurch. Turn S off A473 Pencoed to Bridgend road at large roundabout in Coychurch. Continue along minor road to Treos. Turn L, and at first crossroads R, then first L. Church on L, cross in churchyard, S of church

The arrangement of steps, base, shaft and head is the usual one for crosses of this type, but the base and shaft are modern. This cross is of interest for the survival, albeit in a very worn state, of the lantern head (see also nos 134 and 136). Carved figures under canopied arches can just be made out on each side, with the crucifixion on the east.

Llangan churchyard cross

136
Llangan Churchyard Cross, Llangan
Medieval cross
15th century
OS 170   SS 957778   U1

From Cowbridge take A48 towards Bridgend. At Pentre Meyrick turn R (N) towards Pencoed. After 1ml (1.6km) turn L to Llangan. Turn R, church on RHS, cross S of church in churchyard

The arrangement of this cross is the usual one, but here the steps and probably the base are modern. Beneath the canopied arches on each side of the head are various biblical scenes, with the crucifixion on the west side, the *pieta* on the east, a figure on the south and a headless figure on the north.

137
Coychurch Churchyard Cross, Coychurch
Medieval cross
15th century
OS 170   SS 940797   U1

Take minor road off A473 Bridgend to Pencoed road into Coychurch. Church in centre, S of road. Cross S of church

This cross is unusual in that its steps and base are hexagonal. There are five tall steps, a base with chamfered corners and a tapering octagonal shaft. On top is a more recent square block with a sundial cut into it. The original lantern head is missing. Inside the church, which is dedicated to St Crallo, is a very fine early Christian cross (no. 80).

Coychurch churchyard cross

138
Undy Churchyard Cross, Undy
Medieval cross
15th century
OS 171   ST 440869   U1

Take B4245 to Magor, and continue for 1 ml (1.6km) into Undy. In Undy turn R, over railway, then L. Church on RHS, cross S of church

This is an unusual churchyard cross in that it lacks steps, but has instead a wide stone platform. Its shaft is short and octagonal with a canopy pattern carved on each side. Above the canopies is a band of small circles, and the square base has large broached stops at the angles. It has been suggested that the shaft might be a reused church pinnacle, as the form is unknown elsewhere.

Cross in Undy churchyard

139
Llanddewy Rhydderch Churchyard Cross-Base, Llanddewy Rhydderch

Medieval cross

15th century

OS 161   SO 350129   U1

Take B4233 Abergavenny to Rockfield road. 2ml (3.2km) from Abergavenny fork R to Llanddewy Rhydderch. Church in centre, cross S of church

This churchyard cross is included for its exceptionally fine and well preserved base. The steps, base and first metre of the shaft are medieval, the crucifix is modern, added in 1923. It is the large, bold, ornamental broached stops in the corners of the base which mark it out as one of the finest cross-bases in south-east Wales.

Mitchel Troy churchyard cross

140
Mitchel Troy Churchyard Cross, Mitchel Troy

Medieval cross

15th century

OS 162   SO 492103   U1

Take B4293 Monmouth to Trellech road. 1ml (1.6km) S of Monmouth keep straight on (not up hill) to Mitchel Troy. Church on RHS, cross S of church

The curious feature of this cross is its unusual tapering shaft. The head is missing, and the steps and base are unexceptional. The shaft is in three pieces, and has an elongated octagonal cross-section. Up the four narrow sides run alternating ball flowers and very worn small shields. The only shaft in the area at all similar is that at Undy (no. 138).

141
Trellech Churchyard Cross, Trellech

Medieval cross

15th century

OS 162   SO 500055   U1

Take B4293 Monmouth to Chepstow road to Trellech. Church in centre, cross S of church

This churchyard cross is almost complete and is unusual in that the shaft is surmounted by a cross and not a lantern head. The five steps and base with large chamfered stops in the corners are massive. The slender octagonal shaft and small cross above look out of proportion in comparison, and the way the top section of shaft tapers suddenly suggests that perhaps there was originally a central section which is now missing.

Cross in Trellech churchyard

142
Raglan Churchyard Cross-Base, Raglan

Medieval cross
15th century
OS 161   SO 414077   U1

Raglan is 7ml (11km) SW of Monmouth, and can be reached on the A40 from Abergavenny and Monmouth or A449 from Newport. Church in centre, cross S of church

The steps and shaft of this cross are modern, but the fine base is original and is the most ornamental cross-base in the area. It is square, with prominent chamfered stops in the corners. The rest of the sides are unusually ornamented with Gothic tracery designs, heraldic shields and other now very worn devices. Around the bevelled top is a band of small shields. The richness of the cross-base may be related to the proximity of Raglan Castle (no. 122), held by William ap Thomas and his son William Herbert during the 15th century. The heraldic devices on the base may have depicted their coats of arms.

Raglan churchyard, cross-base

143
Kilwrrwg Churchyard Cross, Devauden
Medieval cross
Medieval
OS 171   ST 462984   U2

Take B4293 Monmouth to Chepstow road. Just S of Devauden turn W towards Newchurch. Take first R down narrow lane, continue to end of road. Footpath across field N to church. Cross S of church

Kilwrrwg church is remote, isolated in the middle of a field. In its churchyard is an

Kilwrrwg churchyard cross, with the Church of the Holy Cross behind

unusual cross whose simplicity seems in harmony with the little church. It is completely different from the preceding ones in this guide, being a simple cross about 2m high carved out of a single lump of stone, on a stone base set into the ground. It is extremely plain, with a rectangular cross-section and a simple cross on top.

144
Chepstow Town Wall and Gate, Chepstow
Medieval town wall
Late 13th century
OS 162   ST 533937   U1

In Chepstow, wall runs roughly S from car park S of castle. Gate in High Street

Knight: Cadw Guide

Chepstow's town wall, sometimes called the Port Wall, is a magnificent survival from the medieval period. The wall was built by Roger Bigod III between 1272 and 1278, when he was also improving the castle (no. 98). It enclosed an area much larger than the medieval town, which only occupied what is now the town centre; the rest of the area enclosed was given over to orchards and meadows.

Originally the wall was continuous, 1,097m (*c*.0.7ml) long and some 3–4m high. It ran from the west end of the castle to the river Wye to the south. A wall-walk ran along the top behind the battlements, and there were 10 semicircular hollow towers at regular intervals along its outer side. On the west side is the Town Gate, still in use. This is a simple archway with a battlemented chamber above. Its form is basically medieval, but it was altered and rebuilt in the 15th and 16th centuries, and was later restored.

Much of the wall survives, albeit hemmed in by the modern town. It can be followed from the car park at its north end to the Town Gate, then along a pedestrian walkway to the new

Chepstow town wall and gate

South Gate, Cowbridge

inner bypass. South of this is a well-preserved stretch of wall along the ridge and down to the railway line. Between here and the river it was demolished to make way for the railway and a shipyard.

145

South Gate, Cowbridge
Medieval town gatehouse
Late 13th to early 14th century
OS 170   SS 993746   U1

Take A48 to Cowbridge. In centre turn S down Church Street. Just beyond church road passes underneath gate

This is the only surviving gateway of the walled medieval borough of Cowbridge. The borough was established by the lords of Glamorgan, the de Clares, in the first half of the 13th century, where the old Roman road between Cardiff and Carmarthen crossed the river Thaw. Its focal position in the Vale of Glamorgan meant that it soon prospered and grew. In its early days it had no protection, but at the end of the 13th or beginning of the 14th century a wall was built around it, said to have been 7.5m high with a wall-walk on top. It had four gateways, one on each side, of

which the south survives. A road still passes under it, and cars can just squeeze through. Heavily restored, it has simple archways at each end, has lost the upper storey which it undoubtedly originally had, and is open to the sky. The Town Gate at Chepstow (no. 144), built at about the same time, may give some idea of its original appearance. There is a short stretch of town wall immediately to its west.

146

Culver Hole Dovecote, Port Eynon, Gower
Medieval dovecote
Medieval
OS 159   SS 465845   U4

Take A4118 to Port Eynon. Continue through village to car park. Culver Hole is a 0.5ml (c.1km) walk. Take track to Youth Hostel straight ahead, then follow track (signed) to R. Fork R, then L over ridge. Drop down to shoreline path below. Follow it to L until cleft in cliff. Clamber down on to rocks, off path to R, from where there is a good view of the Hole. Rope dangles from lowest entrance for the intrepid to climb in. Dovecote approachable only at low tide

Culver Hole dovecote

This must be one of the oddest dovecotes ever built. Its situation is picturesque, in a lonely cleft in the cliff of Port Eynon Point, with a lovely view westwards along the coast. At high tide the sea laps at its foot, at low tide it is a long way out across the rocks.

The dovecote was made by blocking a natural cave at its entrance with a stone wall. The cave extends inwards some 14m at the base. Behind the wall, which is very thick at the base and narrows progressively towards the top, are four stages linked by narrow crude steps. On the inner face of the wall are irregular tiers of nesting boxes. There are three complete openings, the lower two rectangular, the upper one circular. Towards the top the wall is ruined, but two partial openings can be made out, the lower circular, the upper rectangular.

It is not known exactly when the dovecote

was built, but it is very probably medieval, possibly built for the vanished castle of Port Eynon. In the late 15th or early 16th century there is a record that the Lucas family built the Salt House on the other side of the peninsula, and repaired 'Kulvered Hall near thereunto in the rocks'.

By taking the recommended route to Culver Hole, and then returning by a path up the steep slope behind and along to the end of the Point, the visitor can take in the whole of this lovely peninsula, with its wealth of wild flowers, and return by way of the shell of the Salt House on the other side.

147
Monnow Bridge, Monmouth
Medieval bridge
1272–1315
OS 162   SO 504125   U1

In Monmouth, at W end of Monnow Street, over the river Monnow

This is a precious survival, for of the many fortified bridges built in the medieval period in Britain, that at Monmouth is the only one remaining. The narrowness of its archway is quite unsuited to modern traffic and one can see why all the rest have gone.

The bridge itself was built in 1272. It carried the road westward out of Monmouth, and immediately to its west was the suburb of Overmonnow, protected by a deep defensive ditch, the Clawdd Du (which can still be seen). The gatehouse was added some 25 years later for extra protection and as a toll gate; it was built at the same time as the palisade around the town was replaced, at least in part, by stone walls. Royal permission was given to raise tolls on a wide variety of goods including salmon, salt, honey and iron. The gateway was part of the town's outer defences on its most vulnerable side. It is not known if it was used for defensive purposes in the medieval period, but it certainly was during the Civil War when the town was occupied by

Monnow Bridge

Royalists and Parliamentarians in turn.

Originally the bridge was narrower, its width shown by the three medieval arches underneath. The simple, single-arched gatehouse was lower, and was skirted by two wooden walkways. The widening of the bridge and the construction of the passages took place in the early 19th century. Later the gatehouse was heightened a little, and the upper windows were inserted. A newel stair in the upstream side led to a room above the arch, from which the portcullis was worked. Three machicolations allowed the defenders to attack directly from above. A garderobe on the north side discharged straight into the river before the sidewalk was made.

148
The Virtuous Well, Trellech
Medieval holy well
Medieval
OS 162   SO 503051   U2

Just outside Trellech, 4ml (6.5km) S of Monmouth on the B4293. At S end of village turn SE towards Tintern. Well at SE end of second field on LHS. Signposted

According to the Latin inscription on the unusual 1689 sundial, now in the church, this is the greatest of the three 'wonders' of Trellech, the other two being Tump Terrett (no. 86) and Harold's Stones (no. 27). This delightful and unusual spot is well worth a visit.

The holy, or 'Virtuous' well stands in a field just outside the village. Around it is a simple and dignified little stone enclave, approached by steps at its west end. Inside the ground is paved, and there are stone benches along each side. The spring, in a circular stone pool, is enclosed in a horseshoe-shaped recess with an arched top in the middle of the east end. The water is still and crystal clear. On either side are rectangular niches, presumably for offerings.

Exactly when this lovely well was built is not

The Virtuous Well

The visitor's approach to Old Beaupre, down the gentle valley of the river Thaw, gives just the right impression of the rustic idyll, the beautiful retreat, that its Anglo-Norman name suggests. Old Beaupre was a medieval and then Tudor manor house, built around two courtyards. The medieval part, dating from about 1300, consisted of a group of buildings loosely arranged around the southernmost, or Inner Court. In the 16th century an extensive programme of rebuilding was undertaken, started by Sir Rice Mansel, continued by William Bassett and finished by his son Richard. This phase added the northernmost buildings around the middle Court, and included the building of Old Beaupre's most important features, the outer gatehouse and the storeyed porch. These are remarkably well preserved, despite the ruinous state of most of the buildings around them. They demonstrate the Bassetts' wealth and pretensions to grandeur, as was doubtless their intention at the time. The heraldic panels and inscriptions on each leave no doubt as to who built them.

From the outside the manor appears tall and rather gaunt, with few windows; with the exception of the outer gatehouse, it was mainly inward-facing. The visitor enters over a stile into the walled Outer or Fore Court and encounters the three-storeyed outer gatehouse and embattled curtain wall, which were part of the great Tudor rebuilding. The main feature is the arched entrance with its pseudo-classical decorative surround. Over the columns can just be made out the capitals R B (Richard Bassett), C B (Catherine Bassett, his first wife), 1586, and R B. Above the doorway is a heraldic panel which includes the motto of the Bassett family, which reads (translated) 'Better death than dishonour'. The Middle Court within is completely enclosed by a high curtain wall with a wall-walk around the top which was rather curiously suspended between two parallel walls on the east side. Below this side is a raised terrace which was probably a garden feature. The tall, narrow building in the north-east corner is of unknown purpose.

known, but it was certainly here by 1689, and it is probably late medieval. The chalybeate, or iron-rich water, was drunk, as the two glasses on the sundial indicate, for its supposed healing powers. In 1708 Nathan Rogers described it as '*Treleg* Wells, which of late Years have been much frequented, and have been found very Medicinal.'

149
Old Beaupre, Cowbridge
Medieval and Tudor manor house
1300–1600
OS 170   ST 009721   R2   Cadw

1.5ml (2.5km) SE of Cowbridge. Take minor road from Cowbridge towards St Athan. Just after junction with road from St Hilary park on LHS by bridge (signed). Walk c.500m SE across fields. Cadw standard hours every day except Sunday

Hague: Official Guide

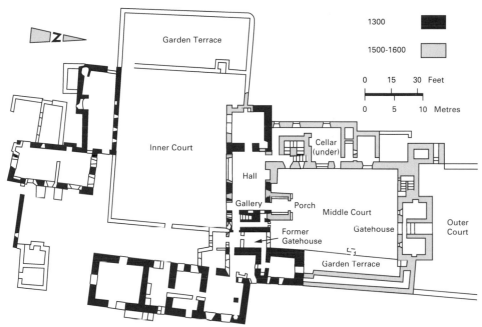

Old Beaupre manor house

In the Middle Court the main feature is the great storeyed porch. As this was the last part to be added it will be discussed at the end. The south range and the tall gabled block to its north-east are the oldest part of the manor. This was originally the northern side of a court to the south, which is now a private garden. The original gatehouse can be made out to the left of the porch where there is a blocked arch with a Tudor window inserted into it. In the Tudor rebuilding this was converted into two rooms. The ground floor is not open to the public, but the first floor can be reached up some steep stairs to the left of the present entrance, or through a Tudor door into the north-east block from the east wall-walk. Tiny stairs here lead to a small privy and a now floorless upper level. The entrance porch leads straight into the 14th-century hall, now open to the sky. Like the rest of this range it was much altered, particularly with the insertion of bigger windows, in the 16th

century, but it retains its magnificent heraldic 14th-century fireplace, possibly moved to its present position from the west wall in the Tudor rebuilding. A modern wooden walkway leads across the east end at first-floor level where there may originally have been a gallery. The fine six-light window facing the Inner Court is 16th-century. The other 14th-century buildings ranged around this court are not open to the public. At the west end of the court, overlooking the valley, is a garden terrace, probably added in the 16th century.

Along the west side of the Middle Court is a large block which is the earliest part of the Tudor additions, built probably by Sir Rice Mansel in about 1540. It is a three-storey building, now roofless and floorless, which was evidently luxurious living accommodation judging from the large windows, fireplaces and in particular the stairs and privies. The stairs were innovatory – their lower, stone treads survive in a great square stair well with a central pillar, which still stands to its full height. The privies were numerous and were all housed at the north end of the building, with a running water drain which still survives.

The last and architecturally most important feature of Old Beaupre is the great storeyed porch. The contrast between the porch's smooth yellow ashlar stonework and the surrounding rough local stone is stark but misleading; originally all the walls were rendered with the same fake ashlar. The porch is built to a very high standard, and its details, except for the lozenges at the base, are very well preserved. In typical Tudor fashion it combines a number of styles, with its Tudor archway, classical columns and strapwork decoration. The north face is divided into three stages, with pairs of columns, in the classically correct ascending order of Doric, Ionic and Corinthian, flanking the entrance. Above them are a heraldic panel and a blocked window. The panel is another celebration of the Bassett family, and below is an inscription in three small panels which states that Richard Bassett built this porch in 1600 at the age of 65. An interesting feature is the bottom left-hand cartouche. Unlike the other three, which are round, this one is square and could be removed to form a spy-hole. The earliest known use of brick in Glamorgan is in the inner facing of the porch, the surface of which is grooved to simulate rustication. Its soft stone has proved too much of a temptation over the years, and it is disfigured by graffiti which go back to the 17th century. Look for 'D.T. 1660' and 'D.W. 1789' on the right-hand side, and 'J.L. 1661' and 'Matthew Biddle Mar 7th 1719' on the left-hand side. The chimney to the right of the

Old Beaupre, the porch

Oxwich Castle, east range and dovecote from the north-west

porch, now lacking its top half, was probably built at the same time. Thereafter Old Beaupre was little altered. After the Civil War the family's fortunes declined, and by the time it was sold at the beginning of the 18th century only part was still habitable.

150
Oxwich Castle, Oxwich, Gower
Tudor manor house
16th century
OS 159   SS 498863   R2   Cadw

Take minor road S off A4118 to Oxwich. In Oxwich continue straight up hill towards Oxwich Green for c.300m. Take backward-
turning track on LHS (signed to Oxwich Point), castle a short distance on LHS. Restricted access at present

This impressively large courtyard house, now mostly ruined, was built by the Mansel family in the 16th century in a lovely situation on the headland overlooking Oxwich Bay. There was probably a medieval house here, referred to in 1459 as being owned by Philip Mansel, but the 16th-century rebuilding has more or less obliterated it. The new house was constructed in two stages. First the gateway and south block were built by Sir Rice (who also built part of Old Beaupre, no. 149) between about 1520 and 1540. Next the huge and more sophisticated east block, opposite the gateway, was added at right-angles to it by his son Sir Edward before 1580.

At the beginning of the 16th century the

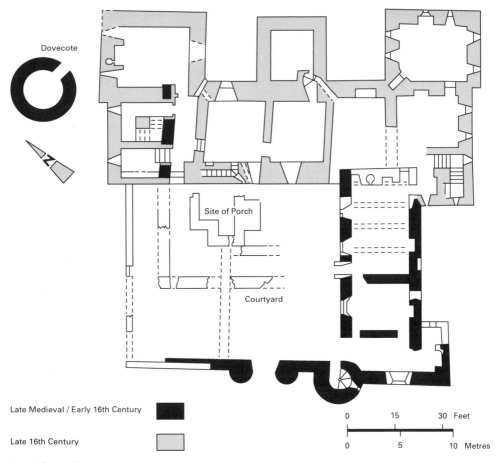

Dovecote

Site of Porch

Courtyard

Late Medieval / Early 16th Century

Late 16th Century

| 0 | 15 | 30 | Feet |
| 0 | 5 | 10 | Metres |

Oxwich Castle

Mansels were a minor landowning family in the Gower. Through royal favour and judicious land purchases they rose rapidly to become one of the most powerful families in Glamorgan. Their spending on Oxwich, and subsequently on Margam Abbey, was commensurate with their new-found wealth and status.

The early part of the house lies on the west and south sides of the courtyard, the north and part of the west sides of which have gone. The mock-military gateway is a simple arch

between solid drum turrets. Over the arch is a heraldic panel bearing the arms of Sir Rice. Next to it, to the south, is part of a round staircase tower which was probably originally matched by a similar one on the north side. The curtain wall has a wall-walk and a ruined parapet. The gateway and curtain wall were anachronisms, for show only, and had no serious defensive function. In 1557, however, they were the scene of a minor affray with the Herberts over looting from a wreck, which cost Edward Mansel's aunt her life. The two-storey south block is much altered, and was being used until quite recently as a farmhouse. The mullioned windows are Tudor, and there is doubt as to the position of the original entrance.

When Sir Rice moved to Margam in about 1540 his eldest son Edward took over Oxwich. His ideas were much more grandiose, but he may have overstretched himself, as within 50 years of its completion Oxwich was leased out. Sir Edward's east block is E-shaped, the arms of the E being three tower-like wings, each with six floors and numerous rooms. Now only the south-east wing stands above ground-floor level. It is an impressive sight, a Tudor sky-scraper, the outside walls honeycombed with small windows, the inside punctuated by fireplaces at all levels. The other two wings are largely ruinous except for two barrel-vaulted basements beneath the middle one. At each end were up-to-date stairs in square stair wells around central piers. The bases of both are still visible. The block was entered through a projecting porch in the courtyard, which is now gone but which stood to the south of the present entrance. It may have looked something like that at Old Beaupre (no. 149). On the first floor was a grand hall lit by two huge windows on the courtyard side. The northernmost one, of 18 lights, survives but is blocked up. Only vestiges remain of the other even larger one, of 24 lights. The window openings of the east block demonstrate the luxurious nature of this part of the house: they were rebated for glass.

At second-floor level, to the south of the hall, was an important chamber, perhaps Sir Edward's, with a fireplace and two tall windows. Above, occupying the whole length of the wing, was that essential ingredient of the grand Tudor house, a long gallery. The bases of its four great windows on the courtyard side survive at the top of the wall. The tall gable-end walls of this part survive, that on the north side with numerous small windows lighting the stair well.

To the north of the house, and almost certainly contemporary with it, is a ruined circular dovecote.

Appendix: Sites of Further Interest

This is a list of fine sites which lie on private land or which are on open ground but are remote and difficult of access. Permission should be sought before visiting sites marked R. It is often difficult to trace the owners of sites, and it is usually best to seek help and information from the owners of the nearest house to the site in question.

Neolithic Period

Cefn Bryn (Nicholaston) chambered cairn, Penmaen, Gower
OS 159   SS 508888   U4

A poorly preserved chambered long cairn, excavated in 1939. An egg-shaped mound of peaty soil, edged by a rough kerb of large stones. In the centre a square chamber of orthostats and dry walling. A small paved area on the NE side with flanking stones, but no access to chamber.

Sweyne's Howes, Rhossili, Gower
OS 159   SS 421898 and 421899   U4

Two poorly preserved chambered cairns, now with only the megalithic chambers surviving. Much of the stone is fallen, making their original layout difficult to determine.

Penmaen Burrows chambered cairn, Penmaen, Gower
OS 159   SS 532881   U2

A chambered cairn in the Severn–Cotswold tradition, partly overwhelmed by sand. Megalithic slabs line an entrance passage and two rectangular chambers, with a large leaning capstone.

Carn Llechart, Llangyfelach
OS 160   SN 697063   U2

A probable chambered cairn on upland moorland, but jumbled slabs are not easy to interpret. The large upright may be the south side of the chamber, with the loose slab to the south the displaced capstone.

Cae-yr-arfau, Pentyrch
OS 170   ST 077821   R2 (in private garden)

The small rectangular chamber of a long cairn, with two uprights and a capstone.

Tythegston long barrow, Tythegston
OS 170   SS 864792   R2

A roughly oval long barrow or cairn with the chamber towards the E end marked by a large capstone lying in a hollow. One upright visible on the S side.

Gaer Llwyd chambered cairn, Shirenewton
OS 171   ST 448967   R2/U3

A much disturbed megalithic burial chamber with a large triangular capstone resting rather giddily on three uprights. Visible from road.

Gwern y Cleppa chambered cairn, Coedkernew
OS 171   ST 276852   R2

A much denuded long mound, with remains of burial chamber at the E end. Seven stones, some upright, with a large capstone tilting towards the S.

Heston Brake long barrow, Portskewett
OS 162   ST 505887   R2

Slight traces of a long mound on top of a small knoll, with the remains of a burial chamber near the SE end. Upright stones define a narrow roughly rectangular chamber, open at the SE end. Two larger uprights stand in line with it. No capstone.

Bronze Age

Ring cairn on Gelligaer Common, Gelligaer
OS 171   SO 098034   U2

An unusual ring cairn below the summit of Gelligaer Common. A low horseshoe-shaped bank with large stones protruding from it, originally upright but now lying flat.

Garn Las, Aberdare
OS 170   SO 029038   U2

One of several round cairns on this ridge, most of which are at present inaccessible in forestry plantations. A circular heap of stones c.1.5m high with a low bank around it.

Carneddi Llwydion, Senghenydd
OS 171   ST 105920   U2

Two round cairns of rounded stones, each with a low central mound and surrounding bank.

Pant Sychbant round cairn and earthworks, Merthyr Tydfil
OS 160   SN 996098   U4

A round cairn of stones, c.2–3m high, in the valley bottom, with above it a low banked enclosure in which are the remains of four circular huts.

Nant Maden round cairn, Penderyn
OS 160   SN 971106   R2

Excavation in 1959/60 showed that this circular cairn had a D-shaped enclosure within a circular kerb of large quartz boulders. In the centre was a rectangular pit with no burial. Four small cremations found between the enclosure and the kerb.

Cairn on Mynydd Drumau, Neath
OS 170   SN 724003   U2

An oval cairn of platform type, with a sunken slab-lined cist in the middle.

Cairn circle on Carn Caca, Resolven
OS 170   SN 822008   U2

A ring cairn high up above the Vale of Neath, with a roughly circular bank lined on its inner side with low upright slabs, of which about 20 remain. Level interior. Only sign of a possible cist is a hollow on the E side.

Tir Lan round barrows, Treharris
OS 171   ST 098991   R2

Three well preserved round barrows aligned NE–SW. The central one is a steep-sided conical mound, whose surface is covered in small stones.

Llanfihangel Rogiet standing stone, Llanfihangel Rogiet
OS 171   ST 444878   R2

A large solitary standing stone, 2.4m high and 1.5m across at the base, tapering to a point at the top.

Carreg Hir, Briton Ferry
OS 170   SS 744954   R1 (apply to school)

A large, pillar-shaped stone of Pennant sandstone, 2.8m high above its concrete plinth. Re-sited in a school playground.

Standing stone on Tŷ'r Coed Farm, Llanrhidian
OS 159   SS 475917   R2

A similar stone to no. 30, and in the same group. Stands 2.5m high. At present partially buried in rubble.

Iron Age

GWENT

Llancayo Camp, Usk
OS 171   SO 378038   R2

A well preserved univallate hillfort. Simple gap entrance on S side, where defences are most massive. An outer area beyond the entrance is enclosed by banks and ditches, and has an inturned entrance, suggesting a later date than the main fort.

Gaer Hill Camp, Penterry
OS 162   ST 517979   U2/R2 (access by public footpath across site)

A large multivallate fort in a commanding position. Outer ramparts survive on NW, W and S sides. A small, square inner enclosure surrounded by a bank and ditch.

Great House Camp, Llansoy
OS 171   SO 432033   U2/R2 (access by public footpath across site)

A large multivallate fort with triple, and in places quadruple ramparts well preserved on all but S side. On steep W side defences reduced to two scarps. Possible entrances on N and E sides.

Gaer Fawr Camp, Llangwm
OS 171   ST 441988   U2/R2 (access by public footpath across site)

A large oblong hillfort in fine hilltop position. Defences now fragmentary, but best preserved at N end, where there is a large curving bank, and S end, where there is a massive bank, ditch and counterscarp bank.

Coed y Defaid, Newport
OS 171   ST 273862   R2

A very well preserved small circular hillfort defended by a single bank and ditch. Original entrance probably the simple gap on the E side.

SOUTH GLAMORGAN

Caer Dynnaf, Cowbridge
OS 170   SS 983743   U2/R2 (access by public footpath across site)

A large multivallate hilltop fort. Outer ramparts fragmentary or reduced to scarps. Complicated, partly inturned entrance on W side. Low banks and platforms in western half of interior delineate houses, yards, lanes, some of late Iron Age–Roman date.

Mynydd Bychan, Pentre Meyrick
OS 170   SS 963756   R2

A small, rectilinear, lowland enclosure surrounded by a bank. Entrance a gap in W side. Excavation in 1949–50 revealed three phases of occupation, 50 BC–AD 50, when the defences were built, AD 50–120, when a group of round drystone wall huts was built, each within a lightly walled yard, and the 11th–12th centuries, when there was a rectangular building in the NE corner.

MID-GLAMORGAN

Rhiw Saeson Caerau, Llantrisant
OS 170   ST 064832   U2/R2

Hilltop fort surrounded by double bank and ditch except on S side. Inturned entrance in SE corner. Small sections of third bank on SW, W and NE sides.

Cwm Bach Camps, Wick
OS 170   SS 897716   U2

Two small clifftop forts. The northernmost is triangular, with a single bank and ditch. There is a wide gap in the middle suggesting that it is unfinished. The second, smaller fort is a narrow triangular area surrounded by a low bank. Both forts have lost much ground through coastal erosion.

WEST GLAMORGAN

Cilifor Top, Llanrhidian, Gower
OS 159   SS 505924   R4

The largest hillfort in the Gower. Defences of multiple scarps along contours of hill.

Entrance on SW side, at oblique angle to ramparts. Three round hut sites near NW end.

Craig Tŷ-Isaf hillfort, Baglan
OS 170   SS 756934   U4

A small, strongly defended fort on a spur of Mynydd y Gaer. Three ramparts defend the E side, and a stony bank runs round the whole site. Entrance is a simple gap on the W side.

Bishopston Valley Fort, Bishopston, Gower
OS 159   SS 569878   U2

An inland promontory fort, with two massive banks across the E side. Entrance at the N end. Excavation in 1939 found an oval hut site in the interior, external revetment of the inner bank, and evidence of a mixed economy. Roman objects found indicated occupation at least into the early 2nd century AD.

Roman Period

Coelbren Fort, Coelbren
OS 160   SN 859107   R2

A medium-sized auxiliary fort dating from c.AD 75, on Roman road from Neath to Brecon. Best preserved on the W side, where surrounding bank and two outer ditches are clearly visible. Excavations revealed a standard layout, with timber buildings inside. To the S are the slight remains of a probably earlier large marching camp. Roads can be traced to the S and E of the fort. Abandoned AD 140–50.

Blaen cwm bach marching camp, Tonna
OS 170   SS 796987   R2

The largest marching camp in the area, big enough to accommodate three legions. A slight surrounding bank and ditch, now discontinuous, best seen on the SW and NE sides, and the E end of the N side. An entrance of titulum type in the middle of the SW side.

Practice camps on Gelligaer Common, Gelligaer
OS 171   ST 116986, 132991, 132994, 138992, 139992   U2

These are miniature marching camps, built as a practice exercise. All are surrounded by a low bank and external ditch. That at ST 132991 has a clavicular entrance on the S side.

Caermead Roman villa, Llantwit Major
OS 170   SS 958699   R2

A rectangular raised area, with turf-covered walls subdividing the interior, is all that can be seen of this large, relatively sophisticated Roman villa. It was occupied between the 2nd and 4th centuries. The main living quarters were along the W side of an inner courtyard. A larger outer courtyard to the E probably housed workshops, servants and stables. About 30 skeletons found in the ruins indicate that the site was used for burial after the villa was abandoned.

Ely Roman villa, Cardiff
OS 171   ST 147762   U2

Park benches define the limits of this villa. All that can be seen are the surrounding banks and ditches which may predate the Roman phase. The villa was a rectangular building with a verandah on the S side, and another separate building to the SW, with baths to its S. It was built in the first half of the 2nd century, and was altered several times before being abandoned in the 4th century. There is evidence for iron working and the use of coal here.

Early Medieval Period

Llangyfelach cross-base, Llangyfelach
OS 159   SS 646989   U1

A late 9th– to early 10th-century quadrangular cross-base covered in plaited and knotted carved decoration.

Pillar-stone in Reynoldston church, Reynoldston, Gower

OS 159   SS 479900   U1

A 10th- to 11th-century rough pillar-stone which once stood on a mound near Stout Hall. On it are incised crosses and worn plaitwork.

Court Herbert pillar-stone, Neath Abbey

OS 170   SS 741976   U2

A 7th- to 9th-century tall stone with a rough Latin cross on the N face and a more refined later one on the S side.

Merthyr Mawr inscribed stones, Merthyr Mawr

OS 170   SS 889780   R2 (in private garden)

Two decorated 11th-century stones, both with inscriptions, in St Roque's chapel. One is a large slab-cross with part of a wheel-head, the other is a simple shaft.

Cwm George Camp, Dinas Powys

OS 171   ST 148722   R4

An important settlement site, excavated in 1954–8, dating from the 5th–7th centuries, situated at the N end of a high narrow ridge. The end of the ridge is cut off by four concentric banks, three of them large. The low discontinuous bank second from the inside is probably the earliest. Inside the banks evidence was found for subrectangular buildings, and a wealth of finds, including pottery and glass from the east Mediterranean, indicates occupants of high status and wealth.

Cefn Morfudd dyke, Tonna

OS 170   SS 787982–790980   U4

A 410m stretch of curving cross-ridge dyke on high moorland. It consists of a discontinuous scarp or bank and ditch. Near it, to the W, is an apparently unfinished oval ringwork, with an entrance on the NE side.

Minchin Hole cave, Pennard, Gower

OS 159   SS 555869   U4

A large cave in the cliffs W of Pwll Du Head. Finds and hearths indicate occupation in the Iron Age, Roman period and early medieval period. From the latter period have been found some fine bronze brooches and 9th-century silver coins.

Lesser Garth cave, Radyr, Cardiff

OS 171   ST 125821   U4

In this cave, on a steep, rocky, south-facing slope, has been found evidence for burials in the Bronze Age and occupation in the Roman and early medieval periods. During the latter period the cave was used as a metal workshop, with finds of crucibles, clinker and bronze, iron and silver objects.

Medieval Period

Mottes and Ringworks

GWENT

Penrhos motte and bailey castle, Llantilio Crossenny

OS 161   SO 409132   R2

A fine motte, surrounded by double bank and ditch, in a commanding position. Traces of bailey to N. Administrative centre of a sublordship of Abergavenny.

Llangibby castle mound, Llangibby

OS 171   ST 369973   R2

A substantial well preserved motte, probably the forerunner of Llangibby Castle (see below) on hill above.

The Berries mound and bailey castle, Caerwent

OS 171   ST 488895   R2

A well preserved small motte with a large, roughly circular bailey to the SW. Motte surrounded by a ditch, bailey surrounded on S and part of N sides by a low bank, and on the E by a higher bank with an entrance in the middle.

Caerleon castle mound, Caerleon
OS 171   ST 342905   R2 (upper part visible from adjacent road)

One of the earliest and largest mottes in south Wales, now in a private garden. Built before 1100 and first held by Turstin fitz Rolf. In 1217 it was captured by William Marshal who built a stone shell-keep on it, probably using stone from the nearby Roman baths. The keep collapsed in the 18th century. The bailey was to the SW and one of its early 13th-century angle-towers can be seen next to the Hanbury Arms public house.

SOUTH GLAMORGAN

Morganstown castle mound, Cardiff
OS 171   ST 128819   U2

A well preserved motte surrounded by a boggy ditch. Bailey bank visible to the E.

Cottrell ringwork, St Nicholas
OS 170   ST 084747   R2

A fine, large raised ringwork surrounded by a ditch, with a causeway across on S side. The outline of a rectangular bailey to the S.

Ystradowen castle mound, Ystradowen
OS 170   ST 011777   U2

A medium-sized motte just W of church, with a quarry hole in the middle. Ditch on N and S sides, stopping abruptly at W end, suggesting that the castle was unfinished. Masonry castle of Tal y Fan 1km to the E (see below).

Llantrithyd ringwork, Llantrithyd
OS 170   ST 045727   R2

An oval enclosure surrounded by a bank and ditch, quarried away in the NW corner. Inside, the stump of a rectangular stone building in the NE corner found on excavation to be an early 12th-century hall. This was the manorial centre of Llantrithyd, held by the de Cardiff family. Abandoned in about 1200, and probably succeeded by Horseland moated site (see below).

MID-GLAMORGAN

Gwern y domen castle mound, Caerphilly
OS 171   ST 175879   R2

A large, steep-sided raised ringwork.

Llangynwyd castle (Tir yr Iarll), Llangynwyd
OS 170   SS 852887   R2

A large, roughly circular mound, surrounded by a deep ditch on all but the NE side, where there is a steep natural slope. Entrance causeway on NW side. A ruined, turfed-over curtain wall, with the foundations of buildings in the interior, and some dressed stone in the entrance passage. A large bailey to the NW, with a bank and ditch along the NW side. An important outpost of the lordship of Glamorgan in the uplands, but vulnerable to Welsh attack. By 1262 'much injured by war', and stormed again in c.1306.

WEST GLAMORGAN

Penlle'r Castell, Ammanford
OS 159   SN 665096   U2

A rectangular mound surrounded by a steep, V-shaped ditch, on high moorland. The remains of walls at the N and S ends suggest small rectangular buildings of drystone walling in the interior.

Old Castle, Bishopston, Gower
OS 159   SS 582900   R2

A small, oval ringwork defended on the N by a ravine and on the remaining sides by a high bank and ditch. Occupied in the 12th century, and a possession of the bishops of Llandaff.

Penmaen Burrows ringwork, Penmaen, Gower
OS 159   SS 534880   U2

A roughly oval ringwork on a headland, opposite Pennard Castle (no. 111), with a substantial bank and ditch on the SW side. Excavation found 12th-century occupation, with a timber gate, entrance keep and interior buildings, followed by 13th-century rebuilding in stone.

Platform houses and deserted medieval villages

GWENT

St Brides Netherwent deserted village, Caerwent
OS 171   ST 428896   R2

Hollows, scarps, platforms and mounds in the field around St Bridget's Church show where houses, roads, enclosures and ponds once were.

Deserted medieval village W of St Mary's Church, Wilcrick, Bishton
OS 171   ST 409880   R2

Group of house sites and enclosures, with four scarped terraces one above the other.

Runston deserted medieval village, Crick
OS 162   ST 495916   R2

The remains of Runston village lie to the S and E of Runston Chapel (see below). Banks and scarps delineate house sites and enclosures, with a hollow way running E–W through the middle.

MID-GLAMORGAN

Platform houses on Mynydd Tŷ Talwyn, Llangynwyd
OS 170   SS 858857   R2

A group of ten platform houses in three pairs, one single and one threesome, associated with a rectangular enclosure at the foot of a steep-sided valley.

Platform houses on Coly Uchaf, Bedlinog
OS 171   SO 092024   R2

Two pairs of platform houses, one not well preserved to the NW of the farm, and one very well preserved to the SW. The southern platform of this pair has stone wall footings and an attached rectangular enclosure.

SOUTH GLAMORGAN

Deserted medieval village NE of Rock Farm, St Athan
OS 170   ST 020682   U2/R2 (public footpath through site)

Some well defined rectangular house platforms, parallel banks of crofts and a hollow trackway running E–W along the S side are all that is left of this village.

Flemingston deserted medieval village, St Athan
OS 170   ST 025698   U2 (public footpath)

Low banks and scarps on the S side of the Thaw valley, some isolated, some enclosing irregular-shaped areas.

Moated sites

Although there are a good many moated sites in lowland south-east Wales they are under-represented in the main site list, as most of them are in private ownership. Apart from Hen Gwrt (no. 91) there are no well preserved moated sites with unrestricted access. Some of the best and most interesting are listed here, such as Doghill and Horseland.

SOUTH GLAMORGAN

Doghill (Worleton) moated site, Dyffryn
OS 171   ST 093720   R2

This is the best-preserved moated site in Glamorgan. A large, square raised island is surrounded by a wide, flat-bottomed ditch, still partly water-filled and boggy. This was the centre of Worleton manor held by the bishops of Llandaff until the 16th century when the Button family bought it.

Horseland moated site, Llantrithyd
OS 170   ST 041724   R2

Building remains are visible on the N side of the interior of this moated site, which is a rectangular raised area surrounded by a ditch, now reed-filled. The W end has been destroyed but the E end is well preserved. The building remains consist of turf-covered stony mounds and stretches of walling. To the S is an area of parallel banks and ditches which may have been for growing a crop needing good drainage. The site probably replaced the ringwork to the NE (see above) as the Llantrithyd manorial centre when that was abandoned in about 1200, and was succeeded by Llantrithyd Place in the 16th century.

GWENT
Pencoed Castle moated site, Langstone
OS 171   ST 404892   R2

A well preserved moated site SW of the castle – square and surrounded by a boggy ditch. A later well, half-way along the NE side.

Goldcliff moated site, Goldcliff
OS 171   ST 361836   R2

A well preserved moated site – a rectangular raised platform surrounded by a wide, flat-bottomed ditch.

Coed Cwnwr moated site, Usk
OS 171   ST 412994   R2

A well preserved small moated site – square, surrounded by a boggy ditch, with a causeway on the W side. A small gem.

Penbidwal moated site, Pandy
OS 161   SO 342222   R2

A well preserved square moated site with a flat-bottomed ditch around all but the S side, which is bounded by a deeply sunken road. Possibly the predecessor of the 16th-century Penbidwal House to the NE, and the centre of a sublordship within the lordship of Abergavenny.

Moated site S of Moynes Court, Mathern
OS 162   ST 520909   R2

A subrectangular area with a well preserved large ditch on the S and W sides. A manor house site, belonging to the bishops of Llandaff, the predecessor of nearby Moyne's Court, which was enlarged in 1609 by Bishop Godwin.

Perth-hir House, Rockfield
OS 161   SO 486159   R2

The remains of a large moated site, with a large ditch on the N and E sides. Within the moated area are the fragmentary remains of the SW angle of Perth-hir House, a 16th-century mansion belonging to the Herbert family.

Miscellaneous earthwork sites
Clawdd Du, Monmouth (Gwent)
OS 162   SO 504122   U1

A large ditch running NW–SE through the suburb of Overmonnow, to the W of the river Monnow in Monmouth. Originally the defensive ditch of the medieval suburb of Overmonnow, which probably became established in the 12th century.

Masonry castles and secular buildings
GWENT
Llangibby Castle, Llangibby
OS 171   ST 364974   R2

An anomalously large, sumptuous and well fortified castle, probably unfinished and never really used. Probably built by Gilbert de Clare (the Last) in about 1300. The curtain wall encloses a rectangular area and stands almost to its full height. There are two keeps at the W end, the southern one a gatehouse, the northern containing the hall.

Cas Troggy Castle, Llantrisant
OS 171   ST 415952   R2

The ruined and much overgrown remains of a large, probably 13th-century castle, with a high upstanding curtain wall with towers at the corners along the S side. The rest of the castle, to the N, is reduced to banks and mounds.

Llanvair Castle, Caerwent
OS 171   ST 445924   R2

A substantial 13th-century castle. The S curtain wall is the best preserved part, with a spectacular, high, circular tower at its E end. There are fragmentary walls within the E end, but the W end has been destroyed and a modern house built on it.

Medieval tower at Hanbury Arms, Caerleon
OS 171   ST 341903   U1

A roofless circular stone tower, incorporating some Roman masonry, dating from the 13th century. It was the SW corner tower of Caerleon Castle, the keep of which was on the large motte to the NE (see above).

Dovecote at Hygga Farm, Trellech
OS 171   SO 486036   R2

A circular stone dovecote, whose tiled roof has fallen in. It has nesting holes with stone sills both inside and out, and remnants of white plaster still adhering to the walls.

SOUTH GLAMORGAN
St Quintin's Castle, Llanblethian
OS 170   SS 989742   R2

A massive, twin-towered gatehouse and high stretch of curtain wall on its N side are the main remnants of this large courtyard castle. A ruinous low wall surrounds the rectilinear ward to the W. In the centre is a mound with the shell of a thick-walled building possibly an earlier keep, on it. The gatehouse and curtain wall are thought to be early 14th century, built by Gilbert de Clare (the Last, d. 1314).

Penmark Castle, Penmark
OS 170   ST 059689   R2

A substantial 13th-century castle. A round tower stands to second-floor level and a

stretch of high curtain walling of the inner ward runs southward from it. Fragmentary remains of other parts, with a large outer ward to the W. Held by the de Umfreville family, and then by the Bawdrips.

East Orchard manor house, St Athan
OS 170   ST 029681   R2

A complex of ruined buildings, standing in places to their full height – a large house, possibly 14th-century, a retainers' hall (now a barn), dovecote, outbuilding (foundations only) and barn (a fragment of a very large one). Originally the property of the de Berkerolles, in 1411 sold to the Stradlings of St Donat's Castle.

MID-GLAMORGAN
Kenfig Castle and medieval town, Kenfig
OS 170   SS 801826   U2

The very ruinous stump of a once important Norman castle, established by Robert, earl of Gloucester in the first half of the 12th century. It has a square, free-standing keep with an entrance at the SW angle and further building remains to the SW. To the S is the bailey, with the remains of a bank and ditch around it. Although 'poor and patched' it was an important administrative centre, and a borough was established to the S by 1183. Throughout the 12th and 13th centuries Kenfig was harried by the Welsh, and from the 13th century was gradually engulfed by sand.

Castell Morgraig, Thornhill
OS 171   ST 160843   R2

A much ruined, and possibly never completed courtyard castle in a commanding position on a ridgetop. The curtain wall is pentagonal, with four angle-towers and one larger rectangular tower jutting out on the E side. The entrance is a simple opening on the W. In general character it is mid-13th-century, and was either built by the Welsh lord of Senghenydd just before being ousted from his territory by Richard de Clare in 1247, or by Richard de Clare himself as a precursor of Caerphilly Castle.

Candleston Castle, Merthyr Mawr
OS 170   SS 871773   U2

A ruined, mainly late 14th-century, small fortified manor house, its name deriving from the Cantelupe family. It originally consisted of a 13th-century tower, to which further wings were added to the N and E. There is a fine 14th-century fireplace at first-floor level in the hall. On the W side a ruined curtain wall encloses an irregular area. Almost all the castle's land is now sand-covered. Occupied into the 19th century.

WEST GLAMORGAN
Penrice Castle, Penrice, Gower
OS 159   SS 497885   R2/U2 (public footpath past it)

A ruined, crudely built courtyard castle above Penrice Castle House, whose curtain wall encloses a very large irregular-shaped area. The earliest part is the late 12th-century circular keep on the NW side. The curtain wall, with solid semicircular towers, is early 13th-century. The gatehouse, of unusual form with two square towers on the outer face and one spanning the passage at the inner end, is mid-13th-century. There are various additions to the basic structure, including a dovecote on the SE side. It succeeded the Penrice ringwork (see above) as the centre of one of the original sublordships of Gower, and its holders were the de Penres family, most of whom appear to have been called Robert.

Ecclesiastical sites
GWENT
Llantarnam Abbey tithe barn, Cwmbran
OS 171   ST 312930   R2

A roofless, but otherwise complete large stone barn, standing N of the present abbey buildings. The Cistercian abbey was founded in 1175 or 1179 by Hywel ab Iorwerth, Welsh lord of Caerleon, and the barn probably dates from the 13th century. It has wide central doorways in the middle of the N and S sides, and three arched buttresses on the outside of the N wall.

Runston chapel, Crick
OS 162   ST 495916   U2   Cadw

A small, simple, roofless 12th-century church dedicated to St Keyna, with round-headed doorway and windows on the N and S sides. In about 1770 services stopped and the village (see above) died. William Coxe saw the church in moonlight at the beginning of the 19th century: 'the roof was falling down . . . a large and broken font was lying on the floor among the weeds'.

SOUTH GLAMORGAN
Blackfriars Dominican Friary, Cardiff
OS 171   ST 178767   U1

The foundations and footings of the church and some claustral buildings exposed by the 3rd marquis of Bute at the end of the 19th century are laid out in a public garden. The friary was founded in 1256 by Richard de Clare, lord of Glamorgan, and is reputedly the burial place of the Welsh leader Llewelyn Bren. The building remains are late 13th- to early 14th-century. The church had a large nave and narrow chancel and to the N were cloisters with buildings ranged round them laid out to the usual Dominican plan.

Remains of Highlight Church, Barry
OS 171   ST 097699   U2

The footings of a small medieval church with nave and narrower chancel, associated with the deserted village of Highlight or 'Uchelolau'. The chancel is probably the oldest part, dating from the early 13th century. A poor S porch was added in the late Middle Ages. Excavated 1964–9.

MID-GLAMORGAN
Capel Gwladys, Gelligaer
OS 171   ST 125993   U2

The restored footings of a small rectangular chapel on high moorland on Gelligaer Common. A modern cross marks the position of the altar. It is thought to have been founded originally by St Gwladys in the 6th century, but the present remains are of a medieval building. The St Gwladys memorial stone (9th–10th-century) is in Gelligaer church.

St Roque's chapel, Merthyr Mawr
OS 170   SS 889780   R2 (in private garden)

A roofless but otherwise well preserved small 15th-century chapel, lying within a small Iron Age hillfort. There are vestiges of a S porch, and a restored belfry. It was originally plastered inside and out. It contains two very fine early Christian stones (see above).

WEST GLAMORGAN

St Baglan's church, Baglan
OS 170   SS 753923   U2

A simple, rectangular, late medieval building, now roofless and partly ruined, with a Perpendicular E window. It was the principal church of the lordship of Afan, and may be pre-Norman in origin.

Hen Eglwys, Margam
OS 170   SS 801865   U2

A simple, rectangular 15th-century chapel on a high, steep-sided knoll above Margam Abbey. Fragments of Perpendicular tracery in E and W windows.

Summary of Dates

Prehistoric monuments in this book are ascribed to archaeological periods based on the conventional three-age system of Stone Age, Bronze Age and Iron Age. This system of classification has served archaeology well through the years, but has recently been criticised for giving too great an emphasis to the materials with which implements were made. Our study of settlements and burial places now makes us realise that the periods of greatest change and upheaval in society do not necessarily coincide with the adoption of new technological improvements.

Accordingly, archaeologists now tend, when they can, to use absolute chronology for descriptive purposes. This has been made possible by the use of radiocarbon dating. Every living thing contains carbon 14, which, after death, decomposes at a known rate. This dating technique measures the amount of carbon 14 remaining in an organic substance, such as charcoal from a burial mound, to give a date for its death – the felling of the tree, for instance. Unfortunately, we now know that radiocarbon dating gives results that are too young, and dates are therefore corrected or 'calibrated' on a set calculation to give a 'calendar' rather than a 'radiocarbon' date.

But the calculation for correcting radiocarbon dates is by no means accepted by all archaeologists, and the very accuracy of radiocarbon dating itself has received criticism in recent years. For this reason, it was decided to retain the conventional three-age system for the basic classification of the monuments in the book. The dates given for each monument in the site heading are designed only to be a rough guide. (When a radiocarbon date is given in the text, it is specifically described as a radiocarbon date and is given corrected in years BC.) From the Roman period onward, radiocarbon dating is not normally appropriate, and calendar years are always given.

The table overleaf outlines the basic chronology over the time span covered by the book, and may help explain some of the terms used in the text.

Approximate Date	Archaeological Period	Characteristic Features
225,000 BC	Lower Palaeolithic (Old Stone Age)	Warm interglacial within Pleistocene Ice Age. First evidence of man in Wales.
100,000 BC	Middle Palaeolithic	
26,000 BC	Early Upper Palaeolithic	First evidence of *Homo sapiens* in Gower caves. Onset of final glaciation.
15,000 BC	Late Upper Palaeolithic	Ice retreats. Creswellian tool types appear.
10,000 BC	Early Mesolithic (Middle Stone Age)	Nomadic hunter-gatherers use finely worked microlithic flints to tip arrows and spears for hunting.
6,000 BC	Late Mesolithic	Seasonal settlements established, especially in coastal areas, by regionalised groups of peoples. Some evidence for manipulation of environment.
3,500 BC	Early Neolithic (New Stone Age)	First farmers arrive. Megalithic tombs built in fertile, low-lying parts of Glamorgan and Gwent. Pottery first used.
2,500 BC	Late Neolithic	Communal tombs decline in importance. Ceremonial henges built. Farming activity spreads to marginal uplands.
2,000 BC	Early Bronze Age	Beaker pottery and first metal objects appear. Burial mounds and cairns and standing stones erected in upland and lower areas in Glamorgan and Gwent.
1,300 BC	Late Bronze Age	Population pressures, deterioration of climate, and soil degradation lead to abandonment of uplands.
600 BC	Iron Age	Hillforts and small, circular defended farms built in increasing numbers. Iron tools first appear. Regionalised groups of people emerge, including Silures of south-east Wales.
AD 43	Roman Period	Wales conquered by Romans. Auxiliary forts established. Roads built. Caerleon legionary fortress, forts and civilian settlement of Caerwent established.
AD 410	Early Medieval Period	Roman withdrawal. Small kingdoms emerge. Spread of Christianity.

Summary of Dates

Approximate Date	Archaeological Period	Characteristic Features
AD 1066	Medieval Period	Normans invade Wales and establish lordships in southern Glamorgan and Gwent. Welsh remain independent in 'pura Wallia' on upland areas to north, subject to overlordship of English king; continental-style monasteries founded.
1276–83		Edwardian conquest of Wales crushes independent Wales.
1400–10		Owain Glyndŵr leads Welsh rebellion.
1485	Post-Medieval Period	Henry VII becomes first Tudor monarch.
1536–40		Dissolution of the Monasteries by Henry VIII.
1536–43		Acts of Union, whereby a unified Wales merges politically with England.
1642–8		Civil War between Royalists and Parliament brings many medieval castles back into use for the last time.

Glossary

Aisle A lateral division of the nave or chancel of a church, usually separated off by columns, and lying to one or both sides.

Apse Semicircular or polygonal end to a chancel, chapel or aisle.

Apsidal Apse-shaped.

Arcade A row of arches usually supported on columns.

Arrowslit, arrowloop A narrow vertical slit in masonry used by archers.

Ashlar Fine masonry using stones dressed to a regular shape, and laid in thin-jointed courses.

Bailey The defended outer courtyard or 'ward' of a castle.

Barbican An outer defence protecting a gateway.

Barrow A mound of earth or earth and stones used, most often during the Bronze Age, to cover burials.

Batter The sloping part of a wall, usually at the bottom of the exterior face of a tower or curtain wall.

Battlements The parapet of a wall or tower equipped with openings ('crenelles') and solid walling ('merlons') and used for defence by archers. Battlements are also known as crenellations.

Berm A strip of ground between the base of the curtain wall and the ditch.

Boss A decorative knob, often on vaulting ribs or on sculptured crosses.

Buttery Store-room for wine and other beverages.

Buttress Projecting mass of masonry giving additional support to a wall, often on corners of churches.

Cairn Mound of stones. Used to cover burials in the Neolithic and Bronze Ages; often had additional ceremonial functions. Clearance cairns are mounds created by clearing agricultural fields of stones.

Cantref The main Welsh administrative unit of land division, used in pre-Norman and later times.

Capital The top or head of a column, often decorated.

Chancel The eastern part of the church, which usually housed the high altar and which was reserved for the clergy.

Chapter house The room in which monks met daily to discuss business and to hear a chapter of the monastic rule.

Choir The part of the church where services were sung, containing the choir stalls.

Cist A stone-lined or slab-built grave.

Cistercian A movement of reformed Benedictine monks, established at Cîteaux in 1098. The 'White Monks', named after their white habits, were especially successful in Wales.

Civitas An area or unit of tribal land under the Romans.

Clas A community of clergy in the pre-Norman Welsh church.

Clavicula An inturned quadrant of bank forming an entrance to a Roman marching camp and facing the attacker's right-hand side.

Cloister A four-sided enclosure, usually at the centre of a monastery, with a covered walk along each side, used for study.

Commote A Welsh administrative unit of land division, used in pre-Norman times. A subdivision of a cantref.

Constable The governor of a castle.

Corbel A projecting stone used for support, often for floor or roof timbers.

Counterscarp Outer defence, a wall or slope of a ditch.

Crossing The central space at the intersection of the east–west axis and north–south transepts of a church. The tower often stands above.

Cross-slab A shaped stone slab on which is, in relief, a cross and often other ornament.

Cruciform Cross-shaped.

Curtain The wall, often strengthened with towers, which encloses the courtyard of a castle.

Decorated The style of Gothic architecture which flourished *c.*1280–1340.

Disc-headed slab-cross Decorated stone slab with round solid head and wide shaft.

Dormitory The sleeping quarters of a monastery.

Drawbridge A wooden bridge across the ditch to the entrance or gateway of a castle. It could be raised or lowered for defensive purposes.

Drystone wall Stone wall built without mortar or clay.

Embrasure A splayed opening, either in a parapet for defensive use by archers, or in walls for windows.

Fret-pattern Typical Celtic motif of classical derivation, and used for decoration on early Christian crosses.

Gunloop, gunport The opening in a wall for a gun.

Hall The room in a castle used for administration of estates and justice, and for entertainment on important occasions. Many castles would also have a smaller hall for less formal everyday use.

Hoard A timber fighting platform projecting from the outside of the top of a castle keep or tower for extra defence.

Interlace A favourite Celtic decorative motif derived from late classical art. Continuous interlacing patterns frequently used on crosses include plaitwork and knotwork.

Jamb The straight side of a doorway or window.

Justiciar The chief minister of the king in the medieval period.

Keep The main, strong, usually free-standing, tower of a castle.

Key-pattern A decorative motif of classical derivation, used on early Christian crosses.

Knotwork see *interlace*.

Lancet A plain slender window with a pointed arch.

Latin cross An upright cross with the lower arm longer than the others, distinguished from the equal-armed Greek cross.

Lintel A supporting wooden beam or stone over an opening in a wall.

Lordship The area ruled by a lord under the supremacy of the king.

Machicolation Openings in the floor of a projecting structure often in front of a castle gatehouse through which missiles could be dropped on to attackers. See also *murder hole*.

Maltese cross A cross with strongly-splayed arms often curved or indented at the ends.

Marches Border or frontier, especially used for the south and east areas of Wales under Norman control.

Megalith Large stone or a structure built of large stones (from the Greek *mega* (great) and *lithos* (stone). Neolithic chambered tombs are often known as megaliths.

Merlon see *battlement*.

Motte A mound of earth constructed to support a tower and palisade.

Mullion The vertical bar between window openings.

Mural tower A tower built on a curtain wall.

Murder hole A hole, often in the vault of a castle gate passage, through which missiles could be dropped on to attackers, or for water to extinguish castle timbers set on fire during an attack. See also *machicolation*.

Nave The part of a church extending from the crossing to the west end.

Newel stair A spiral stair with a central support or 'newel'.

Ogam A system of writing invented in Ireland before the 5th century AD, comprising 20 letters represented by groups of notches, and often used for early medieval inscriptions on stone.

Oriel window A projecting, curved or polygonal window.

Palisade A strong timber fence.

Pent roof A lean-to roof.

Piscina A basin with a drain, usually set into the church wall by the altar, used for washing vessels during Mass.

Plaitwork see *interlace*.

Portcullis Wood and iron gate which could be raised or lowered in grooves in the wall of a castle gate-passage, for defensive purposes.

Postern A small gateway, subsidiary to the main entrance.

Presbytery The part of the church around the high altar, to the east of the choir.

Pulpitum A screen wall dividing the nave from the choir.

Revetment Timber- or stonework built to give support to the side of a bank or ditch.

Ringwork A type of early castle consisting of a defensive enclosure, usually circular, with a surrounding bank and external ditch. A variant is the raised ringwork – a motte with a bank around the top.

Rule The code of religious life followed by a religious order. The two most important in medieval Europe were the Rules of St Benedict and St Augustine.

Sacristy The room for the storage of vestments and sacred vessels.

Shell-keep A defensive stone wall built around the perimeter of a motte.

Slight Damage or destroy a castle.

String course A projecting horizontal decorative band of masonry running around a building.

Tithes A tax payable to the church, comprising one-tenth of agricultural produce.

Titulum A gateway in a Roman marching camp, protected by a short, detached length of bank and ditch.

Tracery Decorative stonework in the upper parts of windows or on walls.

Transept The transverse, short arms of a cruciform church, orientated north–south.

Transom A horizontal bar across the lights of a window.

Tref A Welsh administrative unit of land division, used in pre-Norman times. A subdivision of a commote.

Vault An arched stone roof. A barrel-vault is a vault of semicircular section.

Wall-walk A passage behind the parapet of a castle or town wall, used for defence.

Ward A courtyard within the walls of a castle.

Wheel-headed slab-cross A type of cross on which the head has an inset wheel joining the arms.

Bibliography

Guidebooks

The monuments in the care of Cadw and other conservation bodies often have guidebooks which give a more detailed history and tour of the site. Most of the sites listed below will have guides for sale, but some of the older guides to Cadw sites may now be out of print; these are due to be replaced by new ones in the near future.

Caerleon Roman Fortress J K Knight, Cadw Guidebook (Cardiff 1988).
Caerphilly Castle C N Johns, Official Guidebook (Cardiff 1978).
          D F Renn, Cadw Guidebook (Cardiff 1989).
Caerwent Roman City O E Craster, Official Guidebook (Cardiff 1951).
Caldicot Castle Monmouth District Museums Service Guide leaflet (1979).
Cardiff Castle Cardiff City Council Guidebook.
Castell Coch S Rousham, Cadw Guidebook (Cardiff 1987).
Chepstow Castle J K Knight, Cadw Guidebook (Cardiff 1986).
Ewenny Priory C A R Radford, Official Guidebook (Cardiff 1952).
Grosmont Castle J K Knight, Official Guidebook (Cardiff 1980).
Llanthony Priory O E Craster, Official Guidebook (Cardiff 1963).
Margam Abbey A L Evans, *The Story of Margam Abbey* (1979).
Margam Stones Museum C A R Radford, Official Guidebook (Cardiff 1949).
Monmouth Castle and Great Castle House A J Taylor, Official Guidebook (Cardiff, 1951).
Neath Abbey L A S Butler, Official Guidebook (Cardiff 1976).
Old Beaupre D B Hague, Official Guidebook (Cardiff 1965).
Oystermouth Castle K W B Lightfoot, Guide leaflet.
Raglan Castle A J Taylor, Official Guidebook (Cardiff 1979).
          J R Kenyon, Cadw Guidebook (Cardiff 1988).
Skenfrith Castle O E Craster, Official Guidebook (Cardiff 1970).
The Three Castles J K Knight, Cadw Guidebook (Cardiff 1987).
          J K Knight, Cadw Guidebook (Cardiff 1991).
Tintern Abbey O E Craster, Official Guidebook (Cardiff 1956).
          D Robinson, Cadw Guidebook (Cardiff 1990).
Weobley Castle W G Thomas, Official Guidebook (Cardiff 1971).
          D Robinson, Cadw Guidebook (Cardiff 1987).
White Castle C A R Radford, Official Guidebook (Cardiff 1962).

Further Reading

This is a very selective list of general books which give further information on prehistoric and medieval Wales that is relevant to south-east Wales.

Prehistory

Bradley, R, *The Prehistoric Settlement of Britain* (London 1978).
Cunliffe, B, *Iron Age Communities in Britain* (London 1974).
Daniel, G E, *The Prehistoric Chamber Tombs of England and Wales* (Cambridge 1950).
Johnston, J F, *Hillforts* (London, 1976).
Hogg, A H A, *Hill-Forts of Britain* (London 1975).
Megaw, J V S and Simpson, D D A, (eds), *Introduction to British Prehistory* (Leicester 1979).
Taylor, J A (ed.), *Culture and Environment in Prehistoric Wales* (Oxford 1980).

Roman

Frere, S S, *Britannia: A History of Roman Britain*, (London 1987).
Margary, I D, *Roman Roads in Britain* (London 1973).
Nash-Williams V E, *The Roman Frontier in Wales*, 2nd edn revised by M G Jarrett (Cardiff 1969).
Todd, M, *Roman Britain 55 B.C.–A.D. 400* (London 1981).
Webster, G, *The Roman Imperial Army* (London 1985).
Wilson, R, *Roman Forts* (London 1980).

Early Medieval

Davies, W, *Wales in the Early Middle Ages* (Leicester 1982).
Edwards, N and Lane, A (eds), *Early Medieval Settlements in Wales AD 400–1100* (Bangor and Cardiff 1988).
Nash-Williams, V E, *Early Christian Monuments of Wales* (Cardiff 1950).

Medieval

Butler, L and Given-Wilson, C, *Medieval Monasteries of Great Britain* (London 1979).
Davies, R R, *Conquest, Coexistence and Change: Wales 1063–1415* (Oxford 1987).
Kenyon, J R, *Medieval Fortifications* (Leicester 1990).
Kenyon, J R, and Avent, R, (eds), *Castles in Wales and the Marches* (Cardiff, 1987).
King, D J C, *The Castle in England and Wales* (London 1988).
Knowles, D and Hadcock, R N, *Medieval Religious Houses in England and Wales* (revised edn London 1971).
Renn, D, *Norman Castles in Britain* (London 1973).
Williams, D H, *The Welsh Cistercians* (Caldey Island, 1984).
Williams, G, *The Welsh Church from Conquest to Reformation* (Cardiff, 1976).

The Royal Commission on Ancient and Historical Monuments in Wales

The inventories of the Royal Commission give detailed descriptions of all monuments known at the time of publication. To date there are no inventories for Gwent, but several for Glamorgan.

An Inventory of the Ancient Monuments in Glamorgan I, pt 1: *The Stone and Bronze Ages* (Cardiff 1976).
An Inventory of the Ancient Monuments in Glamorgan, I, pt 2: *The Iron Age and Roman Occupation* (Cardiff 1976).
An Inventory of the Ancient Monuments in Glamorgan, I, pt 3: *The Early Christian Period* (Cardiff, 1976).
An Inventory of the Ancient Monuments in Glamorgan, III, pt 1 (a): *The Early Castles* (Cardiff, 1991).
An Inventory of the Ancient Monuments in Glamorgan, IV, pt 1: *The Greater Houses* (Cardiff, 1981).

Gazetteer References

This is the full list of references added to the relevant site entry in the gazetteer. They are designed to help the interested reader find out more about a specific monument.

Babbidge, A V, 'Excavations at Coed-y-Bwnydd, Bettws Newydd – 1970 Season', *The Monmouthshire Antiquary*, III, pt I (1970–1), pp 59–60.
Babbidge, A V, 'Reconnaissance excavations at Coed-y-Bwnydd, Bettws Newydd, 1969–71', *The Monmouthshire Antiquary*, III, pt III (1977), pp 159–78.
Boon, G, *Isca* (Cardiff, 1972).
Camden, W, *Camden's Britannia, newly translated into English: with large additions and improvements*, (London 1695).
Craster, O E, 'Skenfrith Castle: When was it built?', *Archaeologia Cambrensis*, CXVI (1967), pp 133–58.
Craster, O E, and J M Lewis, 'Hen Gwrt moated site, Llantilio Crossenny, Monmouthshire', *Archaeologia Cambrensis*, CXII (1963), pp 159–83.
Daniel, G E, 'The chambered barrow in Parc le Breos Cwm, South Wales' *Proceedings of the Prehistoric Society*, III (1937), pp 71–86.
Davies, J L, 'An excavation at the Bulwarks, Porthkerry, Glamorgan, 1968', *Archaeologia Cambrensis*, CXXII (1973), pp 85–98.
Evans, D H, 'Excavations at Llanthony Priory, Gwent, 1978', *The Monmouthshire Antiquary*, IV (1980), pp 5–43.
Evans, E, *Swansea Castle and the Medieval Town* (Swansea 1983).
Fox, A, 'An account of John Storrie's excavations on Barry Island in 1894–5', *Transactions of Cardiff Naturalists' Society*, LXIX (1936), pp 12–38.

Fox, A, 'Dinas Noddfa, Gellygaer Common, Glamorgan. Excavations in 1936', *Archaeologia Cambrensis*, XCII (1937), pp 247–68.

Fox, A, 'Early Welsh homesteads on Gelligaer Common, Glamorgan', *Archaeologia Cambrensis*, XCIV (1939), pp 163–99.

Fox, A, 'Hill-slope forts and related earthworks in south-west England and south Wales', *Archaeological Journal*, CIX (1952), pp 1–22.

Fox, C, and A Fox, 'Forts and farms on Margam Mountain, Glamorgan', *Antiquity*, VIII (1934), pp 395–413.

Gardner, I, 'Llanthony Prima', *Archaeologia Cambrensis*, 6th series, XV (1915), pp 343–76.

Gardner, W., 'The Bulwarks: a promontory fort at Porthkerry, Glamorganshire', *Archaeologia Cambrensis*, XC (1935), pp 135–40.

Grant, J P, *Cardiff Castle: Its History and Architecture* (Cardiff, 1923).

Griffith, J, 'Crug yr Avon: Glamorgan's lone sentry-box', *Archaeologia Cambrensis*, 6th series, II, part I (1902), pp 136–40.

Grimes, W F, and H A Hyde, 'A prehistoric hearth at Radyr, Glamorgan, and its bearing on the nativity of beech (*Fagus sylvatica* L.) in Britain', *Transactions of Cardiff Naturalists' Society*, LXVIII (1935), pp 46–54.

Hogg, A H A, 'Castle Ditches, Llancarfan (Glamorgan)', *Archaeologia Cambrensis*, CXXV (1976), pp 13–39.

Kenyon, J R, 'Morlais Castle as viewed by Samuel and Nathaniel Buck', *Archaeologia Cambrensis* CXXXIV (1985), pp 235–7.

Knight, J K, 'Usk Castle and its affinities', in *Ancient Monuments and Their Interpretation*, M R Apted, R Gilyard-Beer and A D Saunders (eds) (London and Chichester 1977).

Knight, J K, 'Excavations at St. Barruc's Chapel, Barry Island, Glamorgan', *Transactions of Cardiff Naturalists' Society*, XCIX (1976–8), pp 28–65.

Lewis, J M, 'Recent excavations at Loughor castle (South Wales)', *Château Gaillard VII* (1975), pp 147–57.

Lubbock, J, 'Description of the Park Cwm tumulus', *Archaeologia Cambrensis*, II, 4th series (1871), pp 168–72.

Lukis, J W, 'On St. Lythan's and St. Nicholas' cromlechs and other remains near Cardiff', *Archaeologia Cambrensis*, VI, 4th series (1875), pp 171–85.

Moore, D, *Caerleon, Fortress of the Legion* (Cardiff, 1979).

Morgan, O, and T Wakeman, *Notes on the Architecture and History of Caldicot Castle, Monmouthshire* (Monmouthshire and Caerleon Antiquarian Association, 1854).

Morgan, W Ll, *The Castle of Swansea*, (Devizes 1914).

Nash-Williams, V E, 'An early Iron Age hill-fort at Llanmelin, near Caerwent, Monmouthshire', *Archaeologia Cambrensis*, LXXXVIII (1933), pp 237–346.

Nash-Williams, V E, 'An early Iron Age coastal camp at Sudbrook, Monmouthshire', *Archaeologia Cambrensis*, XCIV (1939), pp 42–79.

Nash-Williams, V E, *The Early Christian Monuments of Wales* (Cardiff, 1950a).

Nash-Williams, V E, 'The Roman stations at Neath (Glam.) and Caer Gai (Mer.)', *Bulletin of the Board of Celtic Studies*, XIII, iv (1950b), pp 239–43.

Nash-Williams, V E, 'The medieval settlement at Llantwit Major, Glamorganshire', *Bulletin of the Board of Celtic Studies*, XIV, iv (1952a), pp 313–33.

Nash-Williams, V E, *The Roman Legionary Fortress at Caerleon, Monmouthshire* (Cardiff 1952b).

Nash-Williams, V E, *The Roman Frontier in Wales*, revised by M G Jarrett (Cardiff 1969).

Perks, J C, *Chepstow Castle, Monmouthshire* (London 1967).

Probert, L A, 'Twyn-y-Gaer hill-fort, Gwent: an interim assessment', in *Welsh Antiquity*, G C Boon and J M Lewis (eds) (Cardiff 1976), pp 105–20.

Bibliography

Rees, W, *Caerphilly Castle*, (Cardiff 1971).

Robinson, D, 'An aerial survey at Morlais Castle, Merthyr Tydfil, Mid Glamorgan', *Bulletin of the Board of Celtic Studies*, XXX (1983), pp 431–40.

Rodger, J W, 'Llantwit Major, Glamorganshire, excavations', *Archaeologia Cambrensis*, XV, 6th series (1915), pp 141–56.

Simpson, G, 'Caerleon and the Roman forts in Wales in the 2nd century AD. Part 2, southern Wales', *Archaeologia Cambrensis*, CXII (1963), pp 13–76.

Sollas, W J, 'The Paviland Cave – an Aurignacian station in Wales', *Journal of the Royal Anthropological Institute*, XLIII (1913), pp 315–75.

Thurlby, M, 'The Romanesque Priory Church of St. Michael at Ewenny', *Journal of the Society of Architectural Historians*, XLVII (1988), pp 281–94.

Ward, J, 'The Roman fort of Gellygaer', *Transactions of the Cardiff Naturalists' Society*, XXXV (1903), pp 1–104.

Ward, J, 'The Roman fort at Gellygaer – the Baths', *Transactions of the Cardiff Naturalists' Society*, XLII (1909), pp 25–69.

Ward, J, 'The Roman fort of Gellygaer – the Annexe', *Transactions of the Cardiff Naturalists' Society*, XLIV (1911), pp 65–91.

Ward, J, 'The Roman fort at Gellygaer. Discoveries made in 1913', *Transactions of the Cardiff Naturalists' Society*, XLVI (1913), pp 1–20.

Ward, J, 'The St. Nicholas chambered tumulus, Glamorgan', *Archaeologia Cambrensis*, 6th series, XV (1915), pp 253–320.

Ward, J, 'The St. Nicholas chambered tumulus, Glamorgan', *Archaeologia Cambrensis*, XVI (1916), pp 239–67.

Webster, P V, 'Cardiff Castle excavations 1974–81', *Morgannwg*, 25 (1981), pp 201–11.

Wheeler, R E M, and V E Nash-Williams, *Caerleon Roman Amphitheatre* (Cardiff, 1970).

Wilkinson, G, 'Avenue and cairns about Arthur's Stone in Gower', *Archaeologia Cambrensis*, I, 4th series (1870), pp 23–45.

Williams, A, 'Excavations at The Knave promontory fort, Rhossili, Glamorgan', *Archaeologia Cambrensis*, XCIV (1939), pp 210–19.

Williams, A, 'The excavation of High Pennard promontory fort, Glamorgan', *Archaeologia Cambrensis*, XCVI (1941), pp 23–30.

Williams, H W, 'The exploration of a prehistoric camp in Glamorgan', *Archaeologia Cambrensis* II, 6th series, pt I (1902), pp 252–60.

Zienkiewicz, D, *The Legionary Fortress Baths at Caerleon* (Cardiff 1986).

Acknowledgements

Sources of Illustrations

The line drawings were produced by staff of Cartographic Services, Welsh Office. Many were redrawn, with amendments, from plans already published: nos 66, 67, 98, 110, 112, 113, 114, 116, 117, 122, 123, 124 and 127 (Crown copyright plans from Welsh Office or Cadw guidebooks); nos 4, 5, 8, 13, 14, 17, 18, 34, 35, 36, 37, 38, 39, 40, 42, 45, 46, 48, 54, 59, 60, 61, 63, 64, 68, 70, 72, 90, 96, 128, 129, 149 and 150 (Royal Commission on Ancient and Historical Monuments in Wales); nos 49, 51, 52, 54, 71, 83, 92, 94, 97 (Ordnance Survey); no. 50 (Probert 1976); no. 56 (Nash-Williams 1933); no. 57 (Nash-Williams 1939); no. 69 (Webster 1981); no. 91 (Fox 1939); no. 100 (Knight 1977); no. 115 (Monmouth District Museums Service); no. 126 (Evans 1980); no. 129 (Nash-Williams 1952a); no. 132 (Knight 1976–8).

I am most grateful to the National Museum of Wales and the University of Wales Press for permission to reproduce from Nash-Williams (1950) a drawing of the Cross of Cynfelyn (Introduction to chapter 6); and to the National Museum of Wales for permission to reproduce the five reconstruction drawings in the introductory sections to chapters 1, 2, 3 and 4.

Copyright acknowledgements are due to the following photographic sources: Cadw, Welsh Historic Monuments: nos 43, 44, 53, 66 (amphitheatre), 67 (aerial photo), 84, 85, 95, 98, 101, 102, 104 (general), 106, 108, 110, 112, 113, 114, 115, 116, 117, 123 (west end of church), 124 (monks' living quarters), 127, 150 (general). Elisabeth Whittle: nos 1, 2, 3, 4, 5, 6, 7, 9, 10, 22, 25, 27, 30, 31, 32, 33, 66 (barracks), 67 (south wall), 74 (general), 75, 77, 78, 79, 80, 81, 86, 99, 103, 109 (general and chapel window), 111, 116 (Introduction to chapter 7), 119, 120, 125, 129, 130, 134, 136, 137, 138, 140, 141, 142, 143, 144, 145, 146, 149. National Museum of Wales: nos 69, 124. National Monuments Record collection in the Royal Commission on Ancient and Historical Monuments in Wales: nos 73, 107. Wales Tourist Board: no. 147. Cardiff City Council: no. 83. Kate Holt-Wilson: nos 100, 121, 122, 126, 148. D.A.T.: no. 58.

Index

Note: gazetteer entries are listed in bold, by their **page** numbers.

Aberdare
  Garn Las round cairn 187
  Rhos-Gwawr cairn cemetery (no. 21) 13, **22**
Abergavenny
  Benedictine priory 109
  Castle (no. 101) 86, 89, 94, **108–10**
  Museum viii
  St Michael's Chapel, Ysgyryd Fawr (Skirrid Mountain) (no.133) 151, **170–1**
Abergwynfi, Pebyll ring cairn (no. 14) **18–19**
Ammanford, Penlle'r Castell 191
Arthur's Stone, round cairn near (no. 10) 12, **17**
Arthur's Stone chambered cairn (no. 7) 7, **12**, 17
Audele, d', family, earls of Stafford 143

Babbidge, A V 44
Baglan
  Craig Ty-Isaf hillfort 189
  St Baglan's Church 196
Ballon, de, Hamelin 109
Barry
  Castle (no. 120) **142**, 170
  Highlight Church 195
  Knap Roman site (no. 71) **71–2**, 142
  St Barruc's Chapel, Barry Island (no. 132) 142, **169–70**
Barry, de, family 142
Bassett family 180, 182
Bawdrip family 194
Beacons Round Barrows, The (no. 23) **23**
Beauchamp family 88, 92
Beaumont, de, Henry, earl of Warwick 86, 116, 123
Bedlinog, Coly Uchaf platform houses 192
Begwns round barrow (no. 24) **23**, 24
Belinstock see Lodge Wood hillfort (no. 52)
Bere, de la, family 121
Berkerolle, de, family 113, 194
Bettws Newydd, Coed y Bwnydd hillfort (no. 51) 30, **44–5**
Biddle, Matthew 182

Bigod III, Roger 103–4, 151, 152, 153, 176
Bishopston
  Bishopston Valley fort 189
  High Pennard promontory fort (no. 62) 29, 30, 41, **52–3**
  Old Castle 191
Bishton, deserted village, Wilcrick 192
Blaenavon, Carn y Defaid round cairns (no. 11) **17–18**
Blaenrhondda ancient village (no. 63) 30, **53**, 55
Bluet family 144
Bohun, de, family, lords of Brecon 87, 131, 133, 141
Bonvilston, Castell Moel (no. 96) **100**
Boon, G 59
Bovium/Bomium 58
Braose, de, family 86, 94, 106, 109, 116, 119, 168
Brecon, Roman road and fort 56, 58, 67
Brecon Gaer Roman fort, Powys 59
Bridgend
  Newcastle (no. 102) 86, **110–11**, 112, 113, 116
  standing stone (no. 29) **25**
Briton Ferry, Carreg Hir 187
Bronllys Castle, Powys 129, 131
Buarth Maen ancient village (no. 64) 30, **53–4**
Buck, Samuel and Nathaniel 142
Buckland, William 4–5
Bulwark, The, hillfort, Llanmadoc (no. 40) 28, 30, 32, **36**
Bulwarks, The, hillfort, Chepstow (no. 54) **47**, 49
Bulwarks, The, hillfort, Rhoose (no. 46) 37, **41**
Burges, William 92, 138, 140
Burgh, de, family 86, 108, 125–6, 127, 129
Burrium see Usk
Burry, menhir and standing stones (nos. 31–3) 15, **26–7**
Burry Holms promontory fort (no. 58) 29, 41, **49–50**
Bute, 3rd and 4th marquesses of 68, 70, 92, 137, 138, 140, 195
Button family 192

Bwlch yr Avan Dyke (no. 82) **84**

Cadw, Welsh Historic Monuments *vi, viii,*
  59–63, 63–6, 76–8, 90–2, 101–4, 104–5,
  119–21, 121–3, 124–6, 126–9, 129–31,
  131–4, 134–8, 138–40, 144–8, 151–5, 155–
  9, 159–61, 161–3, 163–6, 180–3
Caer Dynnaf hillfort, Cowbridge 59, 188
Caerau
  Castle ringwork (no. 90) 33, 93, **95**
  hillfort (no. 37) **33–4**
  Mynydd Caerau round cairns (no. 12) **18**
Caerleon
  castle mound 86, 191
  Lodge Wood hillfort (no. 52) 28, 30, **45**
  medieval tower at Hanbury Arms 194
  Roman Legionary Fortress (no. 66) 56,
    58, **59–63**, 66
  Roman Legionary Museum 60, 62, 63
Caerphilly
  Castle (no. 116) 87, 88, 93, **134–8**, 141
  Gwern y Domen castle mound 191
  Roman fort 67
Caerwent
  Berries, The, mound and bailey
    castle 190–1
  Llanmelin Wood hillforts (no. 56) 30,
    48–9, 63
  Llanvair Castle 194
  Roman town (no. 67) 48, 56, 59, **63–6**
  St Brides Netherwent deserted
    village 192
Caldicot
  Bronze Age remains 13
  Castle (no. 115) 86, 95, 105, 107, 129,
    131–4
Camden, William 1, 10, 19, 49, 63, 109
Cardiff
  Blackfriars Dominican friary 195
  Caerau Castle ringwork (no. 90) 33, 93,
    95
  Caerau hillfort (no. 37) **33–4**
  Castell Coch (no. 117) 87, 93, 134,
    138–40, 141
  Castle (no. 83) 68, 86, 89, **90–2**, 95, 131,
    138
  Ely Roman villa 59, 189
  Lesser Garth cave, Radyr 73, 190
  Llandaff
    bishops of 89, 99, 168, 191, 192
    Cathedral 158
      bell tower (no. 131) 151, **169**
      Early Christian stone (no. 76) **81**
    Old Bishop's Palace (no. 130) 88, 151,
      168–9

Morganstown castle mound 191
National Museum of Wales *viii,* 28
  Roman fort and road (no. 69) 56, 58, 59,
    64, 67, **68–70**
  Taff Terrace cooking mound (no. 65) 30,
    55
Cardiff, de, family 191
Carmarthen, Roman road 56, 63, 70
Carn Bugail round cairn (no. 8) 13, 15, **16**
Carn Llechart stone circle (ring cairn) (no.
  15) 15, **19–20**
Carn y Defaid round cairns (no. 11) **17–18**
Carn y Wiwer platform houses (no. 94) **98–9**
Carne, Edward and John 165
Carreg Bica standing stone (no. 28) **25**
Castell Arnallt 109
Castell Coch (no. 117) 87, 93, 134, **138–40**,
  141
Castell Moel (no. 96) **100**
Castle Ditches hillfort, Llancarfan (no. 34) 30,
  31
Castle Ditches hillfort, Llantwit Major (no.
  44) 37, **39–40**
Cat Hole cave (no. 3) 4, **6**
Cefn Ffordd trackway 84
Cefn Sychbant round cairns (no. 13) **18**
Cefn y Brithdir platform houses (no. 93) **98**
Charles I, king of England 148
Chateau Gaillard, France 135
Chepstow
  Bulwarks, The, hillfort (no. 54) **47**, 49
  medieval castle (no. 98) 85, 86, 88, 89,
    101–4, 106, 124
  Museum *viii*
  Pierce Wood hillforts (no. 55) **47–8**
  Priory 149
  town wall and gate (no. 144) 151, **176–7**
Chester Roman legionary fortress 60
Clare, de
  family 86, 87, 102, 106, 151
  Gilbert, 'red earl' of Gloucester, lord of
    Glamorgan 87, 91–2, 93, 107–8, 134,
    138, 140, 141
  Gilbert (the Last) 193, 194
  Richard 140, 194, 195
Clark, G T 110
Clwyd 29
Cobb, J R 134
Coed y Bwnydd hillfort (no. 51) 30, **44–5**
Coed y Cymdda hillfort settlement 15
Coedkernew, Gwern y Cleppa chambered
  cairn 186
Coelbren, Powys, Roman road and fort 56,
  189

Coity Castle (no. 104)   86, 88, 89, 110, 111, 112, **113–15**, 116
Colosseum, Rome   61
Colt Hoare, Sir Richard   49, 162
Cowbridge
    Caer Dynnaf hillfort   59, 188
    Old Beaupre manor house (no. 149)   88, 151, **180–3**, 185
    Roman   58
    South Gate medieval gatehouse (no. 145)   151, **177**
Coxe, William   195
Coychurch
    Celtic cross-shaft (no. 80)   **83**, 172
    medieval cross (no. 137)   83, **172**
Craig y Dinas hillfort (no. 41) **36–7**
Craster, O E   63, 99, 129, 161
Crick, Runston chapel and deserted village   192, 195
Crug Hywel hillfort, Powys   42
Crug yr Afan round cairn (no. 9)   13, **16–17**, 18, 24
Culver Hole dovecote (no. 146)   151, **177–8**
Cwm Bach camps, Wick   188
Cwm George camp medieval settlement   73, 115, 190
Cwmbran, Llantarnam Abbey tithe barn   195

Dafydd Gam   99
Daniel, Glyn   9, 39
Davies, J L   41
Deborah's Hole camp *see* Knave Promontory Fort
Despenser family   88, 118, 135, 137
Devauden, Kilwrrwg churchyard cross (no. 143)   **176**
Dinas Powys
    Castle (no. 105)   86, **115–16**
    Cwm George camp medieval settlement   73, 115, 190
Dingestow, Mill Wood castle mound (no. 87)   **94**, 109
Doghill moated site, Dyffryn   89, 192
Domesday Book   86, 161
Dover Castle, Kent   135
Dunraven hillfort (no. 42)   30, **37**, 39
Dyfed   30, 132
Dyffryn, Doghill moated site   89, 192

Edmund 'Crouchback', earl of Lancaster   105, 126
Edward I, king of England   88, 116, 119, 121, 126, 127, 129, 131, 137, 141
Edward II, king of England   134, 137
Edward IV, king of England   131, 144

Ely Roman villa, Cardiff   59, 189
Evans, A L   159
Evans, E   116
Ewenny Priory (no. 127)   149, **163–6**

Ferndale, Twyn y Bridallt marching camp (no. 72)   56, **72**
Ffos Ton Cenglau earthwork (no. 81)   53, 73, **83–4**
fitz Osbern, William, lord of Breteuil, earl of Hereford   85, 101, 105, 106, 124–5, 127, 129, 149
fitz Richard, Walter   149
fitz Roger, Walter   131
fitz Rolf, Turstin   191
Fitzhamon, Robert   90, 110, 113
Fountains Abbey, Yorkshire   153
Fox, C   34
Fox, Lady A   34, 96, 97, 170

Gadlys moated site (no. 97)   94, **100–1**
Gamage family   113
Gardner, W   41
Garth Hill round barrows (no. 22)   **22**, 23
Gavrinis, Brittany, Neolithic tomb   15
Gelligaer
    Capel Gwladys   195–6
    Carn Bugail round cairn (no. 8)   13, 15, **16**
    early Christian standing stone (no. 79)   **82**
    medieval platform houses (nos 91 and 92)   **96–7**, 98
    ring cairn   187
    Roman fort (no. 68)   58, **66–8**, 82
    Roman marching camps and road   56, 189
Gerdinen, Graig Fawr ring cairn (no. 17)   **20–1**
Gilpin, William   105, 155
Giraldus Cambrensis   161, 170
Glamorgan, Robert, earl of Gloucester, lord of   90, 92, 118, 149, 159
Gloucester
    Roman road   56, 63
    St Peter's Abbey   164
Godwin, Bishop   193
Goldcliff moated site   193
Gower, de, Bishop Henry   117
Graig Fawr ring cairn (no. 17)   **20–1**
Grant, J P   90
Granville, de, Sir Richard   149, 155
Gray Hill stone circle (ring cairn) (no. 16)   15, **20**
Griffith, J   16
Grimes, W F   55
Grosmont, Henry and Ralph of   105, 125

Grosmont Castle (no. 112)   87, 88, 113, **124–6**, 127, 129, 131
Gruffydd ap Rhys   139
Gwent, regional kingdom of   75
Gwynlliog, lordship of   143

Hague, D B   180
Hardings Down hillforts (no. 36)   **32–3**
Harold's Stones (no. 27)   15, **24–5**, 93, 179
Hastings family 109
Hen Gwrt moated site (no. 95)   89, **99–100**, 192
Hendre'r Gelli settlement   53
Henry I, king of England   90, 116, 155
Henry II, king of England   102, 110
Henry III, king of England   87, 105, 107, 134
Henry IV, king of England   113, 133
Henry V, king of England   105, 113, 126
Henry VII, king of England   123, 144
Herbert family   184, 193
Herbert, Sir William, of Raglan   108, 131, 144, 148, 155, 175
High Pennard promontory fort (no. 62)   29, 30, 41, **52–3**
Hirwaun, Llyn Fawr reservoir   28
Hogg, A H A   31
Horse Cliff camp   52
Horseland moated site   89, 191, 192, 193
Hyde, H A   55
Hywel ab Iorwerth   94, 106, 109, 195

Isca see Caerleon

Julius Frontinus, Roman governor   56

Kenfig
   Castle and medieval town   86, 194
   Roman   58
Kenyon, J R   141, 144
Kilwrrwg churchyard cross, Devauden (no. 143)   **176**
Knap Roman site (no. 71)   **71–2**, 142
Knave promontory fort, The (no. 60)   29, 30, 41, **51–2**
Knelston *see* Burry, menhir and standing stones
Knight, J K   66, 101, 106, 124, 126, 129, 170, 176

Lacy, de, family   161
Lamphey bishop's palace   117
Landor, Walter Savage   163
Langstone, Pencoed Castle moated site   193
Leland, John   109, 159, 170
Lesser Garth cave   73, 190

Leucarum see Loughor
Lewis, J M   99
Lewis, Thomas, of the Van   137–8
Lhuyd, Edward   10
Liege Castle *see* Castell Moel
Llanblethian, St Quintin's Castle   194
Llancarfan
   Castle Ditches hillfort (no. 34)   30, **31**
   monastery   73, 74
Llandaff *see* Cardiff, Llandaff
Llanddewy Rhydderch churchyard cross-base (no. 139)   **174**
Llandough churchyard, early Christian pillar-cross (no. 78)   81, **82**
Llanfihangel Crucorney
   Llanthony Priory (no. 126)   149, 155, **161–3**
   Pen-twyn hillfort (no. 49)   **42–3**
   Twyn y Gaer hillfort (no. 50)   29, 30, 42, **43–4**
Llanfihangel Rogiet standing stone   187
Llangan
   Celtic cross (no. 77)   **81**
   churchyard cross (no. 136)   81, 151, **172**
Llangennith
   Burry Holms promontory fort (no. 58)   29, 41, **49–50**
   Druids Moor   33
   Hardings Down hillforts (no. 36)   **32–3**
Llangibby Castle and mound   190, 193
Llangwm, Gaer Fawr camp   188
Llangyfelach
   Carn Llechart chambered cairn   186
   cross-base   189
Llangynwyd
   Castle (Tir yr Iarll)   87, 191
   Mynydd Ty Talwyn platform houses   192
   Y Bwlwarcau hillfort (no. 38)   28, 29, **34–5**, 46
Llanharan, The Beacons round barrows (no. 23)   **23**
Llanilid
   Castle Mound (no. 88)   93, **94**
   Gadlys moated site (no. 97)   94, **100–1**
Llanmadoc, The Bulwark, hillfort (no. 40)   28, 30, 32, **36**
Llanmelin Wood hillforts (no. 56)   30, **48–9**, 63
Llanrhidian
   Cilifor or North Hill Tor   121
   Cilifor Top hillfort   188
   Sampson's Jack (no. 30)   15, **25–6**
   Ty'r Coed Farm standing stone   187
   Weobley Castle (no. 110)   **121–3**

Llansoy, Great House camp   188
Llantarnam Abbey tithe barn, Cwmbran   195
Llanthony Priory (no. 126)   149, 155, **161–3**
Llantilio Crossenny
  Hen Gwrt moated site (no. 95)   89,
    99–100, 192
  Penrhos motte-and-bailey castle   190
  White Castle (no. 113)   88, 99, 105, 124,
    126–9, 131
Llantrisant
  Cas Troggy Castle   193
  Castle (no. 118)   87, **140**
  Rhiw Saeson Caerau hillfort   188
Llantrithyd
  Horseland moated site   89, 193
  ringwork   191
Llantwit Major
  Caermead Roman villa   189
  Castle Ditches hillfort (no. 44)   37, **39–40**
  early Christian stones (no. 74)   74, 74–5,
    79–80, 83
  Grange at Abbot's Llantwit (no. 129)
    167–8
  monastery   73, 74
  Roman villa   59
  Summerhouse Fort (no.45)   28, 30, 37,
    40, 45
Llanvair Discoed
  Gray Hill stone circle (no. 16)   15, **20**
  Wentwood round barrows (no. 25)   **23–4**
Llwchwr Castle *see* Loughor Castle
Llywelyn ab Iorwerth ('the Great')   87, 118
Llywelyn ap Gruffudd ('the Last')   87, 93, 134,
  135
Llewelyn Bren   195
Lodge Wood hillfort (no. 52)   28, 30, **45**
Londres, de, family   119, 149, 164, 165
Long Hole cave, Port Eynon (no. 2)   4, **5–6**
Loughor Castle (no. 108)   **118–19**
Lubbock, J   9
Lukis, J W   11
Lydney hillfort, Gloucestershire   48, 49

Machen
  Begwns round barrow, Mynydd Machen
    (no. 24)   **23**, 24
  Roman lead mining   59
Maen Ceti *see* Arthur's Stone (no. 7)
Maendy Camp hillfort (no. 39)   28, 29, **35–6**
Maesyfelin *see* St Lythans Burial Chamber
Mansel family   183–5
Mansel, Sir Rice   161, 180, 181, 183, 185
March, earls of   108
Marcross, Nash Point fort (no. 43)   28, 37,
  38–9

Margam
  Abbey (no. 125)   149, 150, 156, **159–61**,
    184, 185
  Hen Eglwys chapel   151, 196
  Margam Stones Museum, early Christian
    stones (no. 73)   74, 75, **76–8**, 159
Margam, Mynydd y Castell hillfort (no. 35)
  31–2
Marshal family   87, 102–3, 104, 107, 152,
  155
Marshal, William   86, 102, 103, 104, 106,
  107, 155, 191
Mathern, Moynes Court moated site   193
Merrick, Rice   100
Merthyr Mawr
  Candleston Castle   195
  early Christian stones (no. 75) **80–1**, 196
  St Roque's chapel and inscribed
    stones   151, 190, 196
Merthyr Tydfil
  Buarth Maen ancient village (no. 64)   30,
    53–4
  Merthyr Common round cairns (no.
    20)   **21–2**
  Morlais Castle (no. 119)   87, 93, 134,
    141–2
  Pant Sychbant round cairn and
    earthworks   187
Mill Wood castle mound (no. 87)   **94**, 109
Minchin Hole cave   73, 190
Mitchel Troy churchyard cross (no. 140)   **174**
Moel y Gaer hillfort, Clwyd   29
Monknash Grange (no. 128)   150, 151,
  166–7
Monmouth
  Castle (no. 99)   85, **104–5**, 124
  Clawdd Du earthwork   193
  Monnow bridge (no. 147)   151, **178–9**
  Museum   *viii*
  Romans   56
Monnow bridge *see under* Monmouth
Moore, D   59
Morgan family of Tredegar House   47
Morgan, O   131
Morgan, W L   116
Morgannwg, regional kingdom of   75
Morlais Castle (no. 119)   87, 93, 134, **141–2**
Mowbray, de, family   117, 121, 124
Mynydd Caerau round cairns (no. 12)   **18**
Mynydd y Castell hillfort (no. 35)   **31–2**
Mynydd y Gaer hillfort (no. 48)   **41–2**

Nash Point fort (no. 43)   28, 37, **38–9**
Nash-Williams, V E   48, 49, 59, 70, 76–83,
  167

Neath
  Abbey (no. 124)   149, 151, **155–9**, 160, 166, 190
  Carreg Bica standing stone (no. 28)   **25**
  Castle (no. 107)   **117–18**
  Mynydd Drumau cairn   187
  Roman fort and road (no. 70)   56, 58, **70–1**, 118
Newcastle, Bridgend (no. 102)   86, **110–11**, 112, 113, 116
Newport
  Castle (no. 121)   89, **143–4**
  Coed y Defaid hillfort   188
  Museum   *viii*, 63
  Tredegar hillfort (no. 53)   **46–7**
Nicholas of Llandaff   154
Nicholaston chambered cairn *see* Penmaen
Nidum see Neath

Offa's Dyke   43, 127
Ogmore Castle (no. 103)   86, 89, 110, **111–113**, 113, 116, 119, 164
Ogmore-by-Sea, Dunraven hillfort (no. 42)   30, **37**, 39
Old Beaupre manor house (no. 149)   88, 151, **180–3**, 185
Old Court moated site *see* Hen Gwrt moated site
Owain Glyndŵr   88, 99, 104, 108, 109, 113, 126, 163, 168
Oxwich Castle (no. 150)   89, 151, 161, **183–5**
Oystermouth Castle (no. 109)   88, **119–21**, 116

Pandy, Penbidwal moated site   193
Parc le Breos chambered cairn (no. 4)   7, **9–10**, 11
Parkmill
  Cat Hole cave (no. 3)   4, **6**
  Parc le Breos chambered cairn (no. 4)   7, **9–10**, 11
  Paviland cave (no. 1)   3, **4–5**, 52
Paviland promontory fort (no. 61)   29, 41, 51, **52**
Pebyll ring cairn (no. 14)   **18–19**
Pembroke Castle, Dyfed   132
Penarth, Llandough churchyard, early Christian pillar-cross (no. 78)   81, **82**
Pencoed
  Langstone, Pencoed Castle moated site   193
  Mynydd y Gaer hillfort (no. 48)   **41–2**
Penderyn
  Cefn Sychbant round cairns (no. 13)   **18**
  Nant Maden round cairn   187

Penlle'rbebyll ring cairn (no. 18)   **21**
Penmaen
  Castle   123–4
  Cefn Bryn (Nicholaston) chambered cairn   186
  Penmaen Burrows chambered cairn and ringwork   186, 191
Penmark Castle   194
Pennard
  Castle (no. 111)   121, **123–4**, 191
  Minchin Hole cave   73, 190
Penres, de, family   195
Penrice Castle   195
Penterry, Gaer Hill camp hillfort   188
Pentre Meyrick, Mynydd Bychan Iron Age enclosure   188
Pen-twyn hillfort (no. 49)   **42–3**
Pentyrch
  Cae-yr-arfau long cairn   186
  Garth Hill round barrows (no. 22)   **22**, 23
Penydarren Roman fort and road   56, 67
Penywyrlod long cairn, Powys   8
Perks, J C   101
Perth-hir House, Rockfield   89, 193
Pierce Wood hillforts (no. 55)   **47–8**
Poer, Ranulf   94
Pontardawe, Carn Llechart stone circle (no. 15)   15, **19–20**
Pontardulais, Penlle'rbebyll ring cairn (no. 18)   **21**
Pontllanfraith, Twyn Tudor, earthwork castle (no. 85)   **93**, 95
Pontneddfechan, Craig y Dinas hillfort (no. 41)   **36–7**
Pontypridd, Tomen y Clawdd earthwork castle (no. 89)   **95**
Port Eynon
  Culver Hole dovecote (no. 146)   151, **177–8**
  Long Hole cave (no. 2)   4, **5–6**
  Paviland cave (no. 1)   3, **4–5**, 52
Portskewett
  Heston Brake long barrow   187
  Sudbrook Fort (no. 57)   30, 47, 48, **49**
Powys   8, 42, 56, 58, 129, 131
Probert, L A   43

Radford, C A R   76, 163
Raglan
  Castle (no. 122)   88–9, 99, 108, 131, **144–8**, 175
  Churchyard cross-base (no. 142)   **175**
Rees, W   134
Renn, D F   134
Resolven, Carn Caca cairn circle   187

Reynoldston
Arthur's Stone (no. 7)   7, **12**, 17
Arthur's Stone round cairn (no. 10)   12,
   17
pillar-stone in church   190
Rhoose, The Bulwarks hillfort (no. 46)   37, **41**
Rhos-Gwawr cairn cemetery (no. 21)   13, **22**
Rhossili
Horse Cliff camp   52
Paviland promontory fort (no. 61)   29, 41,
   51, **52**
Rhossili Down cairn circle (no. 19)   15, **21**
Sweyne's Howes   186
The Knave promontory fort (no. 60)   29,
   30, 41, **51–2**
Thurba promontory fort (no. 59)   29, 41,
   50–1
Rhymney, Cefn y Brithdir platform houses
   (no. 93)   **98**
Richard, duke of York   108
Rievaulx Abbey, Yorkshire   153
Risca, Twmbarlwm earthwork castle (no.
   84)   **92–3**
Robert, duke of Normandy   91
Robert, earl of Gloucester, lord of
   Glamorgan   90, 92, 118, 149, 159
Robinson, D   121, 141, 151
Rockfield, Perth-hir House   89, 193
Rodger, J W   167
Rogers, Nathan   180
Rousham, S   138
Ruthin, Norman sublordship of   94, 101

St Aaron   73
St Athan
East Orchard manor house   194
Flemingston and Rock Farm deserted
   medieval villages   192
St Brides Major, Ogmore Castle (no. 103)   86,
   89, 110, **111–13**, 113, 116, 119, 164
St Cadog   73, 74
St David's bishop's palace   117
St Donat's churchyard cross (no. 134)   151,
   171
St Dyfrig   73
St Illtyd   73, 74
St Julius   73
St Lythans burial chamber (chambered cairn)
   (no. 6)   **11–12**
St Mary Hill, St Mary's churchyard cross (no.
   135)   151, **172**
St Michael's Chapel, Ysgyryd Fawr,
   Abergavenny (no. 133)   151, **170–1**
St Nicholas
Cottrell ringwork   191

Tinkinswood chambered cairn (no. 5)   7,
   10–11
St Quintin's Castle, Llanblethian   194
Sampson's Jack (no. 30)   15, **25–6**
Savigny, France, abbey of   155
Seisyllt ap Dyfnwal   94, 109
Senghenydd   93, 134, 139
Carneddi Llwydion round cairns   187
Shirenewton, Gaer Llwyd chambered
   cairn   186
Silures, tribe   30, 48, 56, 60, 63, 69
Simpson, G   68, 70
Siward family   94
Skenfrith Castle (no. 114)   87, 88, 105, 107,
   124, 126, 127, **129–31**
Skirrid mountain *see under* Abergavenny
Sollas, W J   4
Somerset family   89
Somerset Levels, Bronze Age remains   13
Southgate, Pennard Castle (no. 111)   121,
   123–4, 191
Stafford family, dukes of Buckingham   88,
   143, 144
Stradling family   194
Striguil Castle *see* Chepstow Castle
Sudbrook Fort (no. 57)   30, 47, 48, **49**
Sully Island Fort (no. 47)   37, **41**
Sumeri, de, family   115
Summerhouse Fort (no. 45)   28, 30, 37, **40**,
   45
Swansea Castle (no. 106)   88, 89, **116–17**,
   119

Tacitus   56
Taff Terrace cooking mound (no. 65)   30, **55**
Talgarth, Powys   8
Taylor, A J   105, 144
Tewkesbury Abbey, Gloucestershire   167
Thomas, Abbots of Margam Abbey   159
Thomas, Sir Rhys ap   123
Thomas, Sir William ap   144, 148, 175
Thomas, W G   121
Thomas of Woodstock, duke of
   Gloucester   133, 134
Thornhill, Castell Morgraig   194
Three Castles *see* Caldicot Castle; Skenfrith
   Castle; White Castle
Thurba promontory fort (no. 59)   29, 41,
   50–1
Thurlby, M   163
Tiberius Claudius Paulinus   66
Tinkinswood chambered cairn (no. 5)   7,
   10–11
Tintern Abbey (no. 123)   103, 149, **151–5**,
   158, 160

Tir yr Iarll *see* Llangynwyd Castle
Tomen y Clawdd earthwork castle (no. 89) **95**
Tonna
    Blaen cwm bach marching camp 189
    Cefn Morfudd dyke 190
Tredegar hillfort (no. 53) **46–7**
Treharris, Tir Lan round barrows 187
Treherbert
    Blaenrhondda ancient village (no. 63) 30, **53**, 55
    Ffos Ton Cenglau earthwork (no. 81) 53, 73, **83–4**
Trellech
    Churchyard cross (no. 141) **174**
    dovecote at Hygga Farm 194
    Harold's Stones (no. 27) 15, **24–5**, 93, 179
    The Virtuous Well (no. 148) 93, 151, **179–80**
    Tump Terrett castle mound (no. 86) **93–4**, 179
Treorchy
    Bwlch yr Avan dyke (no. 82) **84**
    Crug yr Afan round cairn (no. 9) 13, **16–17**, 18, 24
    Maendy Camp hillfort (no. 39) 28, 29, **35–6**
Tretower Castle, Powys 129, 131
Trilateral or Three Castles *see* Grosmont Castle; Skenfrith Castle; White Castle
Tudor, Jasper 104, 144
Tump Terrett castle mound (no. 86) **93–4**, 179
Turbervilles, lords of Coity 110, 113
Turner, J M W 155
Twmbarlwm earthwork castle (no. 84) **92–3**
Twyn Cae Hugh round barrow (no. 26) **24**
Twyn Tudor earthwork castle (no. 85) **93**, 95
Twyn y Bridallt marching camp (no. 72) 56, **72**
Twyn y Gaer hillfort (no. 50) 29, 30, 42, **43–4**
Tythegston long barrow 186

Umfreville, de, family 194
Undy churchyard cross (no. 138) **173**
Urban, Bishop 169
Usk
    Castle (no. 100) 86, 87, **106–8**

Coed Cwnwr moated site, Usk 193
Llancayo Camp hillfort 188
Roman legionary fortress 56, 60, 63, 68

Vaughan, Roger 104
Venta Silurum see Caerwent
Villiers, de, Henry 118
Virtuous Well, The (no. 148) 93, 151, **179–80**

Wakeman, T 131
Ward, J 10, 66
Waverley Abbey, Surrey 159
Webster, P V 68
Wellsted, William 155
Wentloog, lordship of 93, 143, 144
Wentwood round barrows (no. 25) **23–4**
Wenvoe, Coed y Cymdda hilltop settlement 15
Weobley Castle (no. 110) **121–3**
Wheeler, R E M 59
White Castle (no. 113) 88, 99, 105, 124, **126–9**, 131
Whitton Roman villa 59
Wilkinson, G 12
William the Conqueror 90, 92, 101
William Rufus 90
Williams, A 51, 52
Williams, H W 35
Williams, Sir Richard and Henry 159
Worcester, earls of, (Raglan Castle) 99, 144–5, 146
Wordsworth, William 155
Worleton *see* Doghill moated site

Y Bwlwarcau hillfort (no. 38) 28, 29, **34–5**, 46
Y Pigwn marching camp, Powys 58
Ynysddu, Twyn Cae Hugh round barrow (no. 26) **24**
Ynyshir, Carn y Wiwer platform houses (no. 94) **98–9**
Ystradowen castle mound 191
Ystradyfodwg Iron Age settlement 53

Zienkiewicz, D 59

Index by Madeleine Combie

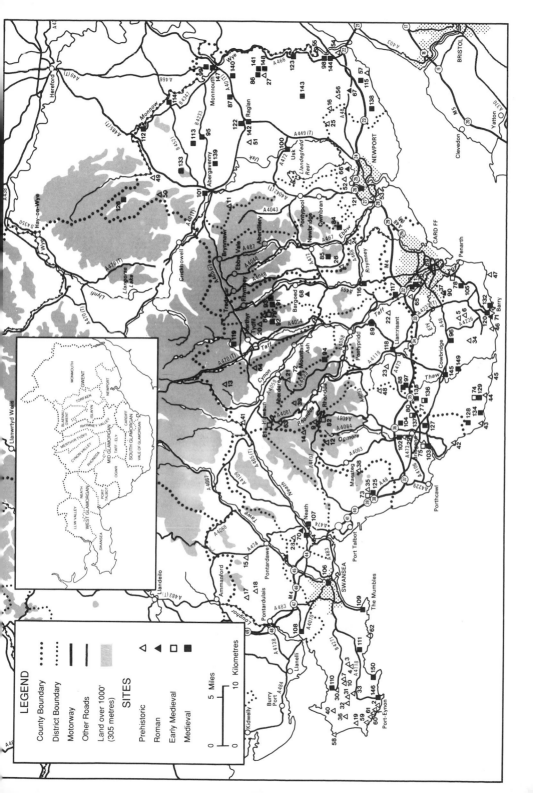